IMAGES
of America

JONESPORT AND BEALS

IMAGES
of America

JONESPORT AND BEALS

Ann Trussell

ARCADIA
PUBLISHING

ISBN 978-0-7385-5463-1

Published by Arcadia Publishing
Charleston, South Carolina

Printed in the United States of America

Library of Congress Catalog Card Number: 2007924194

For all general information contact Arcadia Publishing at:
Telephone 843-853-2070
Fax 843-853-0044
E-mail sales@arcadiapublishing.com
For customer service and orders:
Toll-Free 1-888-313-2665

Visit us on the Internet at www.arcadiapublishing.com

This book is dedicated to my dear mother, Winifred Kasper; my sister, Elaine (Kasper) Spires; my Grandmother Davis, whose love for Jonesport was my inspiration for writing this book; and also to Kasper, who will never be forgotten.
I wish they were still with us to share in the joy of this day.

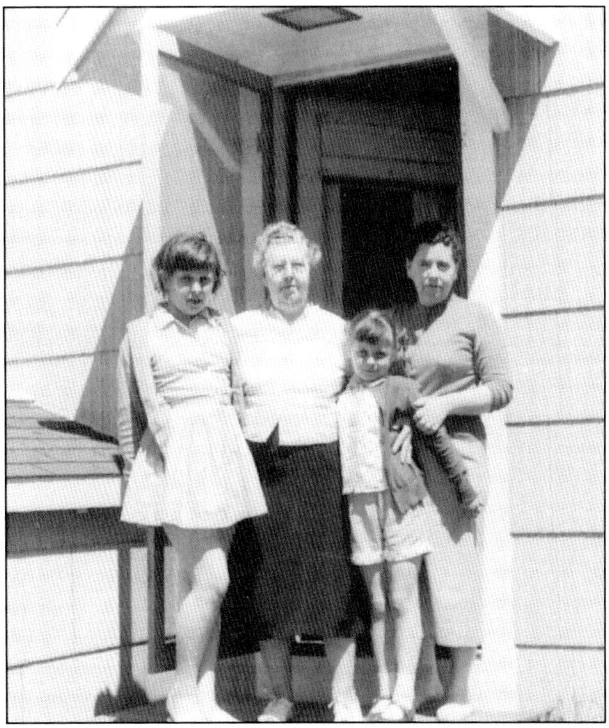

Seen here from left to right, are Elaine (Kasper) Spires (1947–1991), Eva (Faulkingham) Davis (1897–1980), author Ann (Kasper) Trussell, and Winifred (Davis) Kasper (1920–1997) in the front yard of Irene and Clyde Lamson's home.

Contents

INTRODUCTION

I believe my love for Jonesport started when I was very young. My mother and grandmother always talked about Jonesport and Beals Island and how they longed to go home. There were always great stories about Jonesport, which made it seem like a magical place.

From as early as I can remember we would drive up Route 1 on the long journey from Boston, Massachusetts, to Jonesport, Maine. We would leave home very early in the morning. My father would pack the car the night before and put some of the suitcases on the floor near the back seat; then, he would put blankets and pillows on the suitcases and make it like a bed. Elaine would sleep on the back seat and I would sleep on the suitcases. She always had a way of making it seem like I had the best spot in the car. Elaine would say to me, if you sleep on the suitcases and dad has to stop quickly, you won't fall off the seat; she failed to tell me that she would fall on top of me if the car had to stop. My sister Elaine was older and she could talk me into almost anything.

Elaine was petrified of bridges. When we got to the metal drawbridge in Bath, Maine, she would shake and cry, but somehow we made it until we would reach the next bridge. I would get so excited when it would open and we could view the boats passing.

We would always stop in Wiscasset to see the schooners that were abandoned in the harbor. The ghost ships of the *Luther Little* and the *Hesper* were a diversion for my sister and me. Through the years, I have watched them deteriorate to the point that you can't tell they are schooners at all.

We would follow Route 1 through many small villages like Camden and Searsport, seeing the ocean from time to time. When we passed the prison in Thomaston we would hide; we were afraid that one of the prisoners would get lose. Sometimes, we would stop at Perry's Nut House in Belfast. My Dad loved nuts of all types. We would get several types of nuts to snack on until it was time for lunch; the nuts didn't usually last that long though.

Down the road was another bridge and this one was the worst bridge to cross. It was the cable bridge that crosses the Penobscot River from Belfast to Verona Island. That bridge is like being on the roller coaster at Old Orchard Beach and heading up the first hill. It's high and only has a small railing on each side so you can see right down to the river below. You can see Fort Knox really well from there; the fort was built to protect Bangor during the Civil War.

When we came to the big billboard with the sunrises that said welcome to Washington County, my Grandmother Davis would always say, "I'm home again!" My grandmother was born in Jonesport on Beals Island. She would write about Jonesport often in her poetry and in her life's story; she was probably longing to go home. I cherish those poems most of all! Grandma Davis was soft spoken and sweet; everyone who knew her loved her dearly. We made the trip to Jonesport at least twice a year to bring Grandmother Davis up to visit her mother and her daughter, my Auntie Irene. My Auntie Irene and her husband, Clyde, were always glad to see us. Irene would cook all kinds of goodies for us. She would make us fried dough and homemade beans. Just writing about them makes me long for Jonesport; I know my family doesn't understand how strong my ties are to Jonesport; I guess I have a lot of my grandmother's blood in me. If I could split myself in half, half of me would live in Jonesport and the other half would be back at home with my family.

The next big town we would go through was Ellsworth; when we got there, we knew we were getting close. We would turn off of Route 1 onto Route 182 through the Black Woods (that's what my grandmother called them). It's a winding road that goes by several lakes and through the mountains and exits in Cherryfield. From Cherryfield we would continue on our way up Route 1 until we reached Route 187.

Route 187 is a highway off of Route 1; its main purpose is to connect Jonesport to Route 1. The roads were winding and bumpy in those days, unlike the highways that we travel on today. A journey that takes approximately 6 hours along Route 95 now, would have taken 10 to 12 hours back in the 1950s. With the super highways now, you travel so fast that you don't get to see much other then cars whizzing by. It's so nice traveling along the coast through all the small towns; most people are in such a hurry to get somewhere they don't take the time to enjoy themselves along the way.

As you drive down Route 187, the road winds along the sea. As you get closer to town, you can start to smell the ocean and see the seagulls soaring through the air. When it's foggy you can actually feel the fog on your face; it's cool and wet and feels like an angel is touching you. In the spring, you can see the ocean and bays from the road. When summer starts to bloom, the trees start to block the view in some areas. But then you can see all the blueberry fields starting to bud and that's a sight in itself. To see Jonesport in the fall is a beautiful sight, with all the blueberry fields a beautiful shade of crimson. Winters are cold in Jonesport and the ice forms along the bays; as the tides change the ice moves and forms big ice caps that are breathtaking, to say the least. So as you can see, no matter what time of year you chose to go to Jonesport, it's the perfect time of year.

From Tib Point to Machias Bay, there are many quaint village areas that you could spend days exploring and just relaxing in the serenity. Most of the people from the area, like their families before them, have lived there all their lives. They have no reason to leave; it's home. And I can understand why people chose to make it home; it the most beautiful place I've ever been. It such an enchanting area!

I hadn't been back to Jonesport for 25 years; when I returned I was mesmerized all over again. I was busy bring up my sons, then one day I told my husband that I wanted to go to Jonesport. When I returned with my husband and son Shawn, they fell in love with the area; it was everything I had told them. We bought land the next day and have spent every spare minute since then that we can at our camp on Masons Bay.

Jonesport is a lovely fishing village in Washington County; it is called "Sunrise County" because it's the farthest point east in the continental U.S. The sun comes up at about 4 a.m. That's when most of the people get their start. They are a hardy bunch and very hard working. A large percentage live off the sea: fishing, clamming, worming, or crabbing. The clammers and wormers have to work the tides in the hot sun, rain, or the freezing cold. As for the fisherman, that's a hard but rewarding life. They have to weather the wind and fog, and in Jonesport, the fog can be blinding. One time we were going to Jonesport, the fog was so thick you couldn't see the end of your car. We couldn't turn off the road because we couldn't see a driveway to turn into until we had passed it. The only thing we had to follow was the line on the side of the road. To see that line, you had to put your head out the side window and judge you're way along. I know it's hard to believe that story but it's true.

The bridge from Beals Island to Jonesport was built in 1957 and was the talk of the town for many years. When I was seven years old, my father and uncle Clyde took me across the staging from the main land of Jonesport to Beals. Beals Island is off Jonesport, right across Moosabec Reach. Until the early 1950s, you could only get to Beals Island by boat or ferry. Great Wass Island is connected to Beals Island at Flying Place Cove. Beals Island and Great Wass Island are beautiful islands with lots of coves and woods to explore. They have nature walks on the island and beaches to comb. It's a perfect place to go and sit by the sea and reflect on your life. You're never alone when you're on the island; someone is always close to lend a hand. That's such a great feeling. When you drive through Jonesport or on the Island of Beals or Great Wass and you pass someone, they always wave just to say hello! How neighborly that is—I don't know of any other place in the world that people are so friendly. They really make you feel right at home, like you really belong. When my grandmother was young, she would go with her family to their camp on Great Wass Island at Black Duck Cove. They would spend the summer there. Her mother would make school clothes and the children would play on the beach and pick berries.

Manwarren Beal settled Beals Islands, c. 1774. The most colorful of Beals Island legends concerns Barney Beal, the son of Manwarren Beal. Tall Barney was a "downeast" hero that I think everyone should know a little about. The story about him has been passed down from generation to generation. He was strong and gentle; he was also my great-great-great grandfather. I was not born on Beals, or even in Maine for that matter, but the ties I have to the area are as strong as anyone on the island or the mainland of Jonesport. Every time I go there, I feel like I've gone home, just as my grandmother Davis did before me. When I'm no longer around, I hope my sons find comfort in Jonesport just as I have. From the time I was a little girl, I have heard stories about Barney. He would carry a dory on his back and had killed a horse with one punch. It is said that when he sat in a chair, his hands touched the floor.

I have a little house that was made by Charles Doyal of Fisherman's Island; it was a wedding gift for Barney and his wife, Phebe. It has been passed down to me from my mother and to her from her mother. Barney and his wife had 11 children. A lot of islanders are descendents of one of his 11 children. The small white house, built of old ship wood, was where he lived and brought up his children. It still stands on Beals Island on Barney's Cove. The house is so small that he would sleep with his feet out the window.

If you ever have some time to spend and don't know where to go, Jonesport is the perfect place for you to relax and explore. There are some nice bed and breakfast inns with friendly innkeepers who will make you feel just like you've come home again. Plan on spending a little time in Jonesport—it'll be the most memorable experience that you ever have.

One

Beals and the Outer Islands

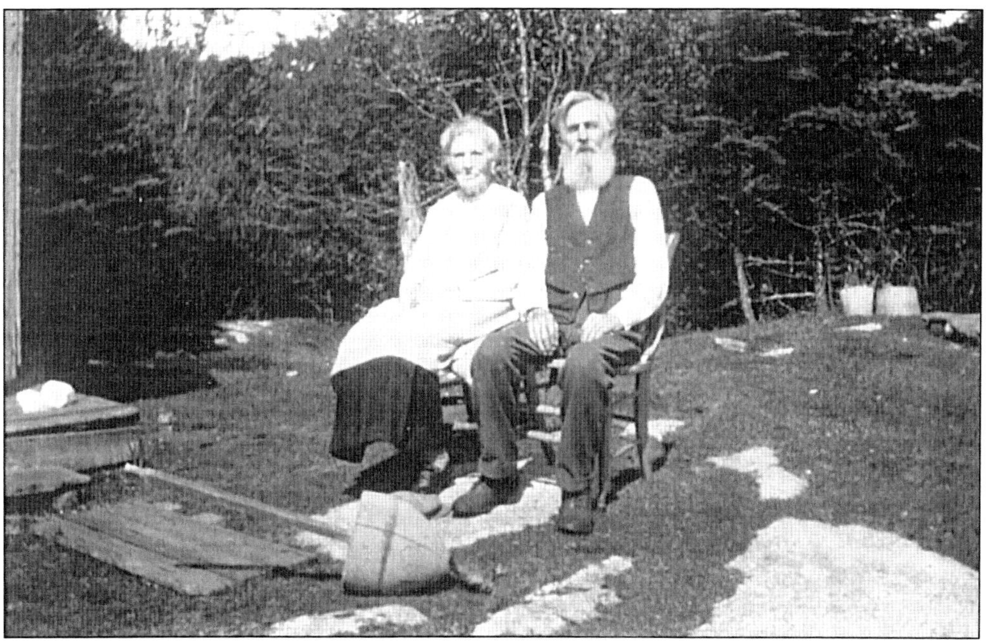

Lucinda Jane Beal and her husband, Eliha Ellis Beal, both born on Beals Island, are sitting outside their home on Beals Island. The picture was taken in the early 1930s.

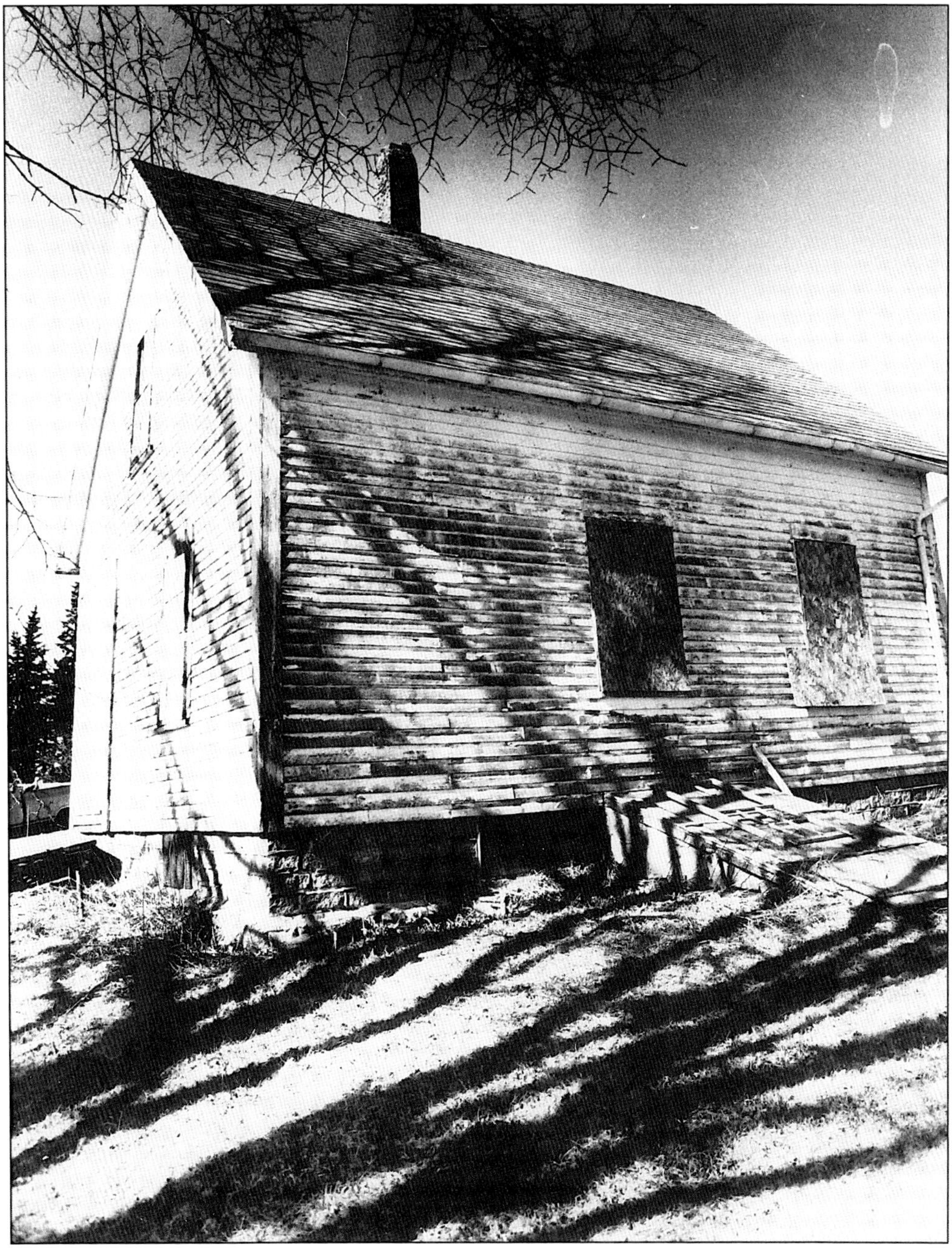

This small white house, built of old ship wood, belonged to Barna Beal. He lived here with his wife, Phoebe, and their 11 children. The building still stands on Beals Island.

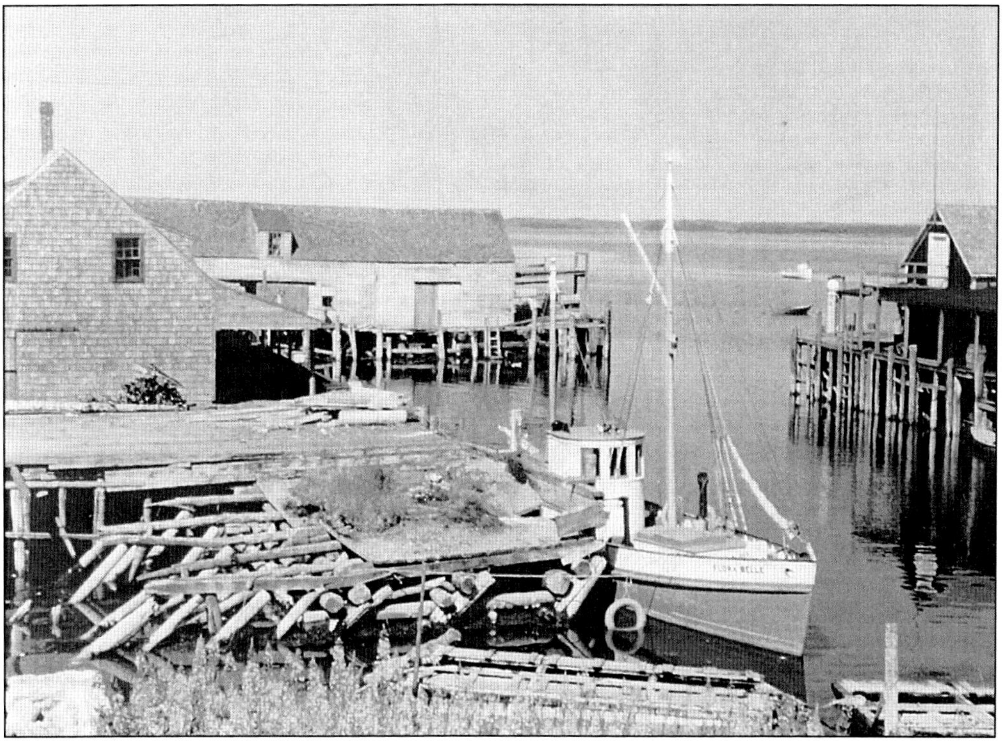

Beals Island was incorporated in 1925. The island is 6 miles long and 2 miles wide. This view from one of the wharves on the island looks across to the main land of Jonesport.

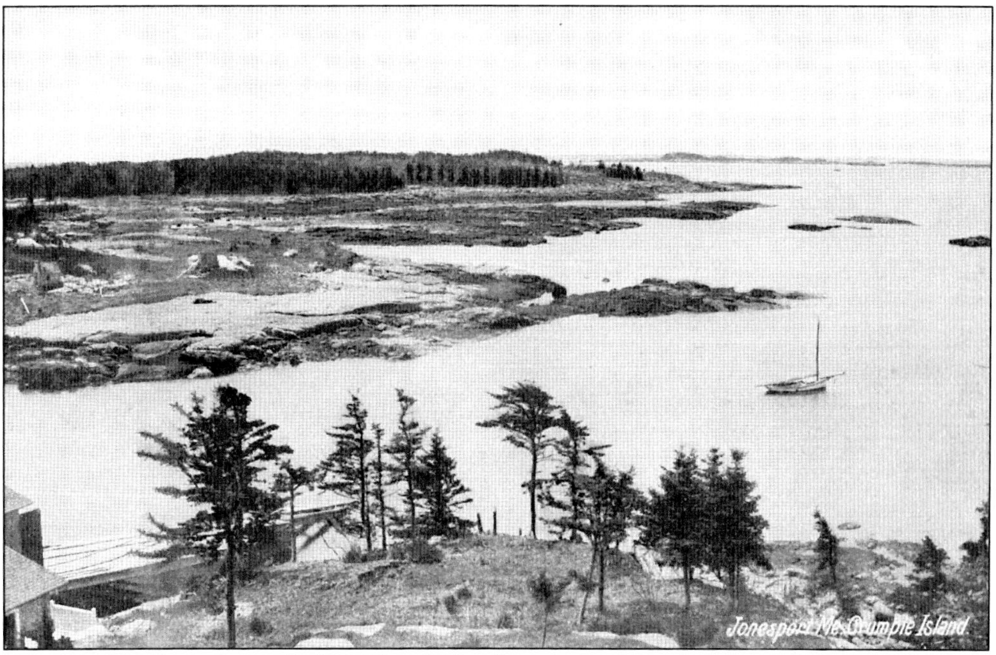

Crumple Island was first called Bluffhead Island in 1785. There was no regular habitation on it until the 1880s. People had summer residences here and would go fishing and duck hunting.

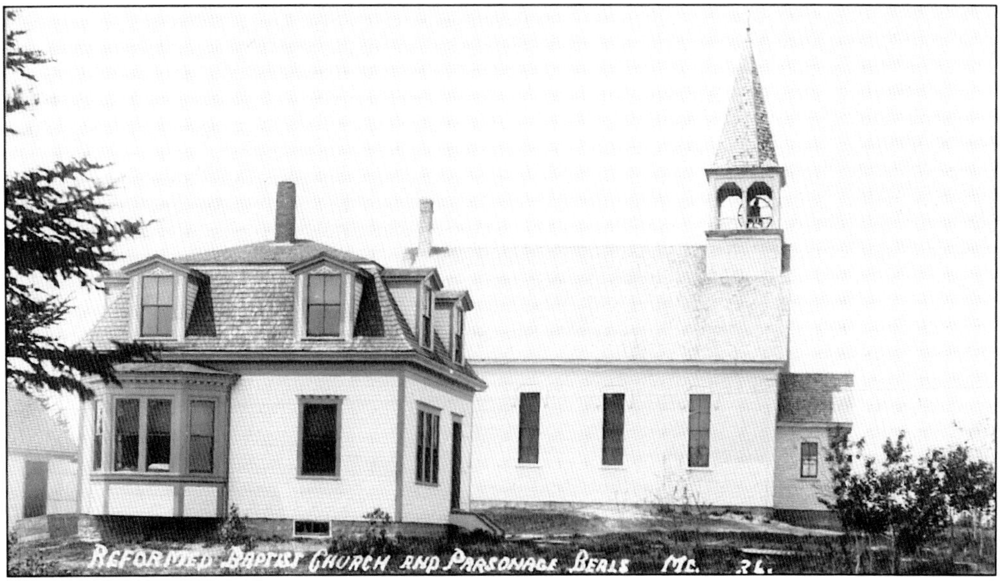

This is one of the churches on Beals Island. Suppers were often held in the churches to make extra money for church repairs. In the winter months, they would serve clam chowder; everyone would attend. A tragedy occurred one evening in the winter of December 1900 as Merta (Beal) Faulkingham and Lewis Faulkingham were leaving church with their family. It was real cold and there was ice on the roof of the church as well as the surrounding buildings. A huge sheet of ice slid off the roof of one of the buildings. They all jumped back away from it and thought they were safe. Grandma reached under the blanket of baby Cinderella to find that her head had been crushed. Baby Cinderella didn't live long and is buried on Beals in the family plot.

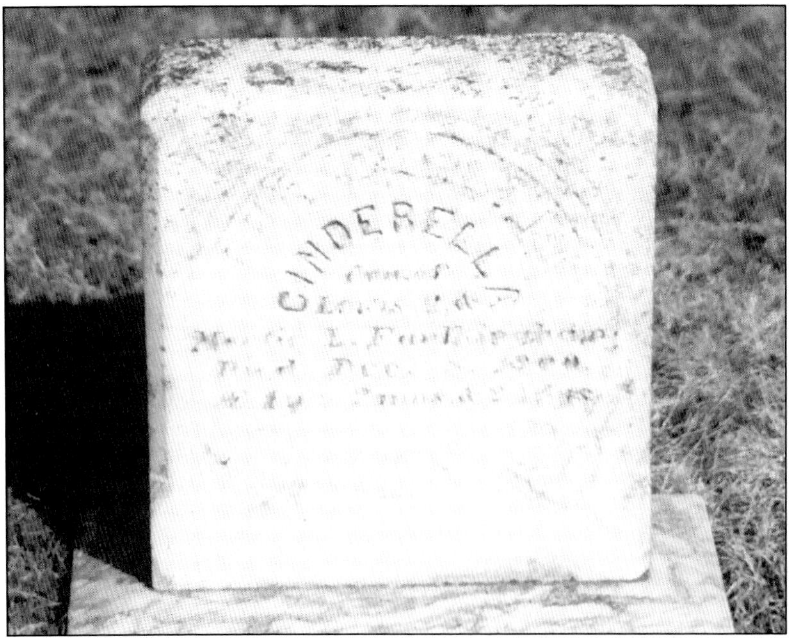

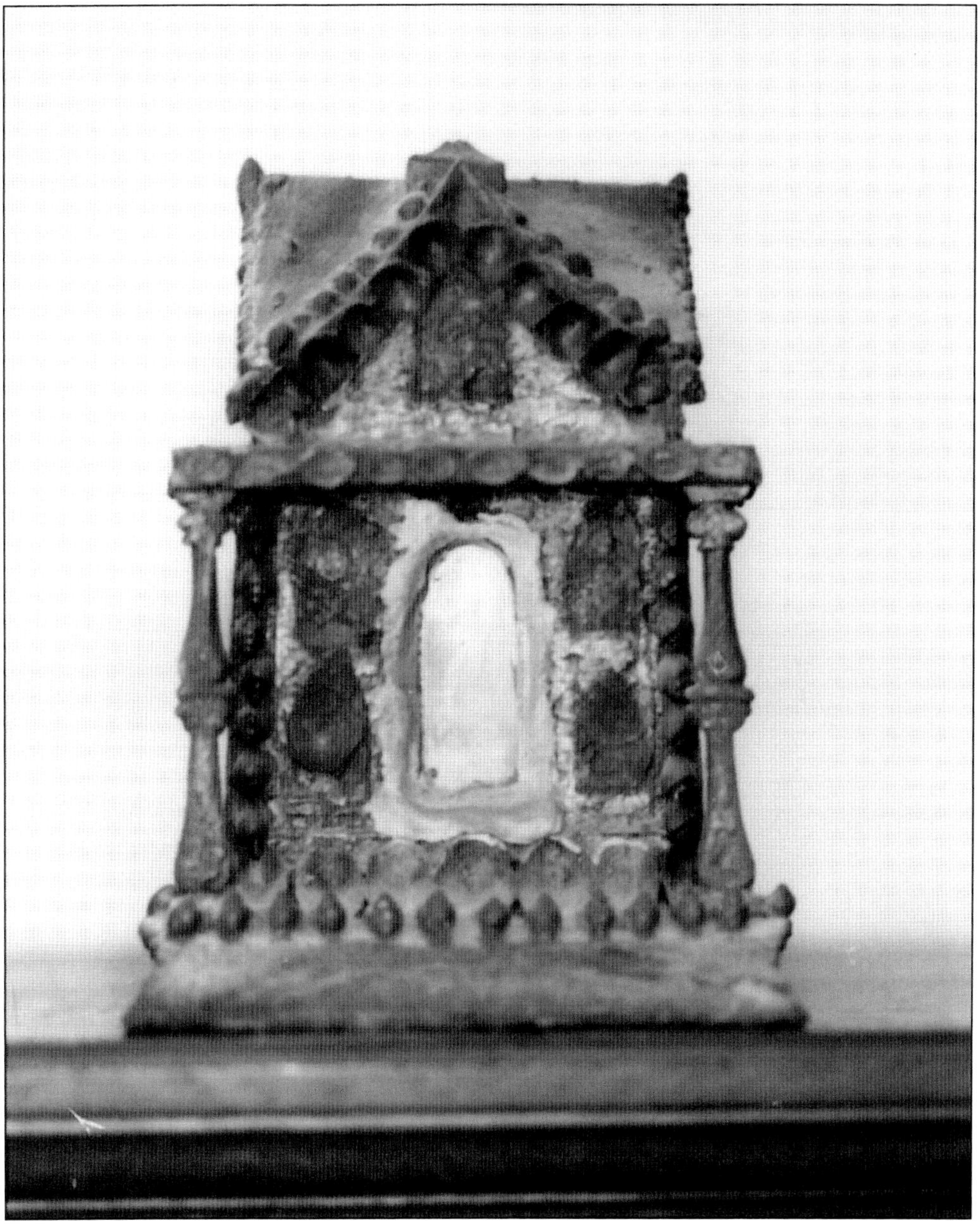

This miniature house stands about 10 inches tall. It's made out of wood and clay and is decorated with small seashells. Through the small glass door in the front of the house, people sit on tiny chairs along both sides of a long table. The people look out the glass as if they are watching you look at them. There are tiny shell dishes on the table and a lace tablecloth. The wallpaper on the walls has faded through the years, but you can still see the motto above the table. It reads "though today may not fulfill all thy hopes, have patience still; for perhaps tomorrow's sun sees thy happier days begun." This house was a wedding gift in 1855 from Charles Doyal of Fisherman Island to my great-great-great-grandmother, Phebe Ann (Stanwood), and great-great-great-grandfather, Barna Beal. It has been a prize possession that has been handed down from generation to generation.

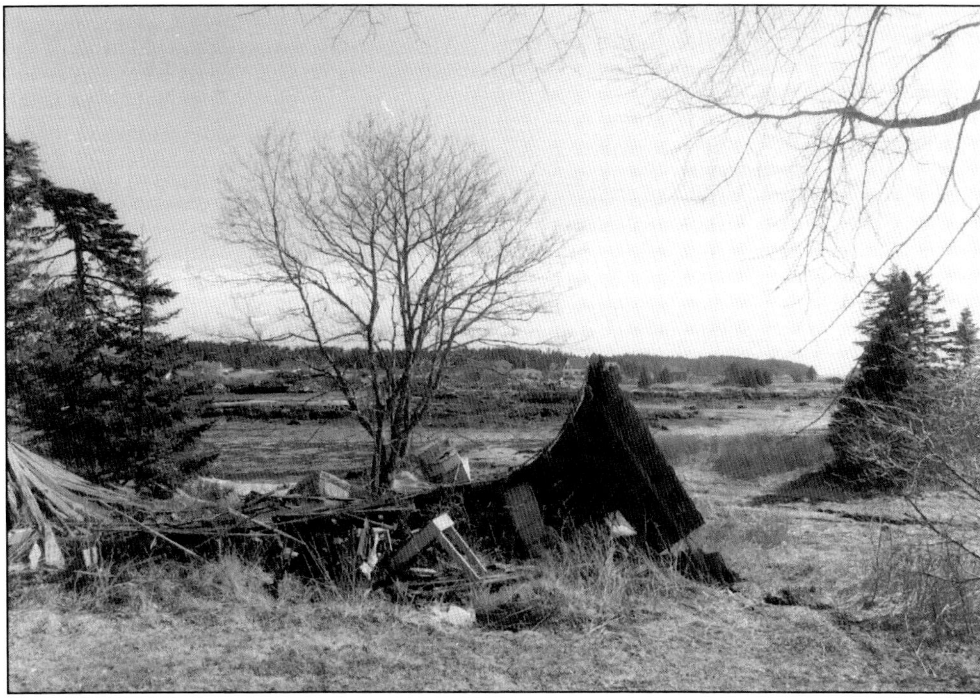

Barney's house is built on Mark Point; Barna and his eldest son, John, built the home *c.* 1875. This view from Barney's house shows the south side of Barney's Cove on Beals Island.

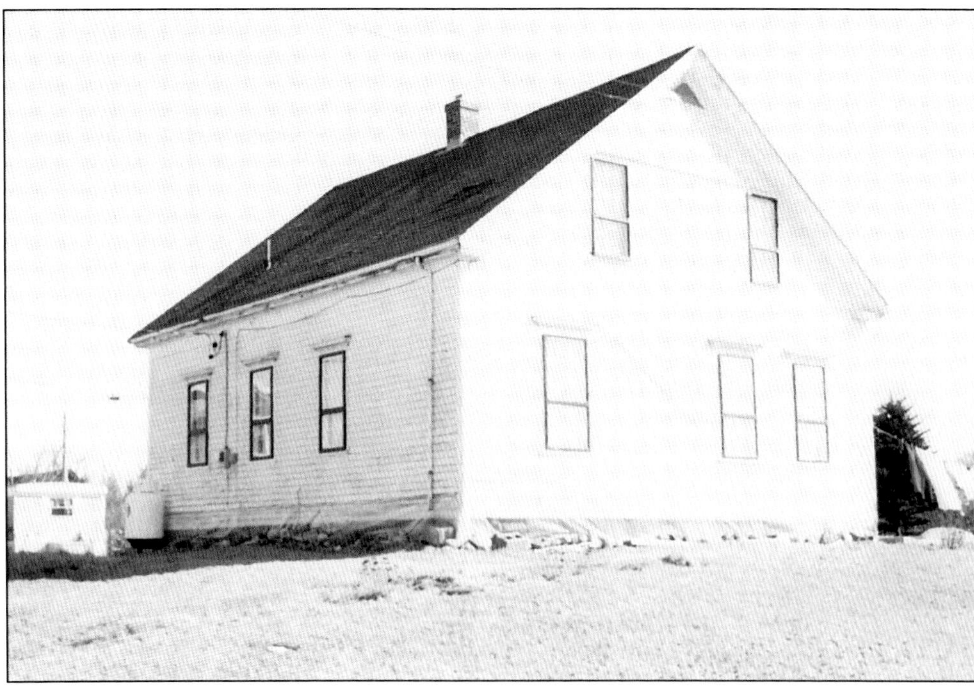

This house is one of the oldest homes on Great Wass Island. It is located on Boat Cove and looks across toward Jonesport.

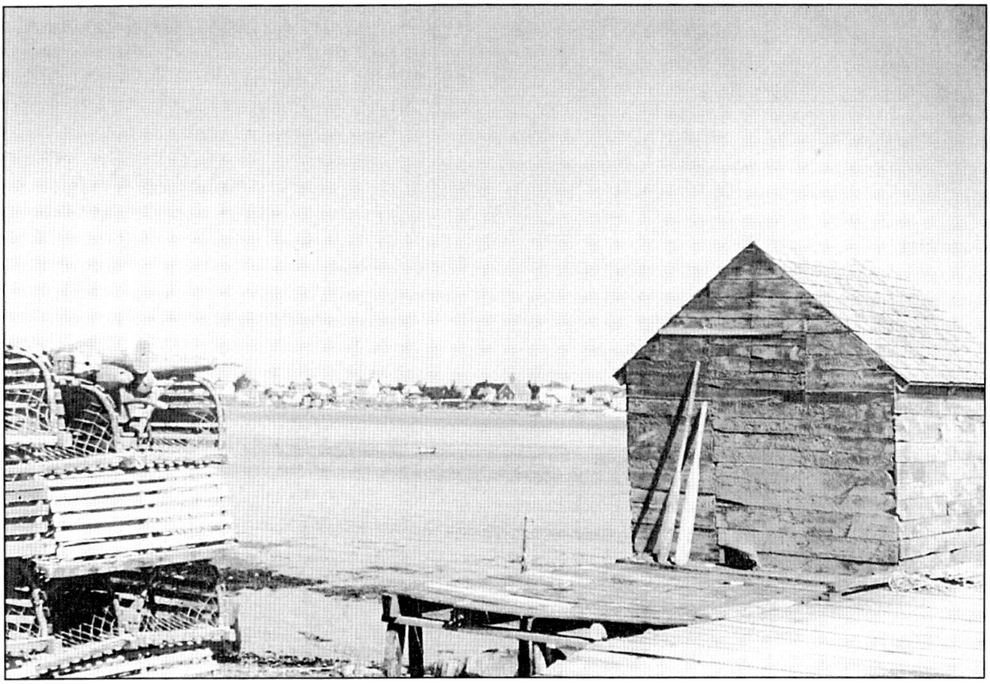

This wharf, located on Beals Island near Barney Point, looks across toward Jonesport. The picture was taken *c.* 1930.

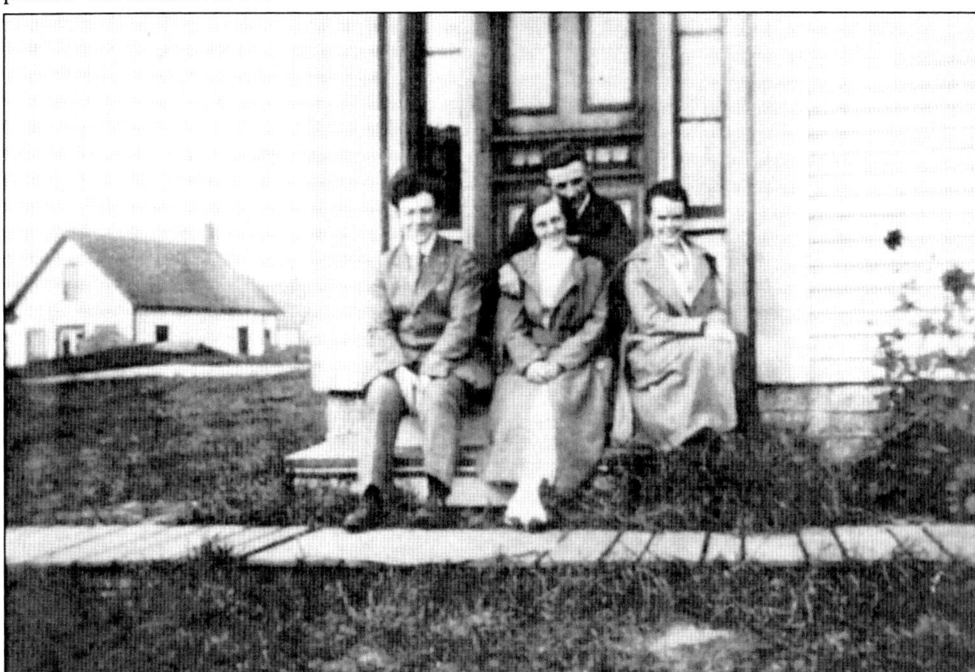

Sitting on the steps in front of their house on Beals Island, from left to right, are Avery Beal, Lillian ?, Authur Emerson (behind her), and Authur's sister Marjorie (Emerson) Beal (wife of Avery on the right).

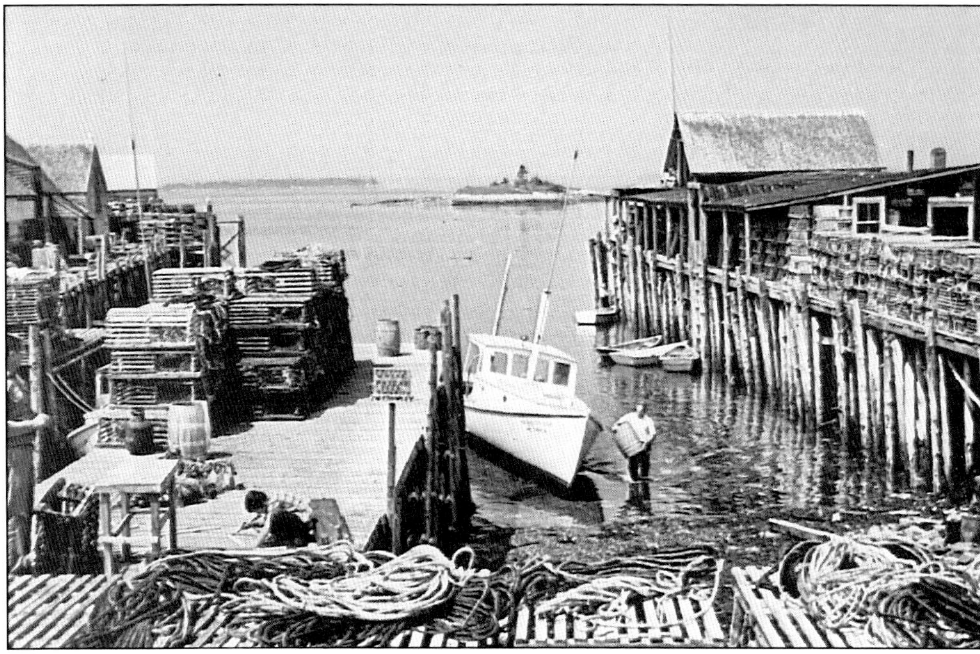

Beals Island is a cozy island surrounded by the sea. I find it no surprise that my grandparents chose to settle here. Looking out from Beals, a small island called Little Barneys Island is visible; in the far distance is Norton Island.

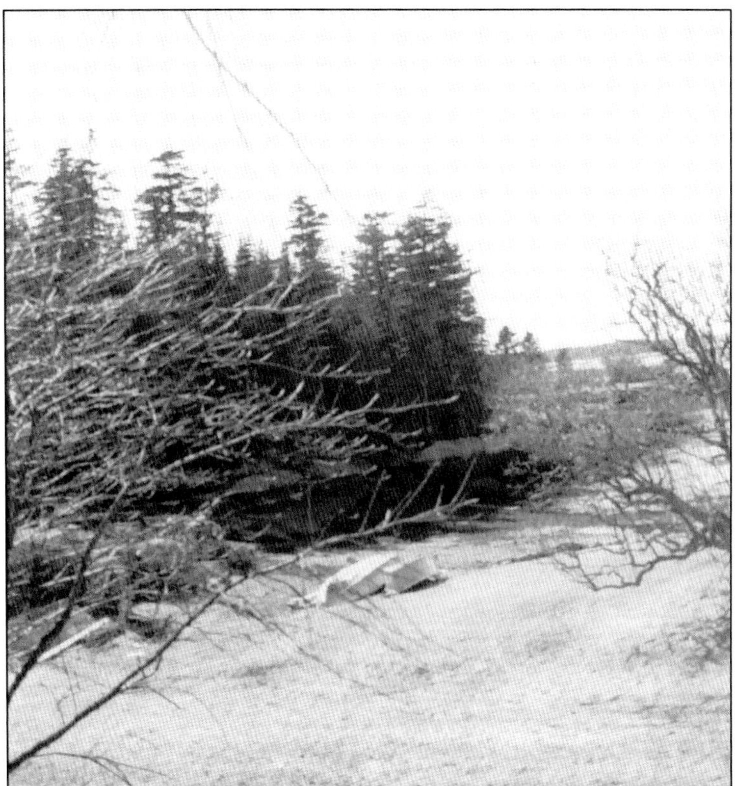

Mills Pond on Beals Island is a large cove that looks out toward Eastern Bay. This inland is not far from Manwarren Beals house, which was robbed during the Revolutionary War by English privateers. Manwarren was sick in bed when a vessel flying an American flag appeared in the harbor. The privateers entered his home, demanded money, and took or destroyed all the family's possessions.

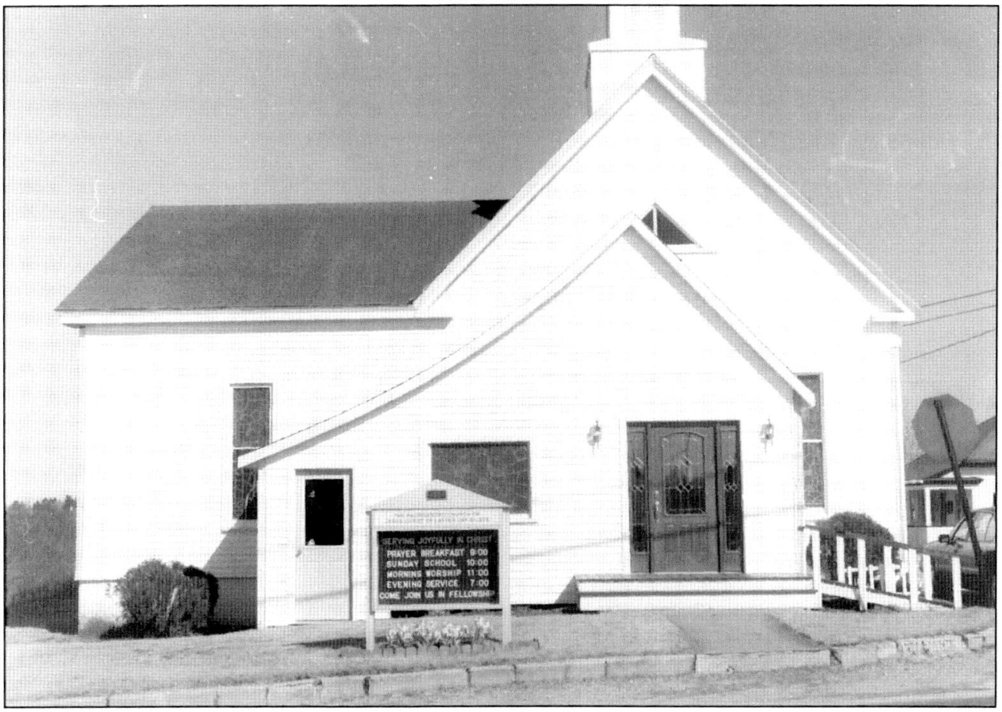

Christmas was always a happy time, especially for children on Beals Island around the turn of the 20th century. There were three churches on the island and all three had large Christmas trees that reached the ceilings. Parents and friends carried their gifts to the church in large boxes or baskets. No one wrapped their gifts; instead, they were labeled with the name of the person for whom they were intended. The presents were hung on the branches of the tree from top to bottom. The tree looked pretty decorated with dolls, mittens, ribbons, and other gifts.

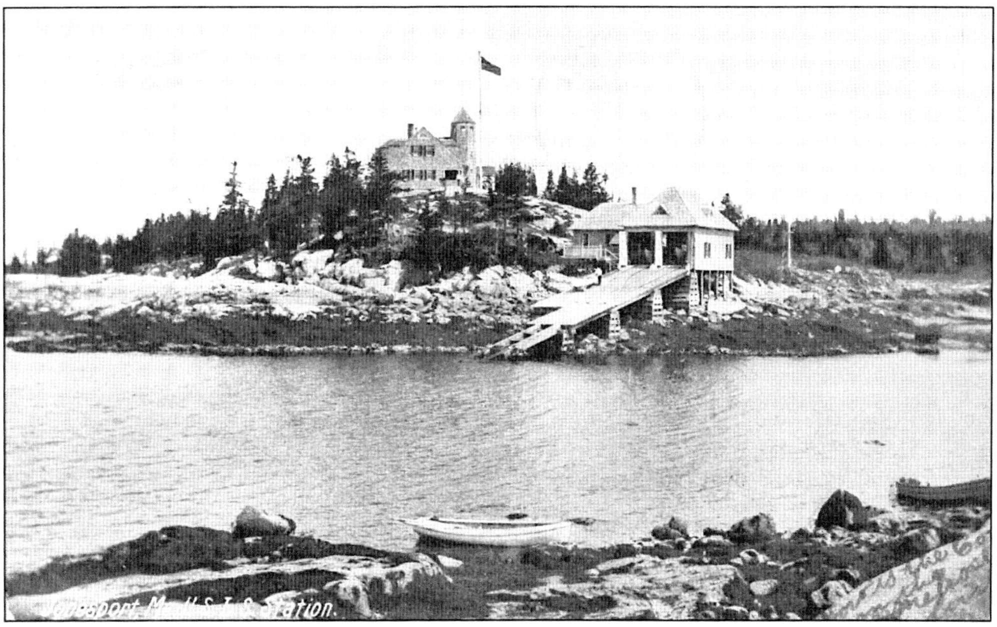

This is a view of Coast Guard station on Beals Island in 1907.

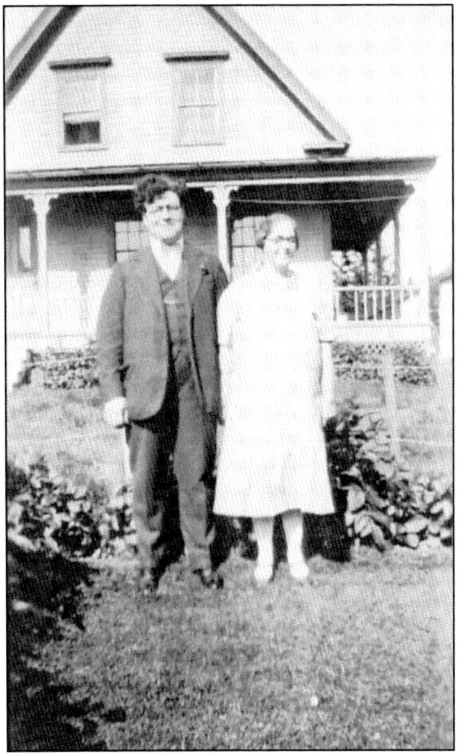

Avery and Marjorie Beal pose in front of their home on Beals Island in the summer of 1927.

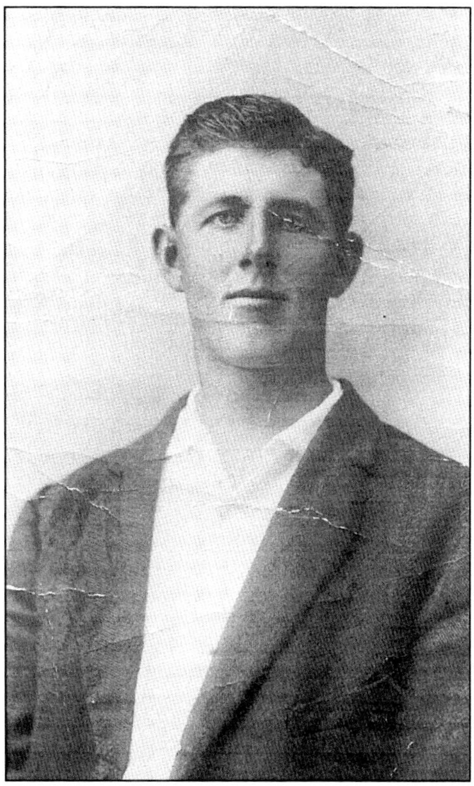

William Riley Beal was born on Beals Island in 1890. This picture of him was taken c. 1920. Riley was a boat builder by trade. At the age of 83, he was still an active member of the community building lobster boats.

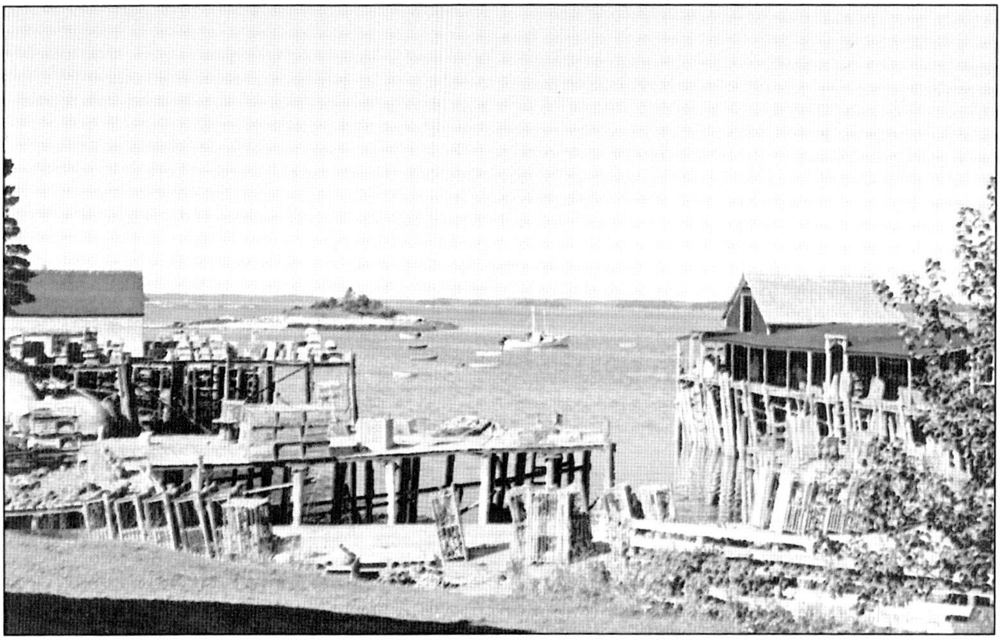

Beals Island is a cozy island surrounded by the sea. You're lulled to rest each evening by the waves hitting the shore. All the sounds are a bit like heaven, so peaceful and serene. I find it no surprise that my grandparents chose to settle here. It's such a peaceful place and the people that live on the island are friendly and courteous.

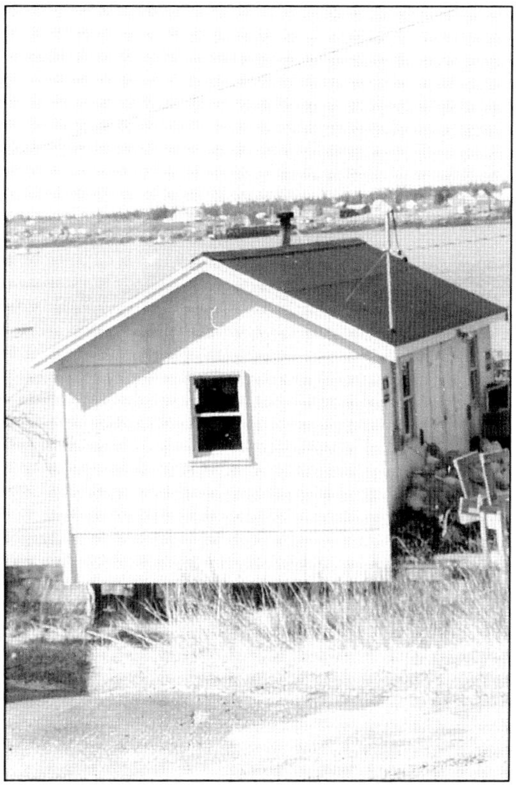

Barney Cove on Beals Island is located on the south side of the island looking across to the mainland of Jonesport. This is one of the many boathouses on the island. In the summer, you can see fish drying on lines as you drive past this area.

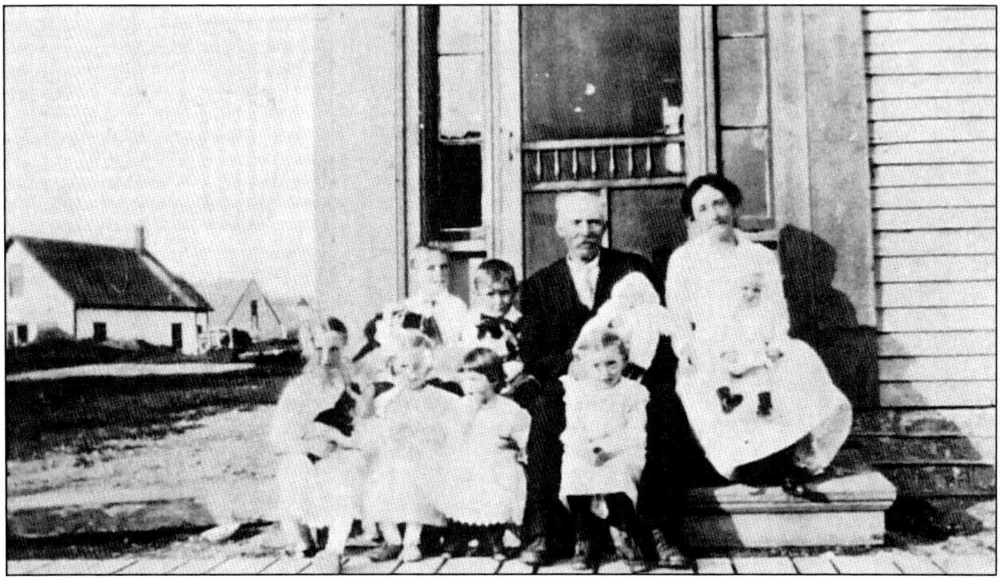

The family sits on the steps of Avery and Marjorie Beal's home on Beals Island in the summer of 1912. Seen here, from left to right, are as follows: (front row) Gertrude, Cora, Agnes, and Ella Drisko; (back row) Donald Drisko, Darrell Emerson, C.P. Emerson (holding Lucy Beal), and his wife, Cora Emerson (holding Tulia Drisko).

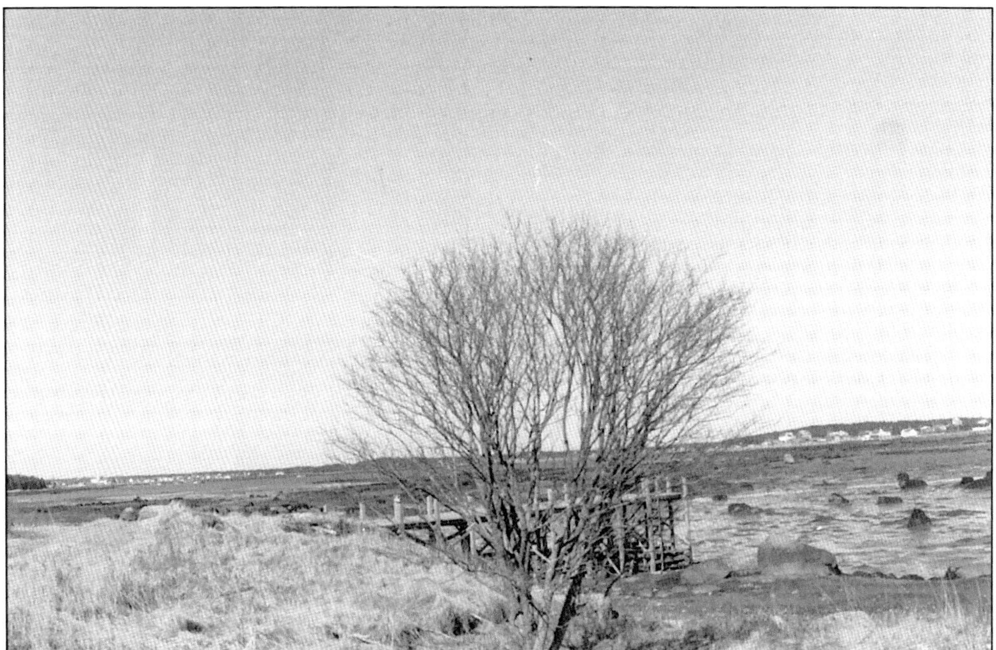

This wharf is at Flying Place Cove on Beals Island. The tide recedes and empties the whole bay. When the tide is out, you can see people clamming on the beach.

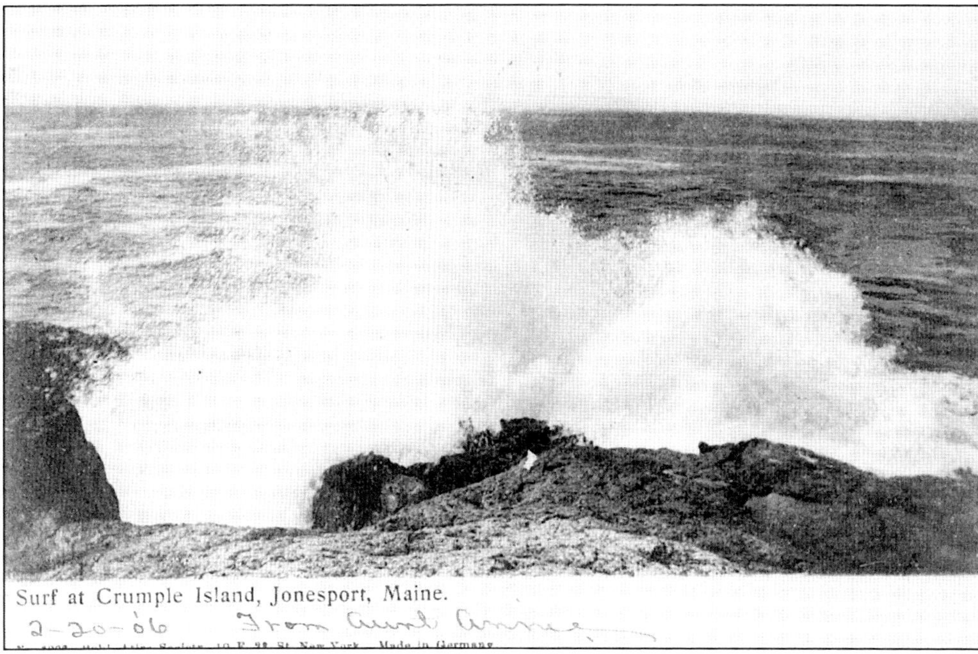

Crumple Island, located to the west of Pond Point off Great Wass Island and east of Fisherman Island in Western Bay, looks out to the Gulf of Maine. It's one of the outer islands of Jonesport. The surf pounding on the rocks is an everyday occurrence; no outer islands protect the island from the sea in this 1905 picture.

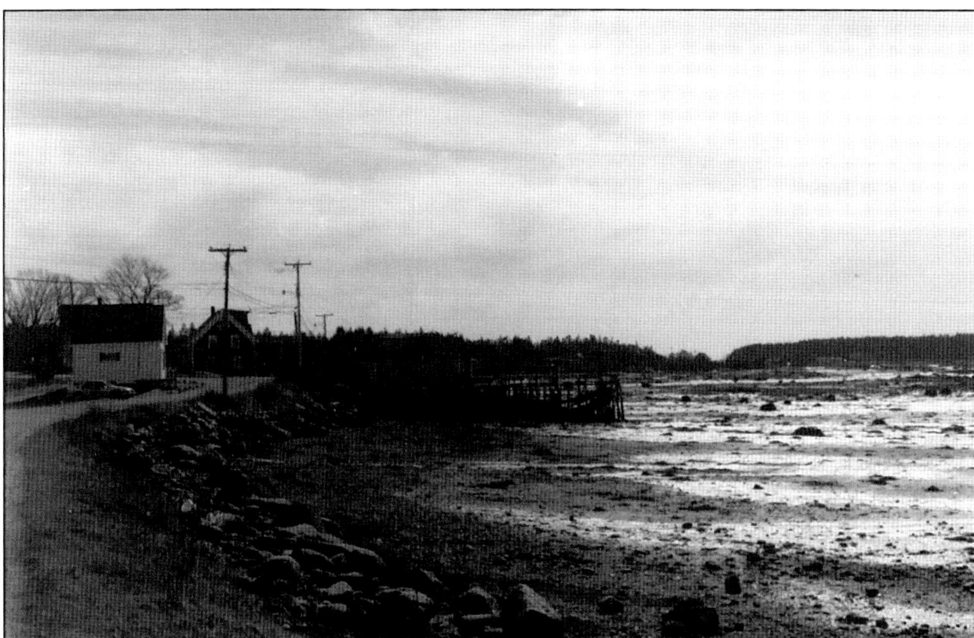

I don't know where Boat Cove on Great Wass Island got its name, but up until in the 1980s, there were several abandoned boats sitting up on the beach. It's kind of sad when you go there and don't see them anymore. It was a boat graveyard, as I called it; whenever we visited, that's one of the first places that we would explore.

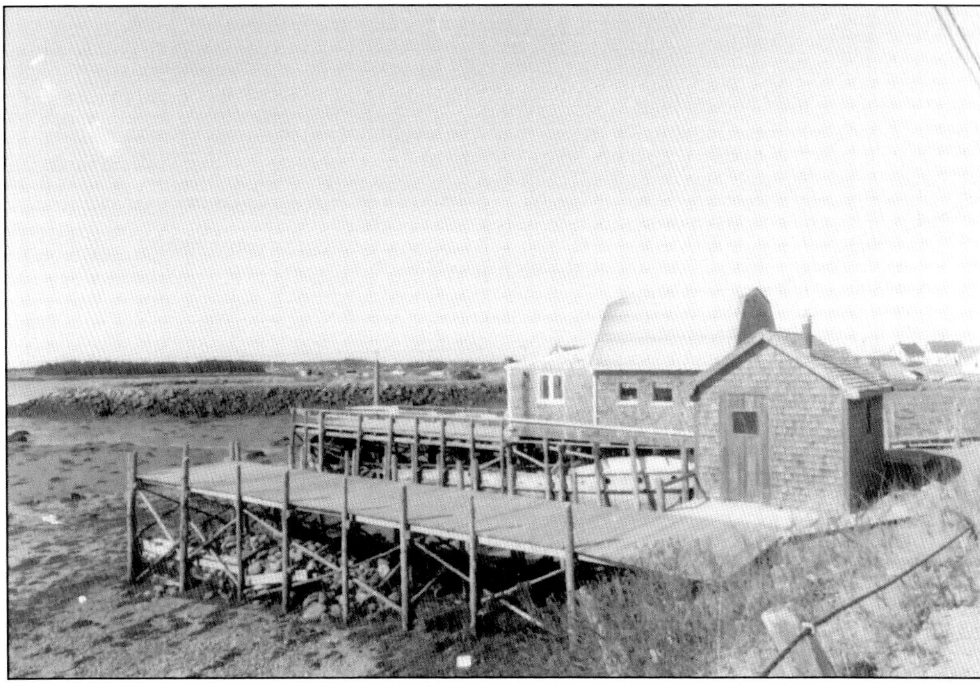

This cottage is built on top of a boat at Boat Cove on Great Wass Island. What a beautiful place to spend your time relaxing and looking out to sea. The boathouse looks across to Henry Point in Jonesport, Maine.

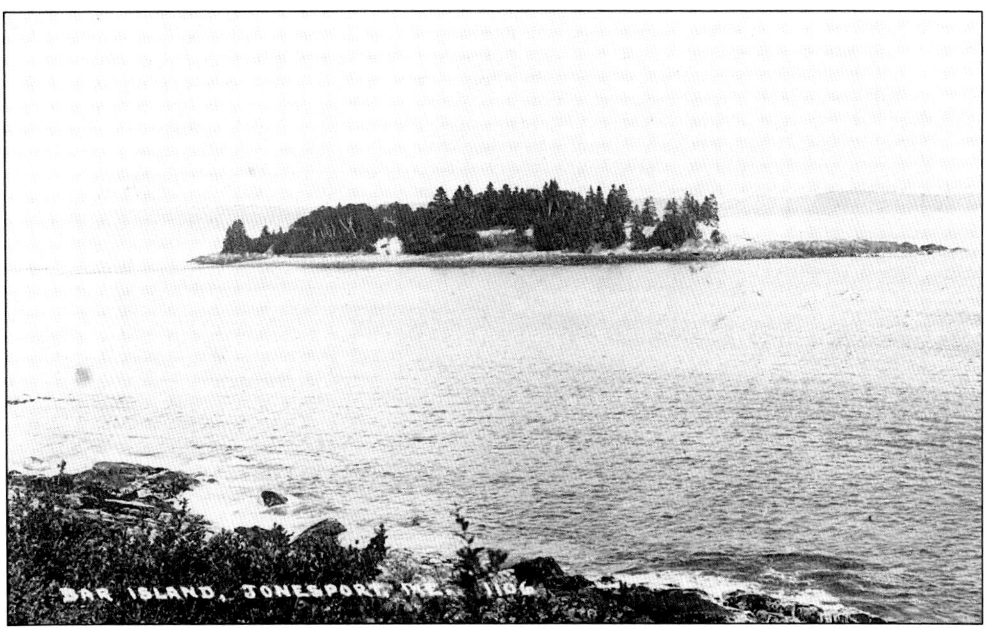

Bar Island was once called Hen Island. It is located off the coast of Jonesport at Wash Out Point, between Popplestone Beach and Sandy River Beach.

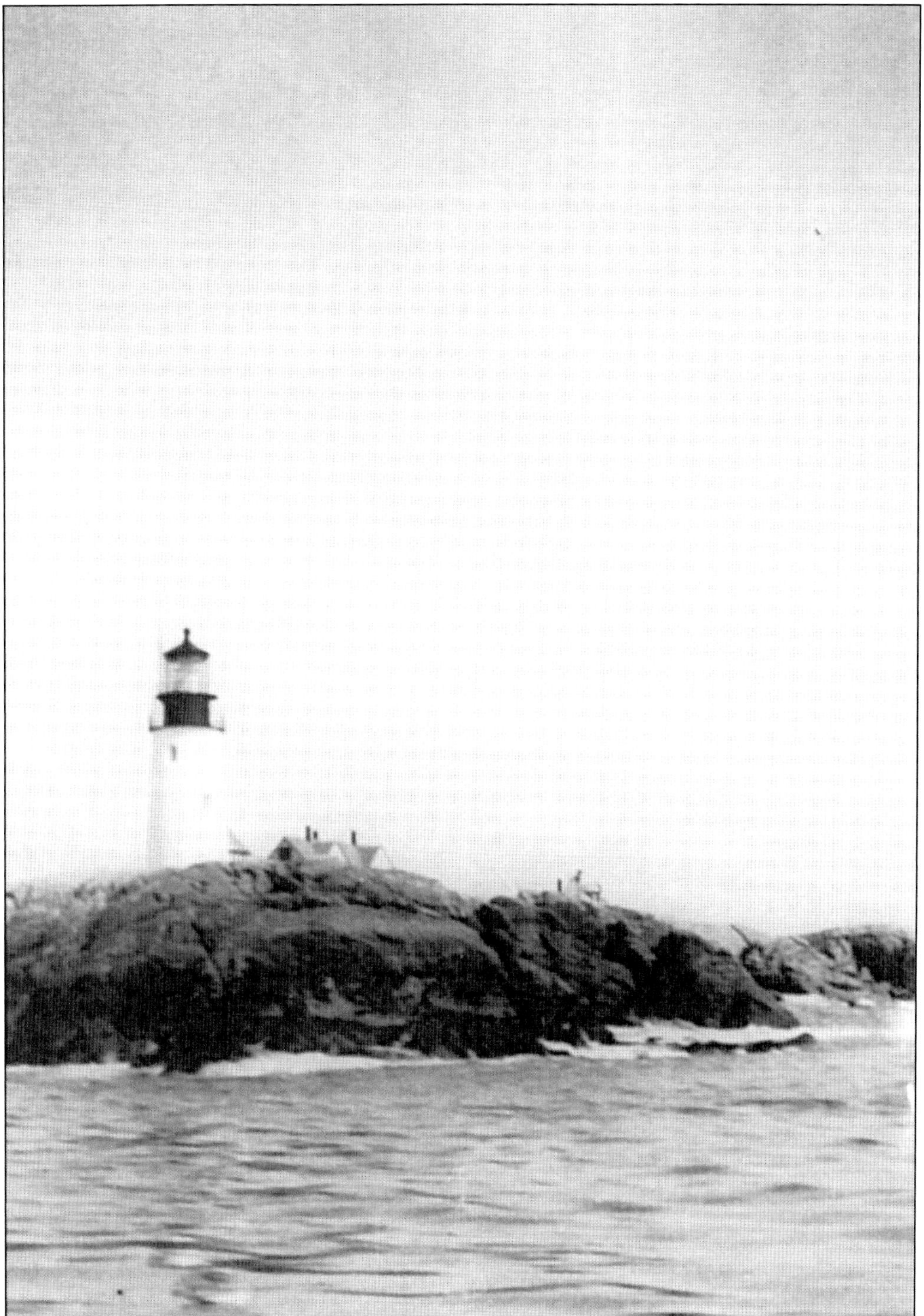

In 1826, 4 acres of land on Mistake Island off the coast of Jonesport in Moosabec Reach was dedicated to the Moosabec Light House. The first lighthouse stood for 74 years and was replaced, in 1903, by a structure that is a landmark today.

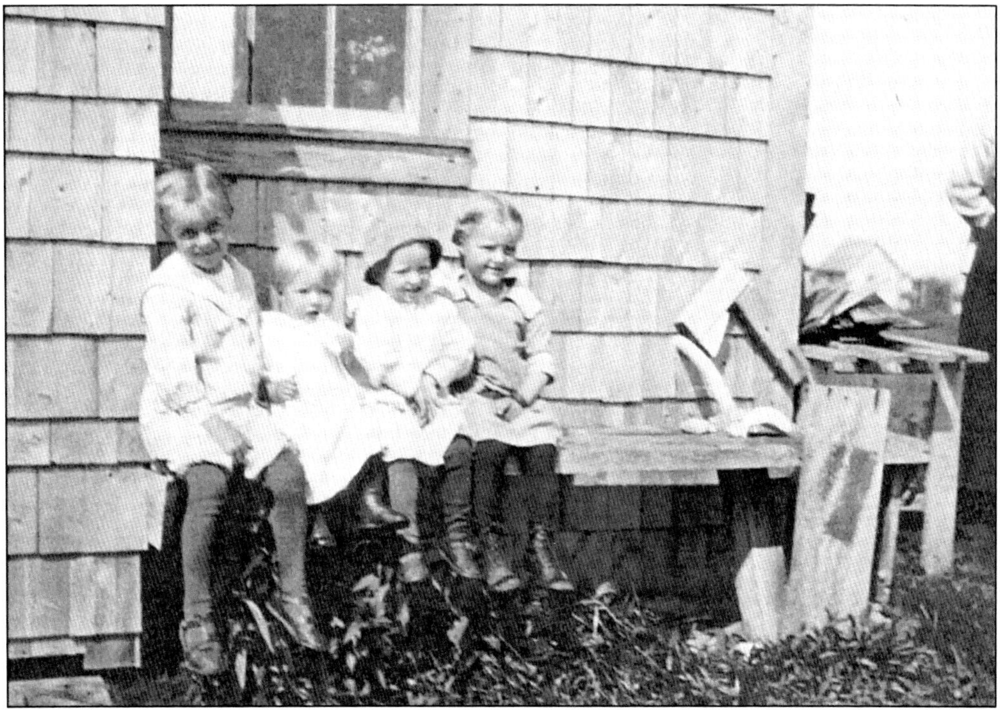

The Drisko children, Donald, Cora, Ella, and Gertrude, can be seen here at their fishing camp on Crumple Island off the coast of Jonesport in the summer of 1916.

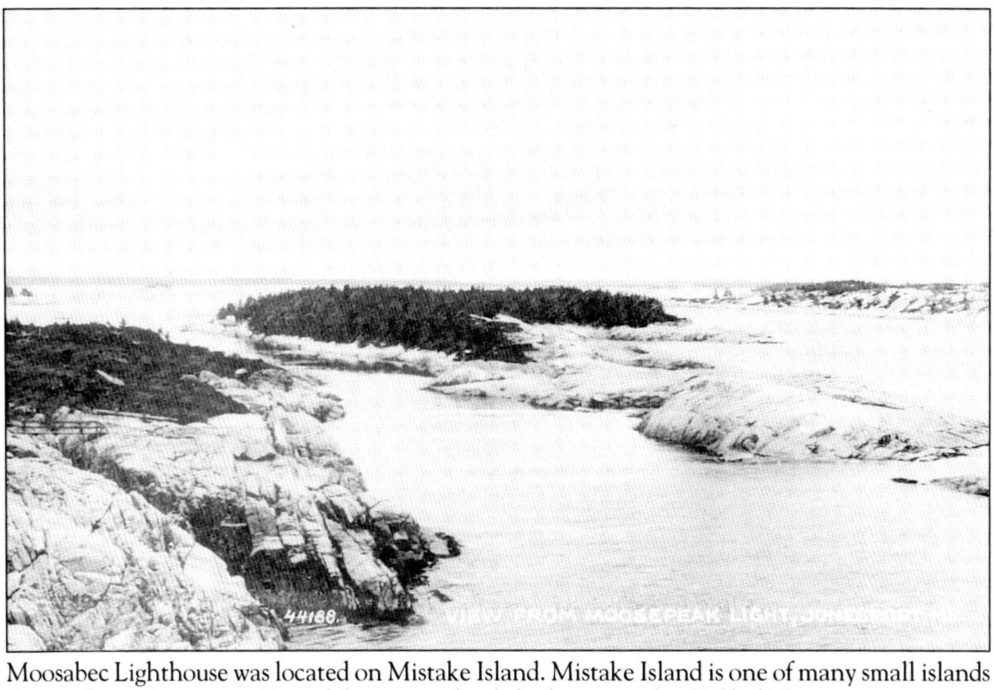

Moosabec Lighthouse was located on Mistake Island. Mistake Island is one of many small islands that make up Jonesport. One of the outer islands looks out to the Gulf of Maine.

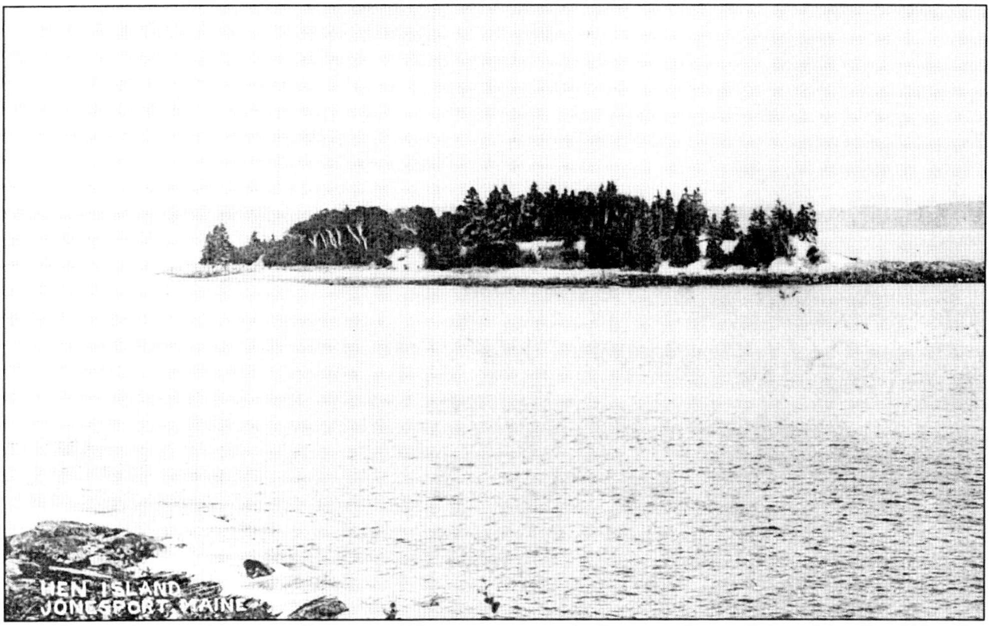

Hen Island is off the coast of Jonesport, Maine, at Wash Out Point. It always has a cool ocean breeze, even when the temperatures reach a 100° in Bangor.

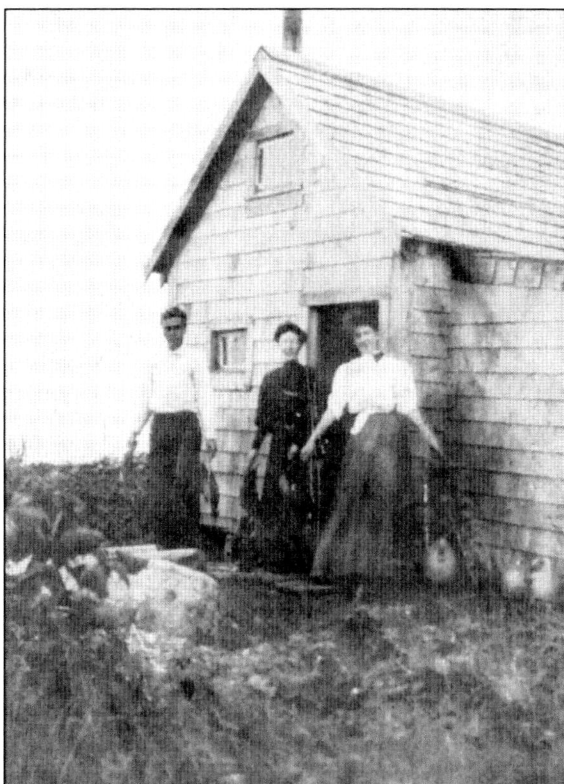

Standing in front of their camp on Fisherman Island in 1907 are Merton Drisko (left), Helen Leighton (center), and Genera Smith.

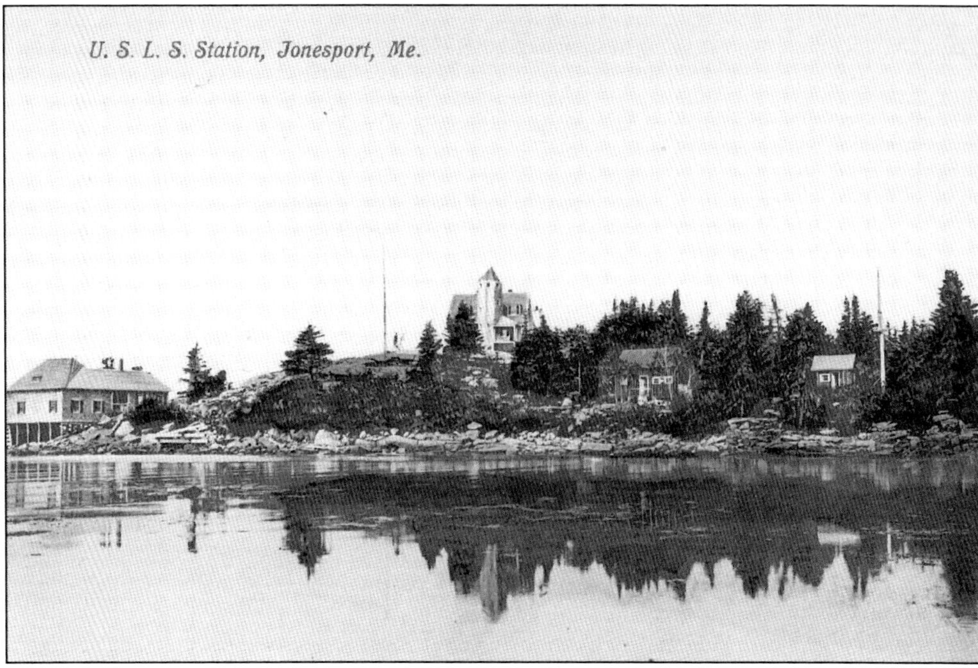

The Coast Guard station on Great Wass Island reported 180 days of fog one year.

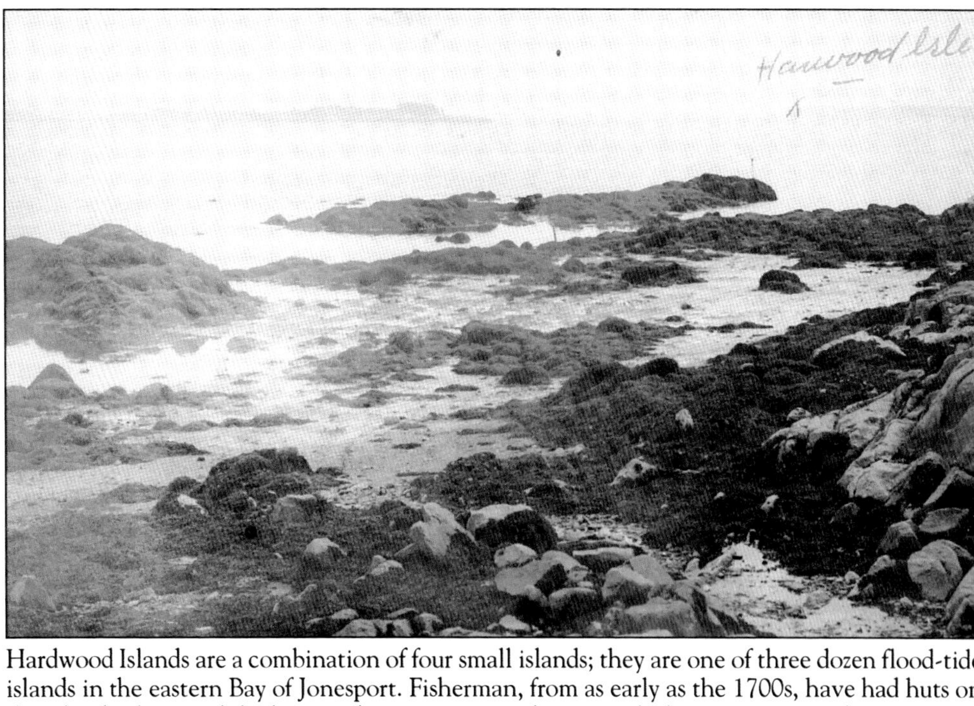

Hardwood Islands are a combination of four small islands; they are one of three dozen flood-tide islands in the eastern Bay of Jonesport. Fisherman, from as early as the 1700s, have had huts on the islands; they used the huts in the summer months to watch their weirs, store their gear, and dry their nets.

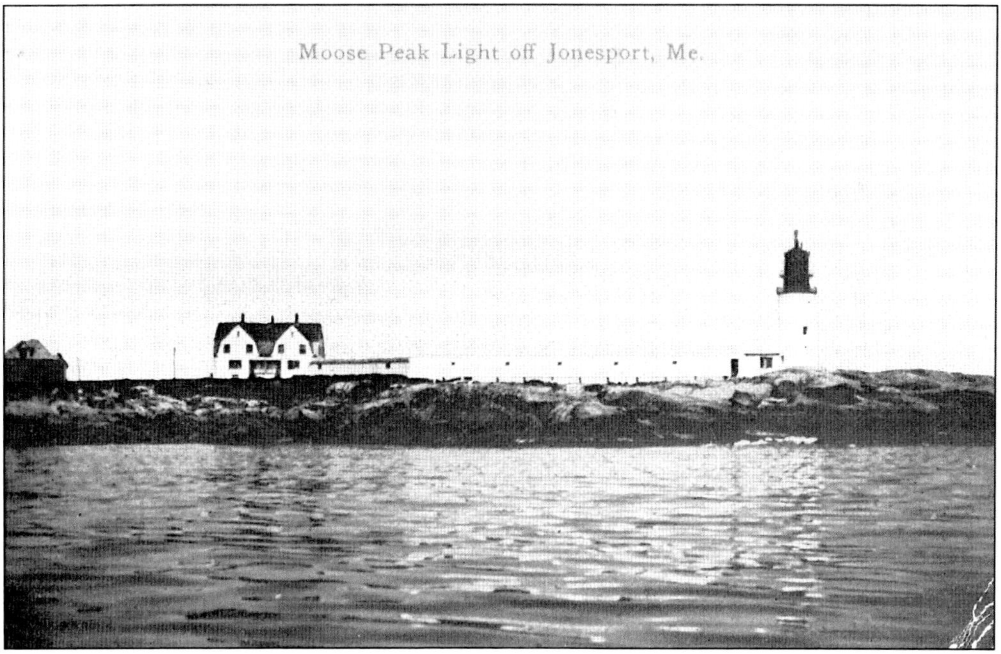

Moose Peck Light, shown here in 1913, was erected in 1826 on Mistake Island and is operated by the Coast Guard. The lighthouse is 72 feet above sea level.

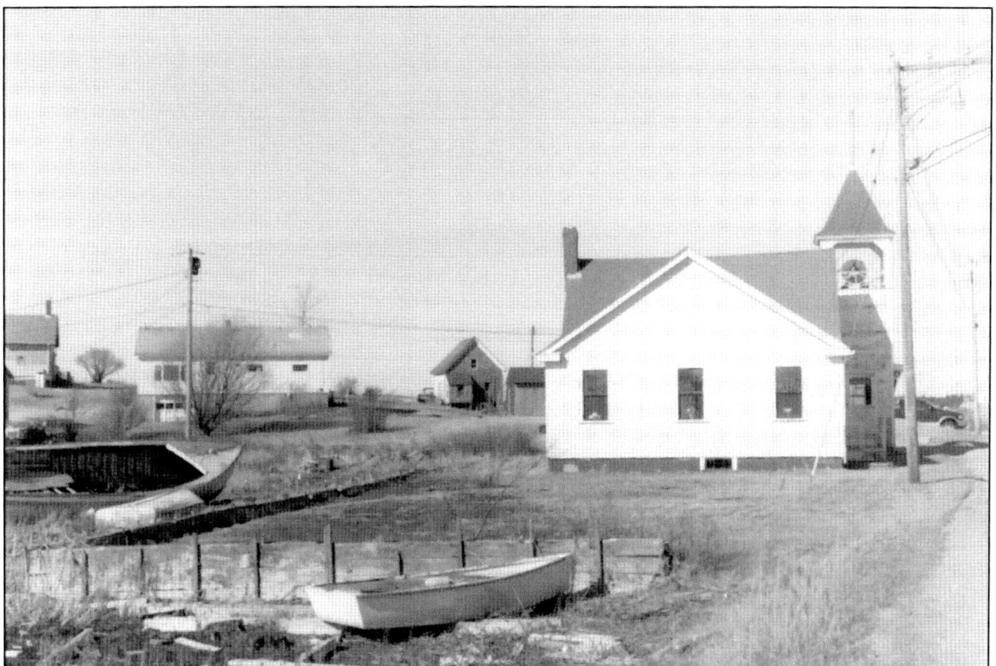

The Advent Christian Church at Boat Cove on Great Wass Island overlooks the ocean, looking toward Jonesport.

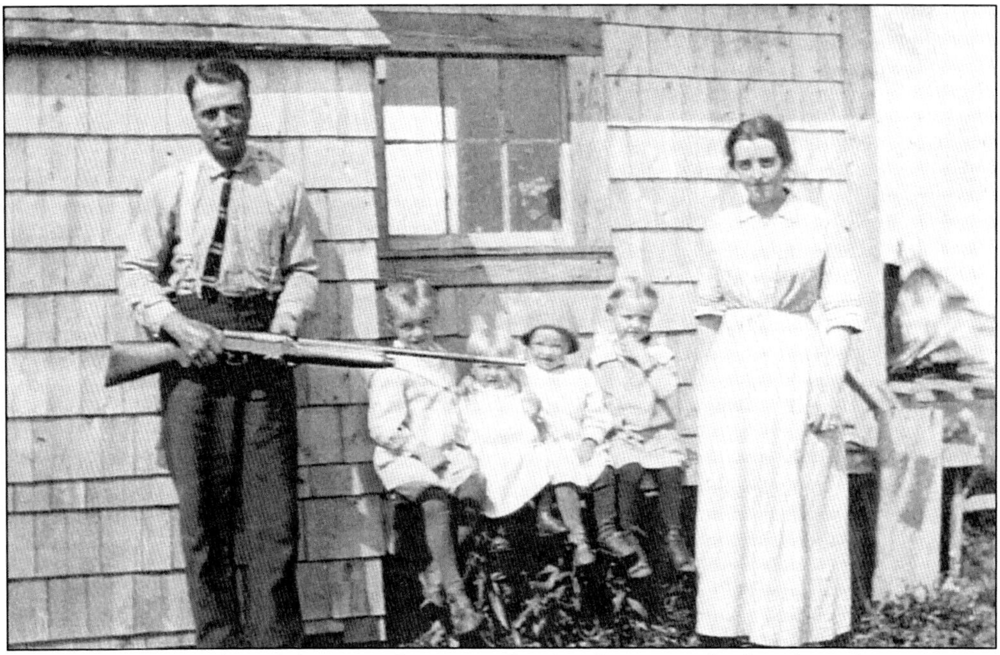

Merton Drisko stands with his new shotgun as his family sits on the bench at their camp on Crumple Island off Jonesport.

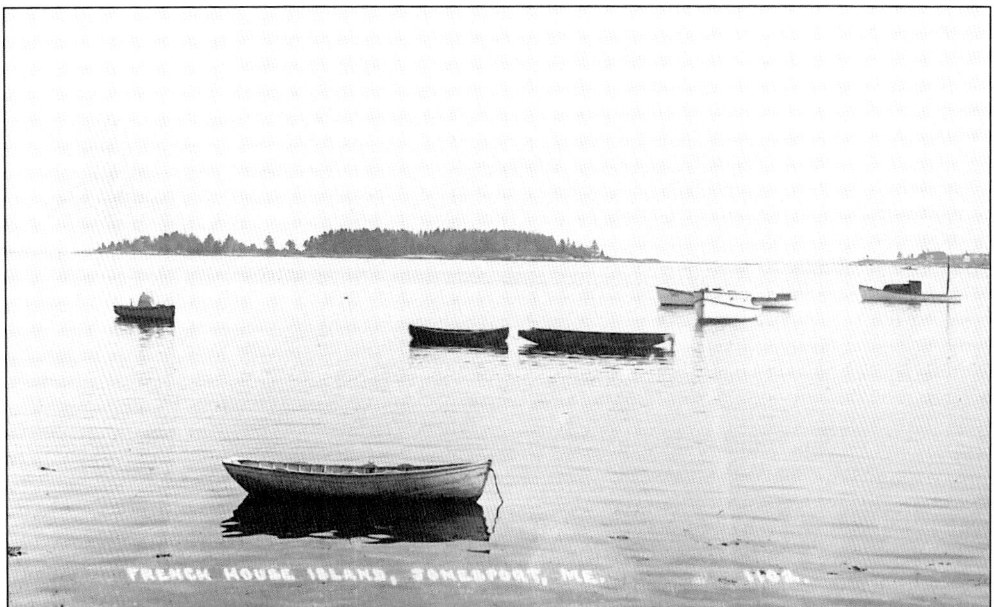

French House Island was named before the Revolution by Manwarren Beal. In the late 1800s, there was a schoolhouse on the island with five pupils. A weiring operation was also on the island along with wharves and drying sheds.

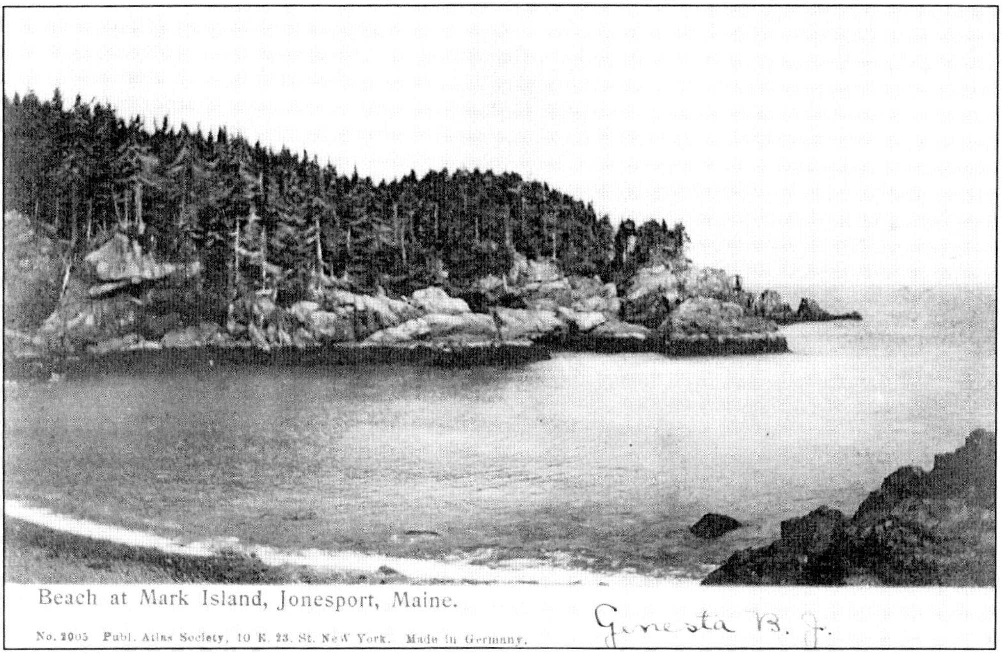

This view of Mark Island, Jonesport, was taken in 1906. Tale has it that Captain Kidd buried treasure on Mark Island.

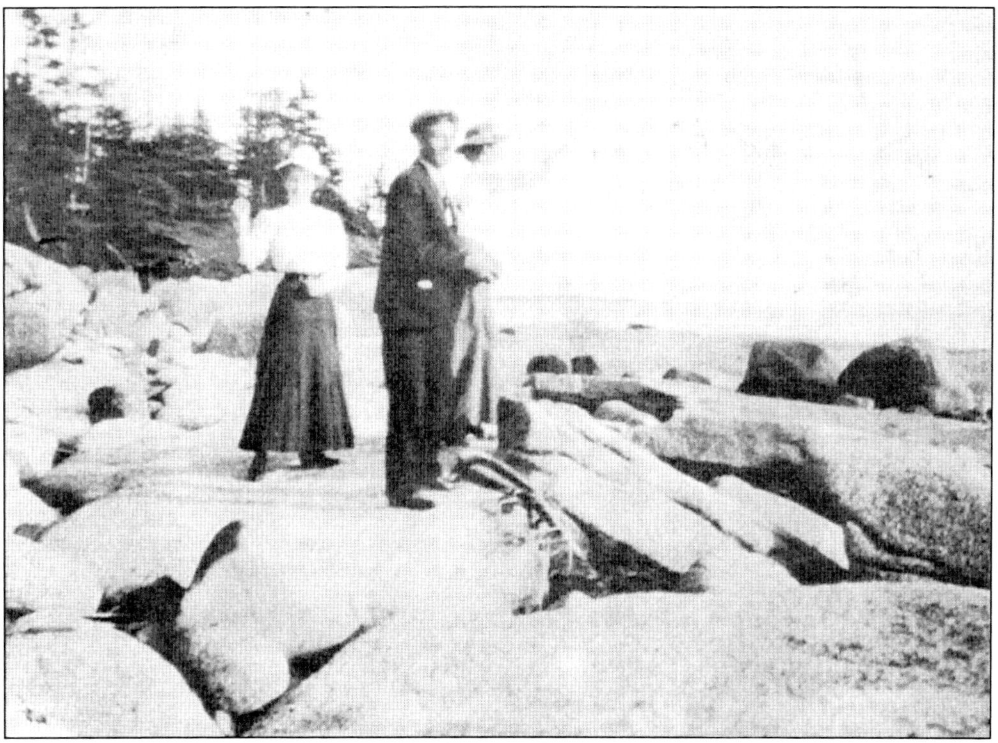

In this picture Merton Drisko, Helen Leighton, and Genera Smith stand on the rocky shore of Fisherman Island in 1907.

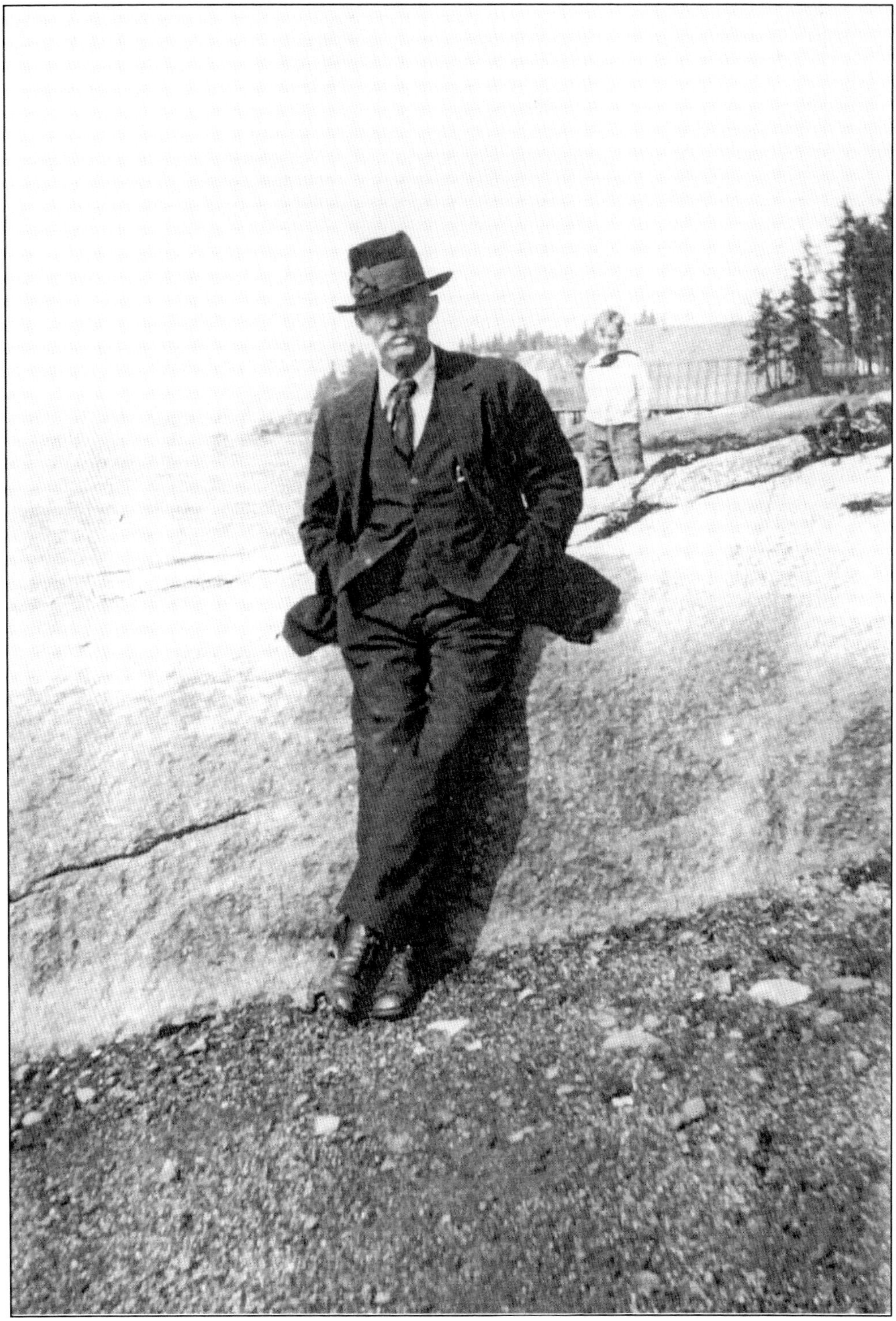

C.F. Emerson stands on Beals Island all dressed up and ready for church; the little boy in the background remains unidentified.

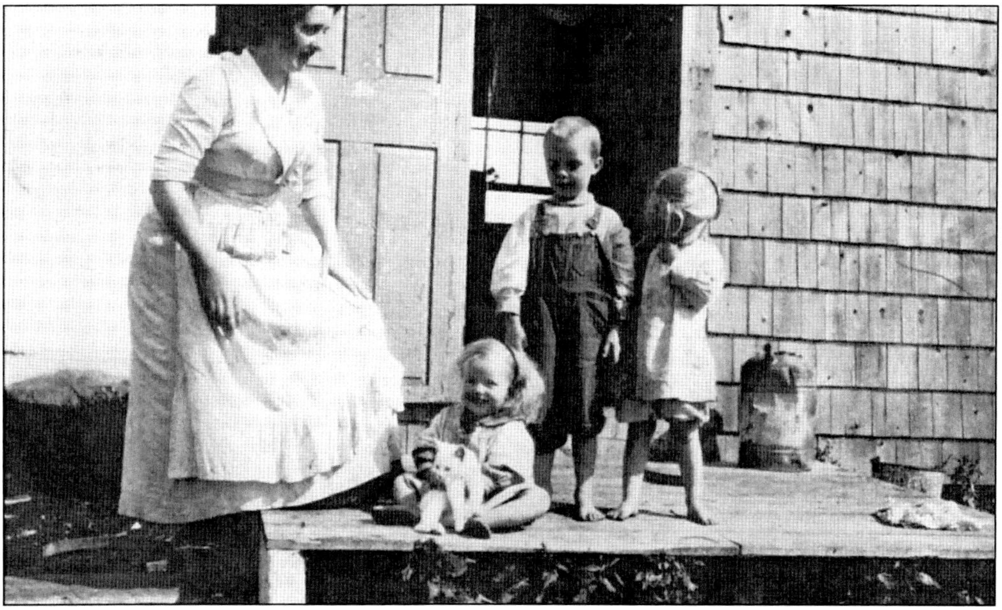

Addie Drisco and her children, Ella, Donald, and Gertrude, pose for a picture at their camp on Crumple Island in 1913.

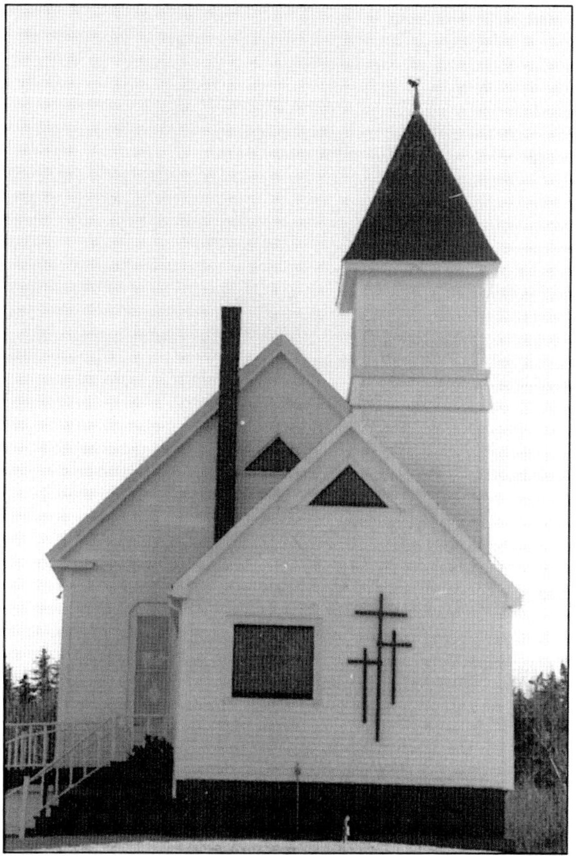

There were three churches on Beals Island around the turn of the 20th century. Christmas was a special time for the children, and they would march up and down the aisles singing songs while the organist played music and the choir sang. A lot of children would recite poems. The girls wore white dresses and bright ribbons in their hair.

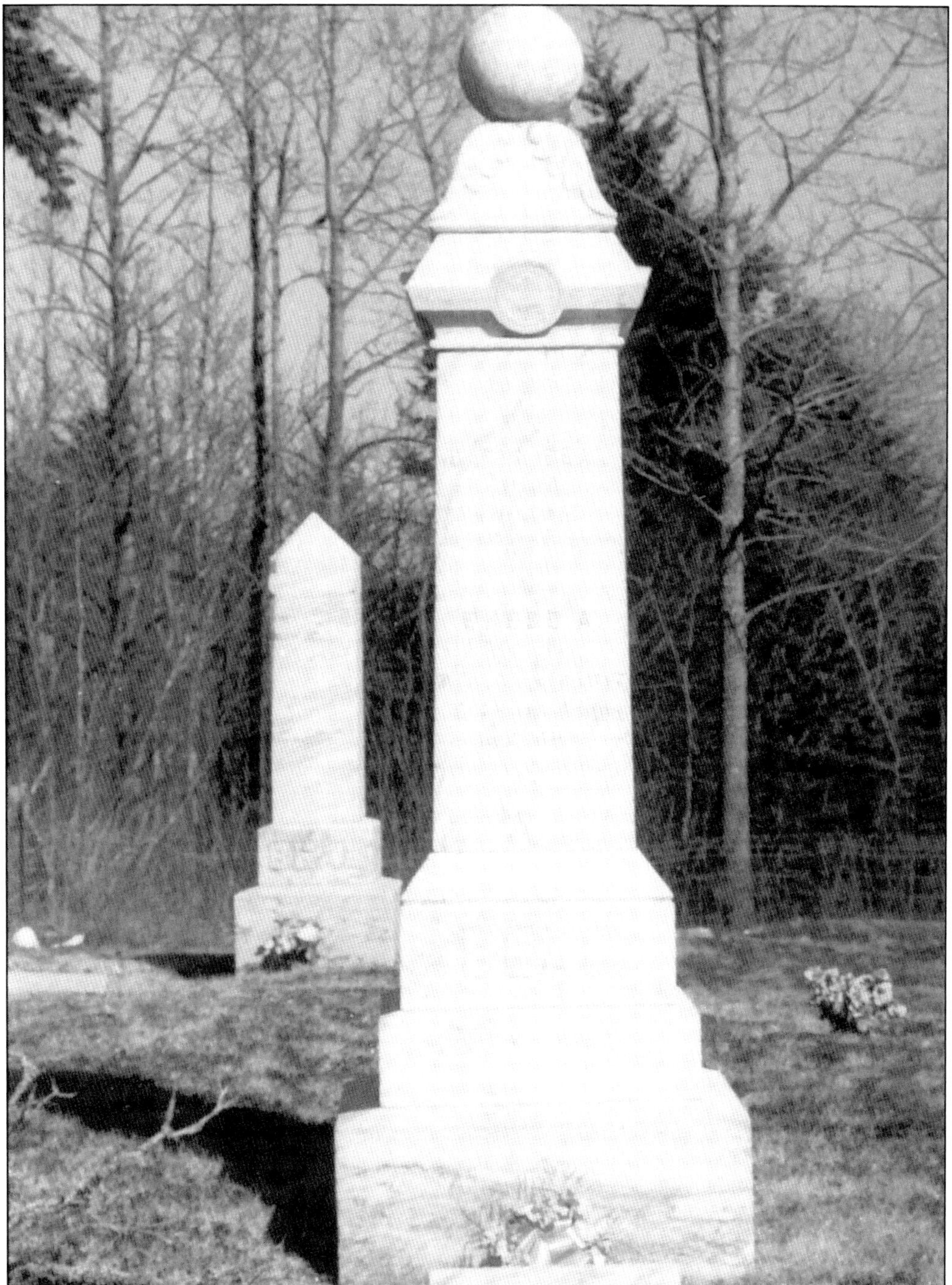

Barna Beal, my great-great-great-grandfather, was born on Beals Island on December 13, 1835, and died on February 1, 1899. He was a "Downeast" hero that I think everyone should know a little about. I heard stories about him from the time I was a little girl. Tall, strong, and gentle, he carried dories on his back and killed a horse once with a punch. Barney and his wife had 11 children. Many islanders are descendents of his children.

Two

Jonesport's Main Street over the Years

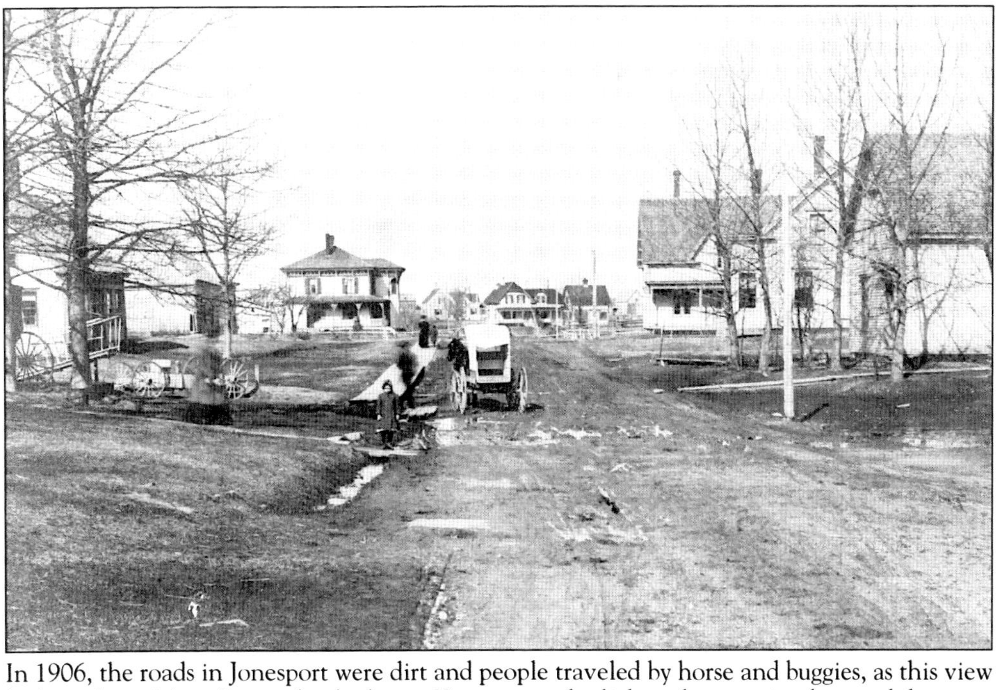

In 1906, the roads in Jonesport were dirt and people traveled by horse and buggies, as this view looking down Main Street clearly shows. You can see the light poles were in place and the town was in the process of having the wires run.

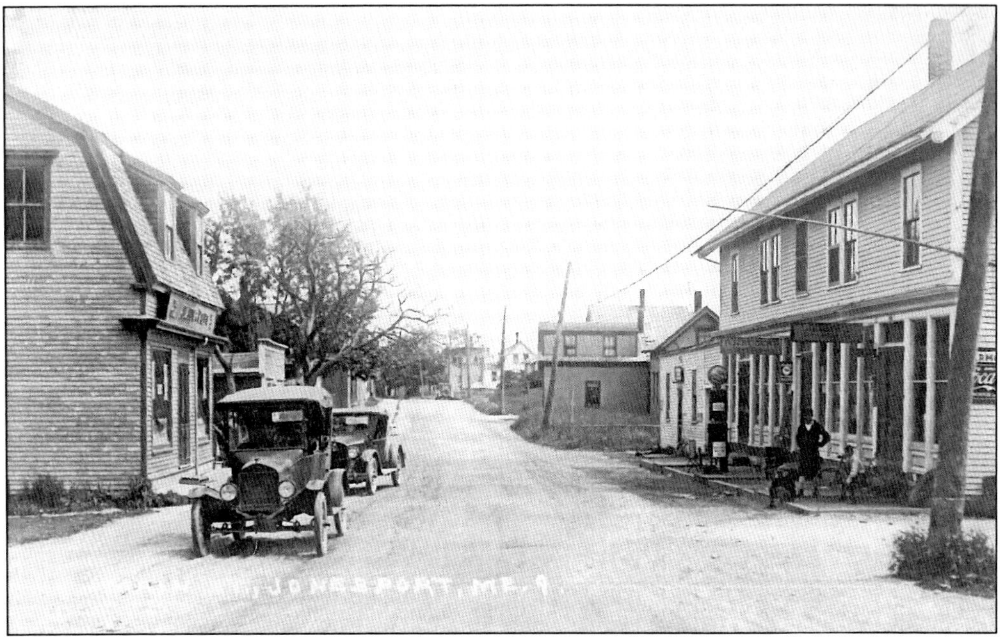

This view of Main Street in 1914 shows the small town charm and atmosphere of Jonesport. The wooden sidewalks and dirt roads created many a dusty traveler.

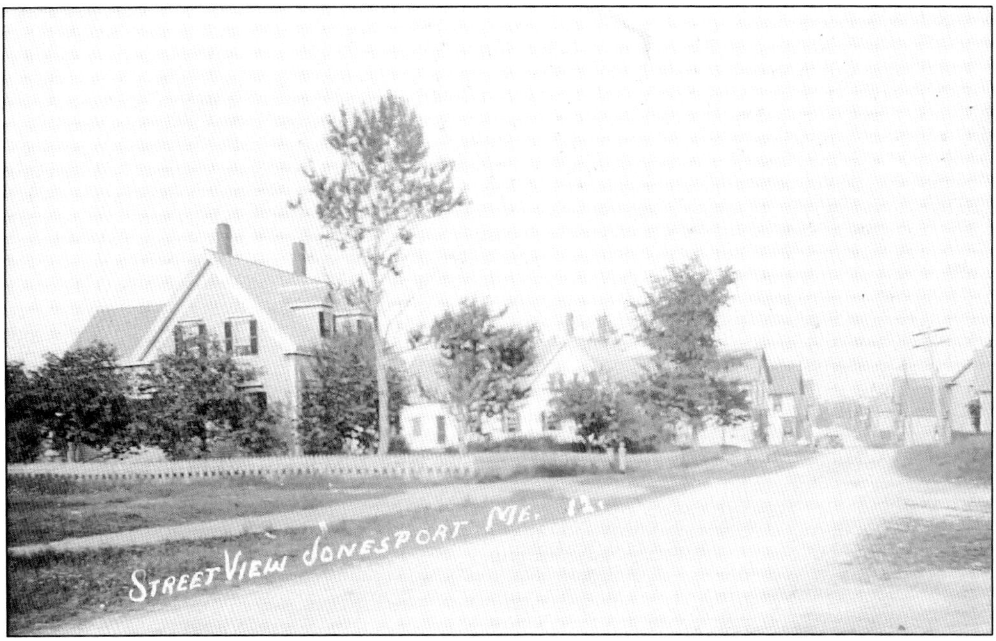

Mrs. C.V. Woodside's ladies' finishing parlor was located on Main Street midway to the business section. She carried stylish headwear, lace, veils, fancy gloves, and other novelties. This picture was taken in 1913.

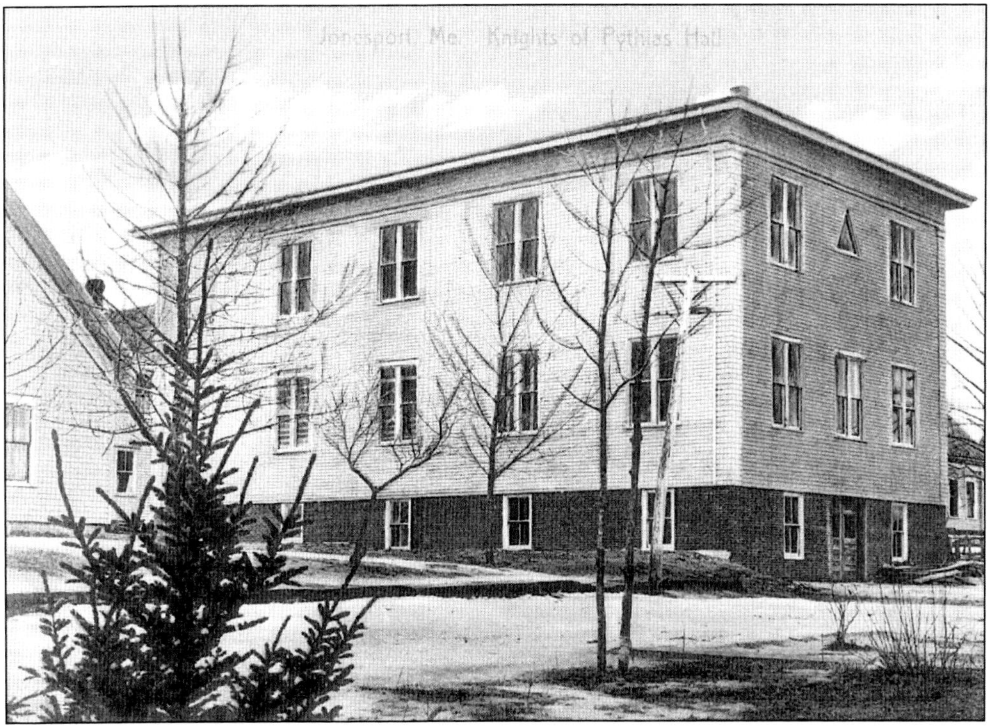

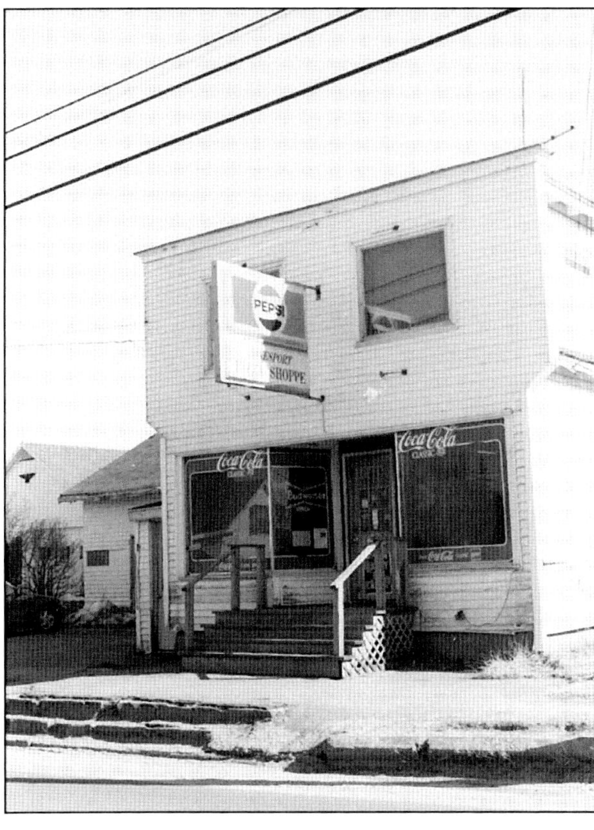

The Knights of Pyhias Hall, located on Main Street, is shown above in 1910. The interior of the building was a beautiful place. After the hall was destroyed by fire, Harmon's Drug was opened on the site. Jonesport Pizza (right) is now located there.

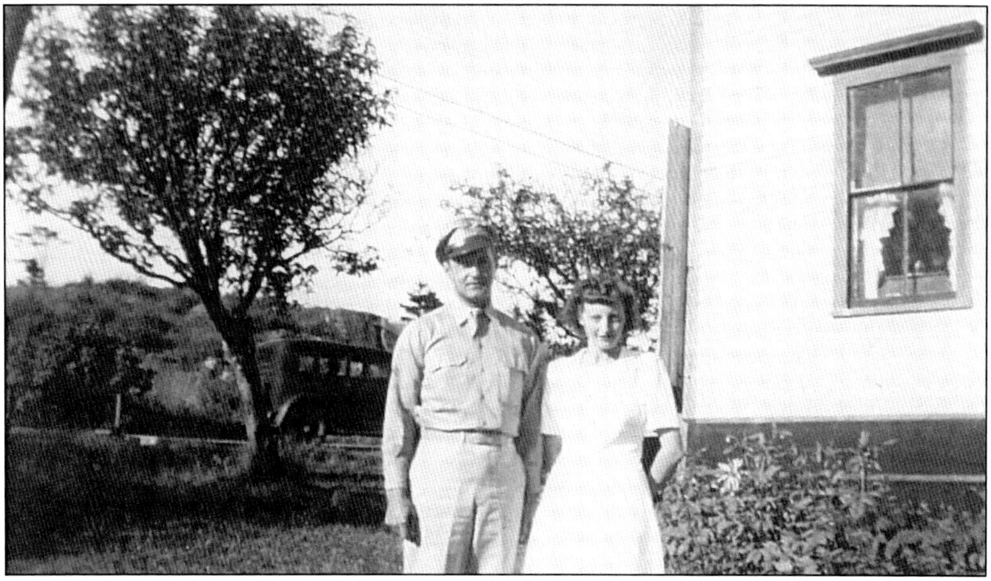

Clyde Lamson and Irene Dobbins pose in front of the Lamson family home in Jonesport, which was located near the Underwood factory. At the time of this early 1940s photograph, Clyde was home on leave from the Air Force and Irene was up visiting her grandmother from Boston, Massachusetts. They married shortly after the picture was taken.

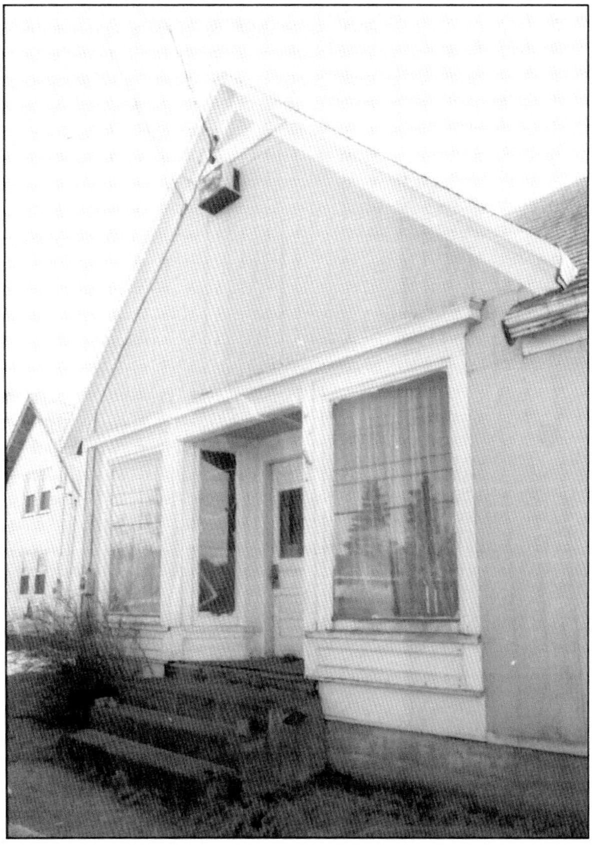

The West Jonesport Post Office on Donovan Cove looks across toward Beals Island. The post office closed in the mid-1970s.

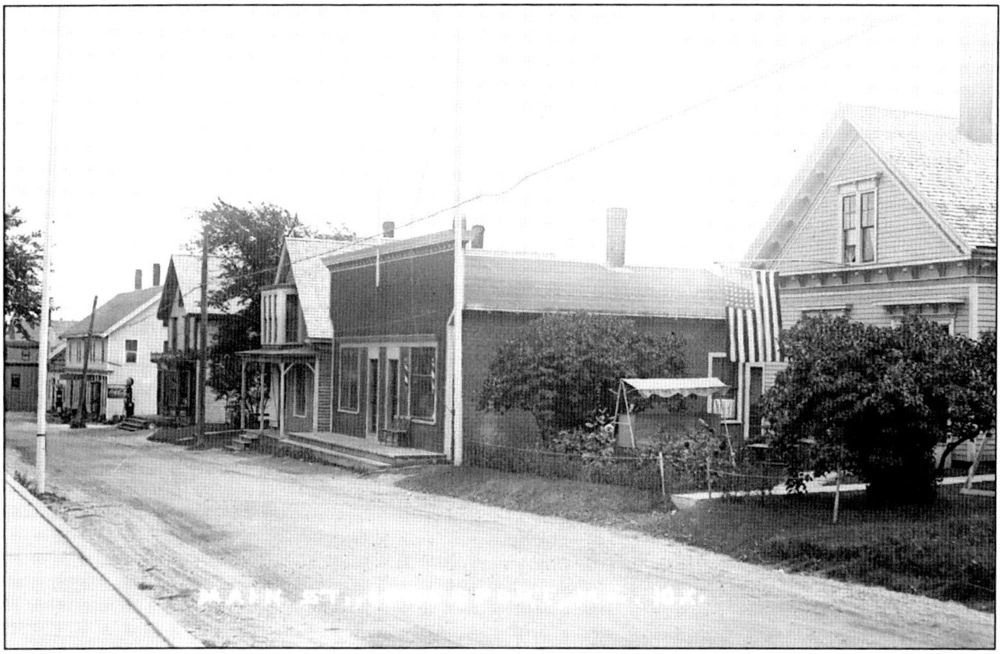

Main Street was a busy part of town around the turn of the 20th century. The Roy Lamson Bakery and lunchroom was located midway between the post office and the opera house (now the IGA Supermarket). Roy served hot and cold lunches; he made bread, pastry in all forms, cakes, and carried a full line of groceries.

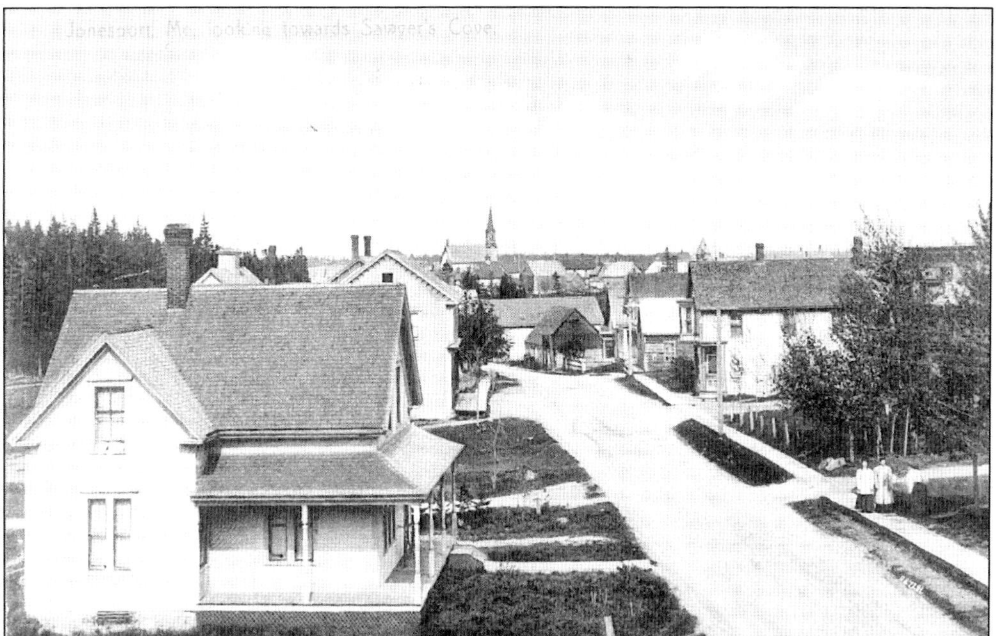

This c. 1910 view of Main Street in Jonesport looks toward Sawyers Cove. On the left was the home of Harry Rogers; it is now the Jonesport by the Sea Inn. The vacant lot on the right is the site of the current Jonesport Post Office.

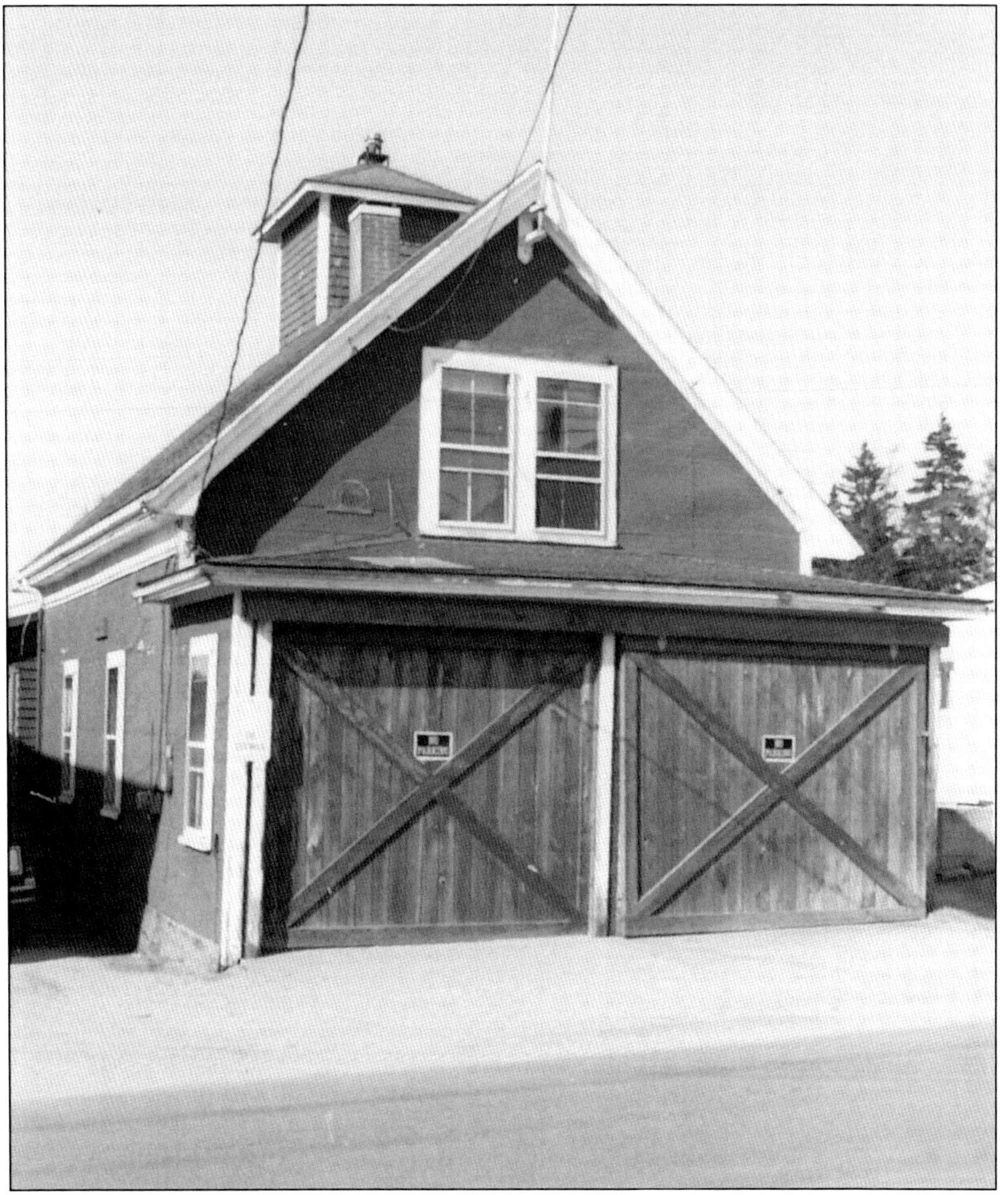

The first fire department was started in 1916 by the selectmen of the town. It was located on the L.S. Kelley Block on Main Street. The superintendent of schools had an office on the second floor of the building.

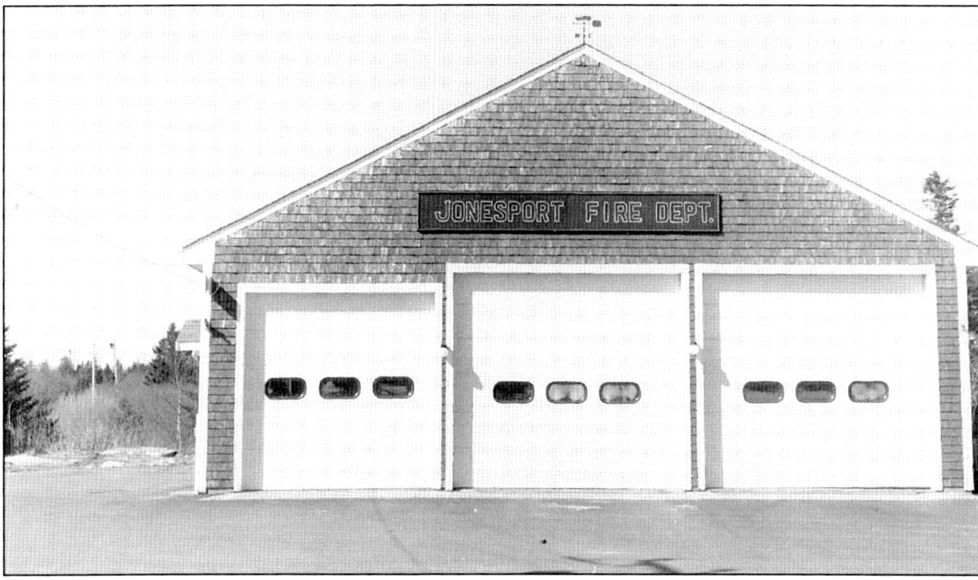

The fire department is now located on Main Street not far from the old West Jonesport Post Office. The building is also the home of the town office and town clerk. Up until 1977, the town clerk was located at Carroll and Arletta Crowley's home on Main Street in Jonesport. Carroll Crowley was the town clerk from 1950 until the time of his death in 1961. His wife, Arletta Crowley, then took over the job as town clerk until she retired in December of 1979.

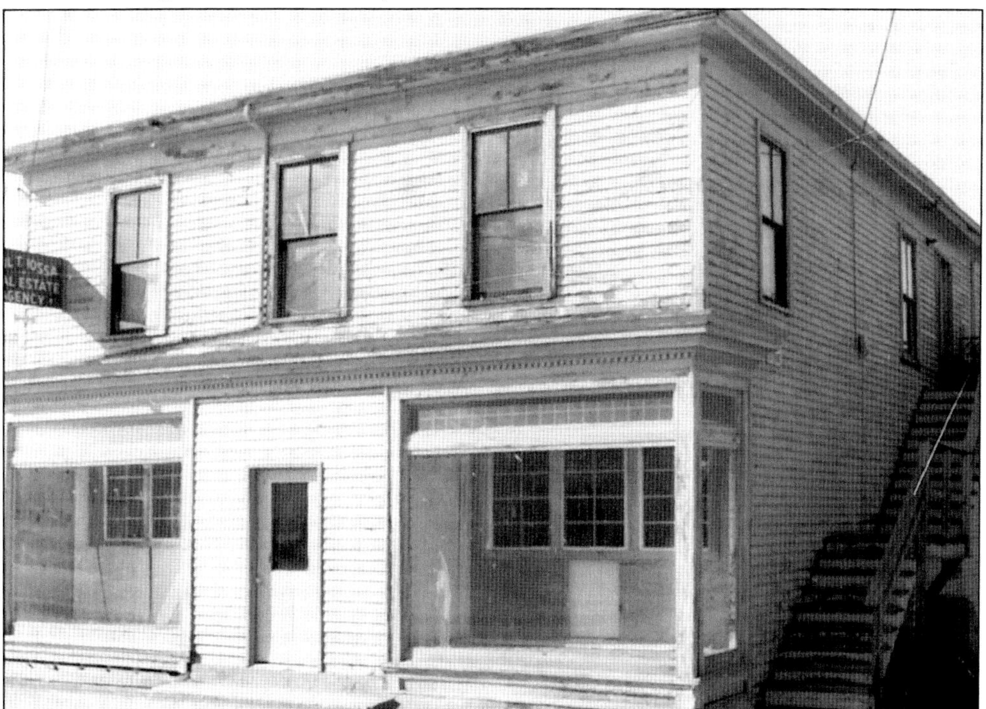

Ervin Ray operated the System Store in this building for many years. The store sold clothing, cloth, and personal items. It was located on Main Street near Churches Hardware. The building has been the home of many businesses over the years.

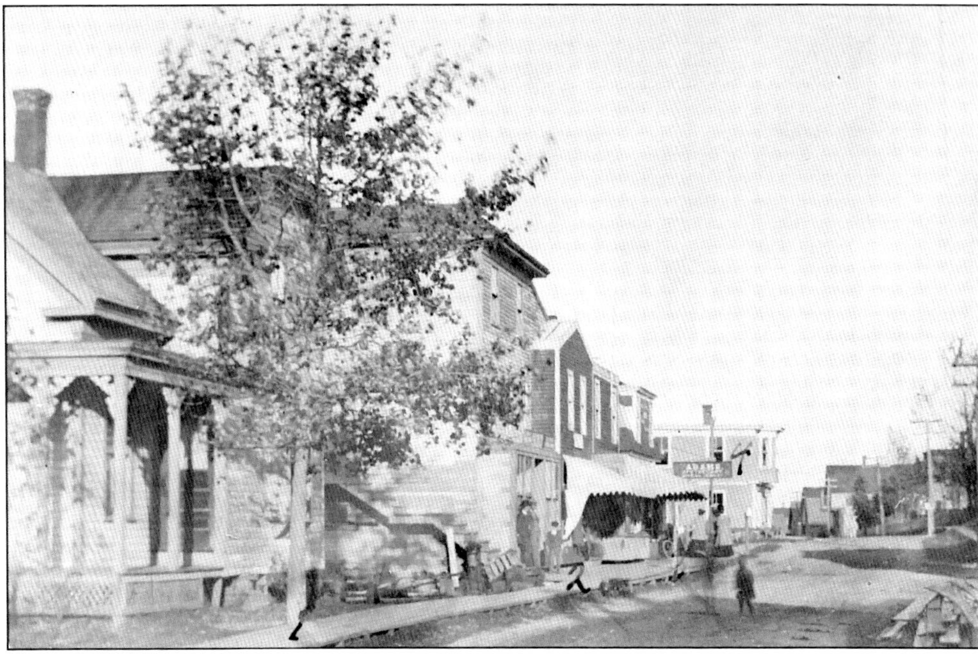

This view of Main Street in Jonesport was taken around the turn of the 20th century. You can see Adams Pharmacy, which was in the L.S. Kelly Block about midway down Main Street. Adams Pharmacy was very modern for its time. Some of the items that you could purchase there included holiday goods, jewelry, and art and photography supplies—an interesting combination for a pharmacy.

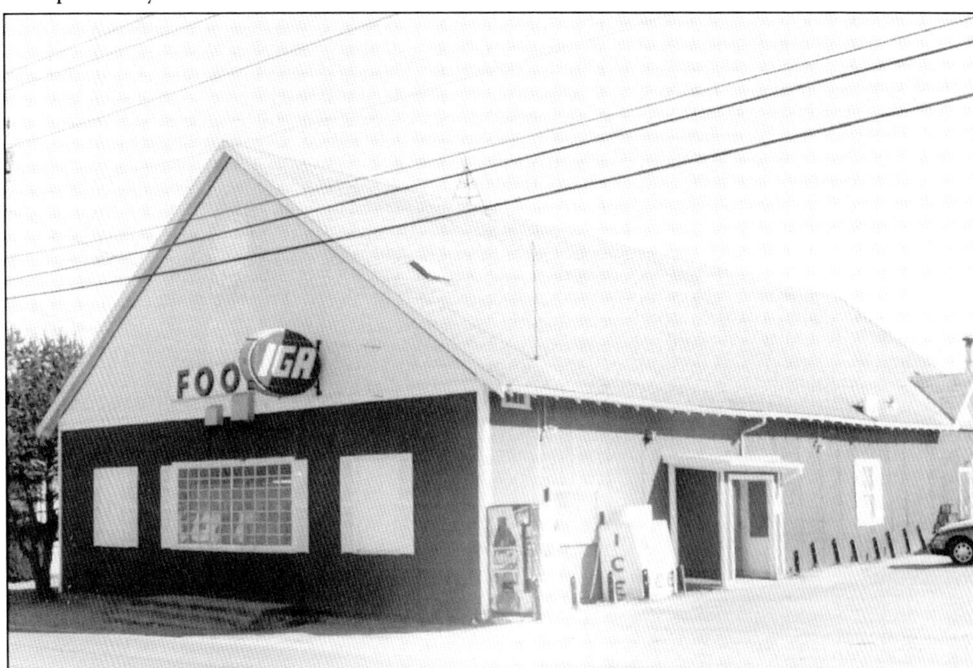

The IGA Supermarket opened in 1968 in the old Jonesport Opera House. The Jonesport Opera House hosted many bands, including the Islanders from Beals and the Illusions of Machias.

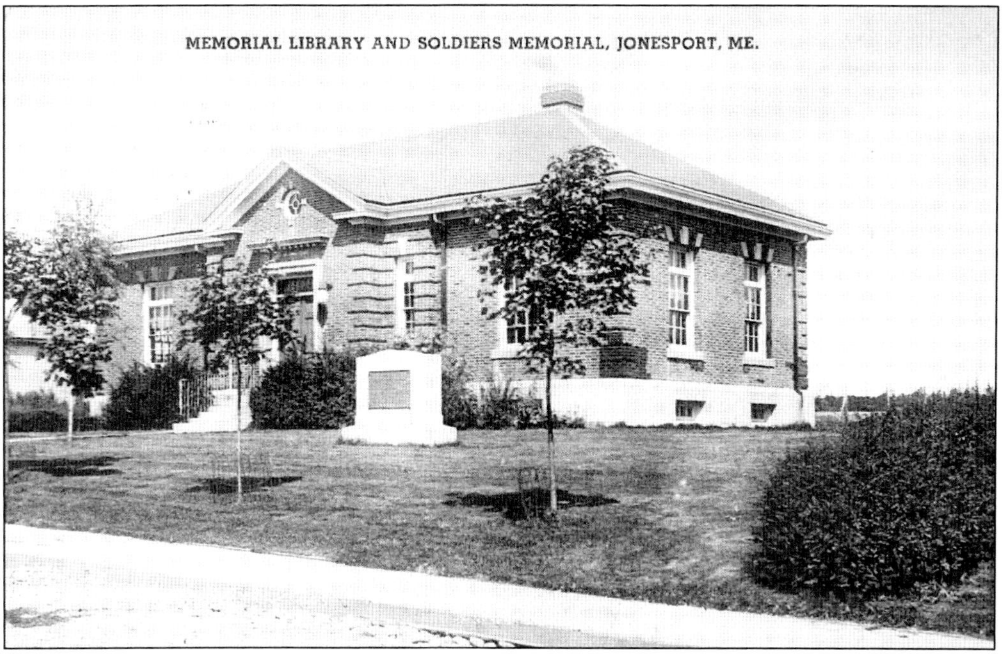

The Peabody Library was erected in 1915. Mary Peabody donated it to the town in memory of her husband and brother. This picture was taken c. 1937.

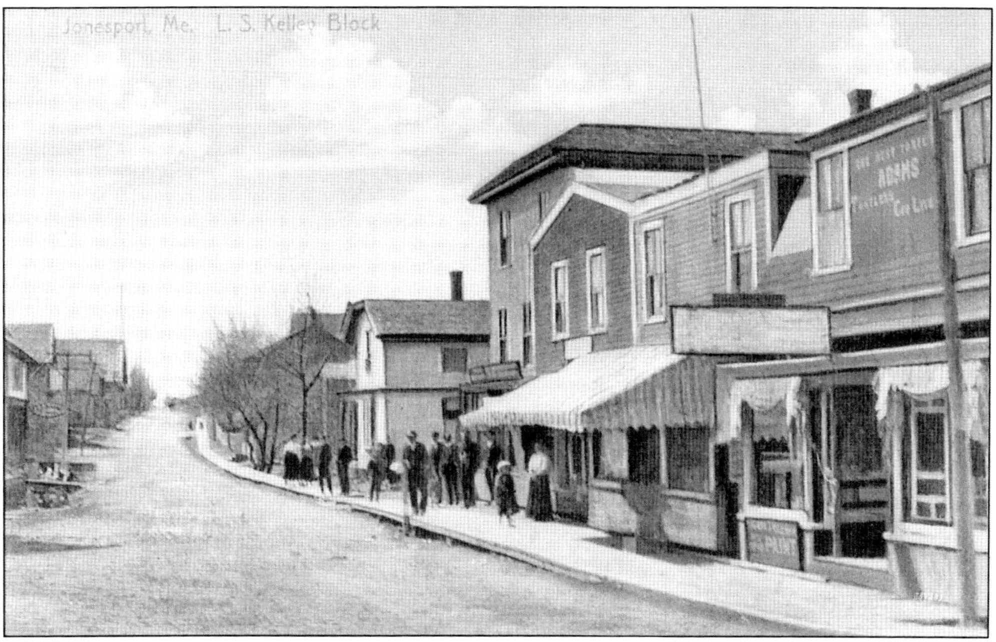

Main Street in Jonesport in 1910 was lined with stores that made up the L.S. Kelly Block. Through the years, fires have demolished the buildings.

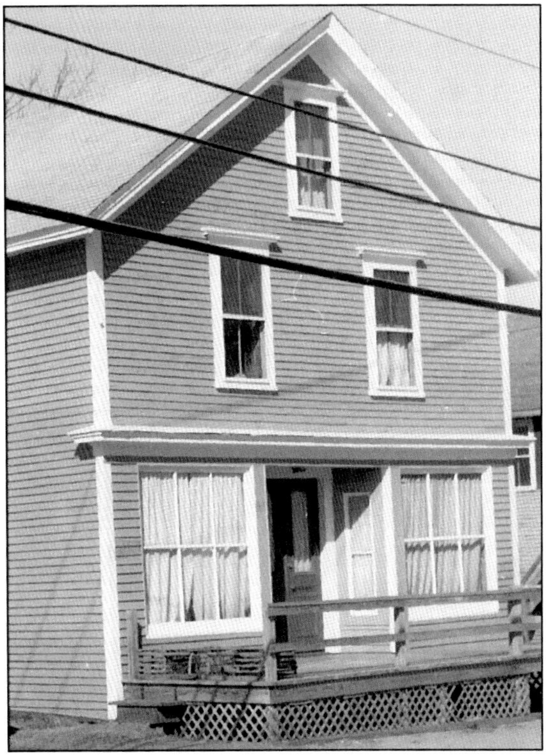

The Jonesport Fire Department is on one side of this building; Cummings Hardware Store was on the other. The building was the home of Cummings and Norton Grocery and is located on Main Street in Jonesport. The store was owned and operated by Ed Cummings and Less Norton from the early 1920s until *c.* 1958, when it closed.

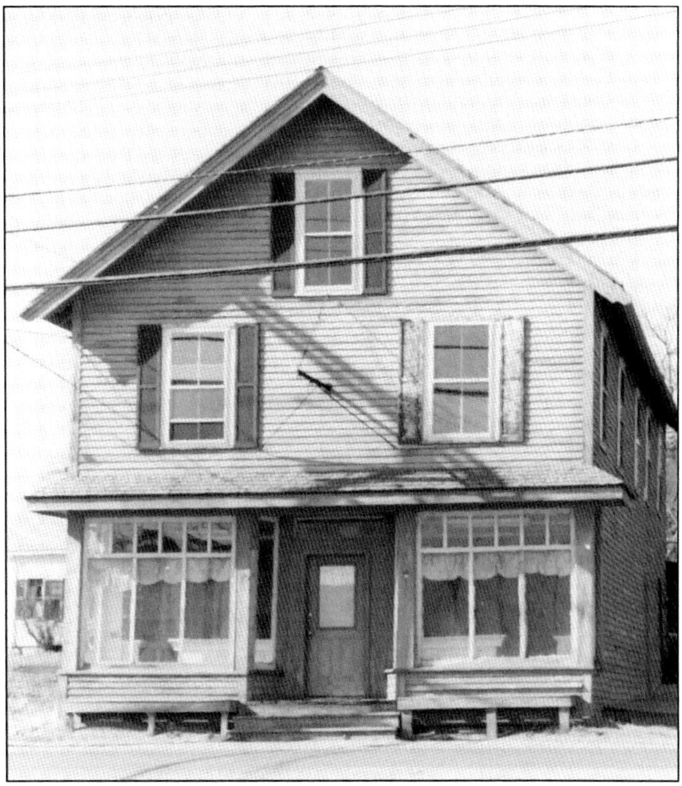

This is a full view of Harry Cummings Hardware, located directly across from the Jonesport-Beals Bridge and the Coast Guard station.

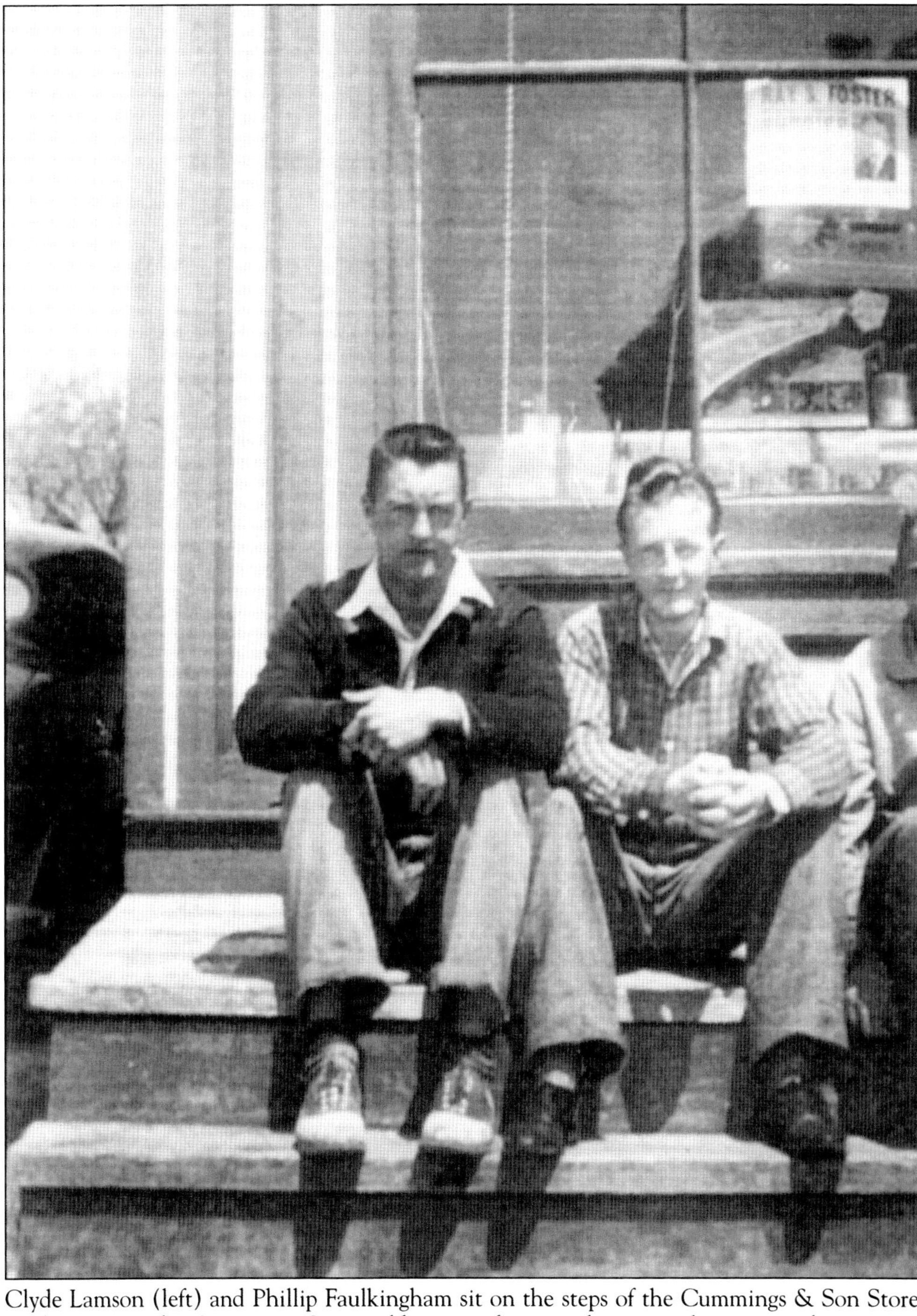

Clyde Lamson (left) and Phillip Faulkingham sit on the steps of the Cummings & Son Store in the 1930s. The Cummings Store sold ranges, furnaces, hot water heaters, appliances, tin ware, and kitchen furnishing. There was also a workshop and tinsmith in the building. The Cummings building on Main Street looks toward the Jonesport-Beals Bridge. The building is still in use with a redemption center on the first floor and apartments on the second; it is located next to Tall Barney's Restaurant.

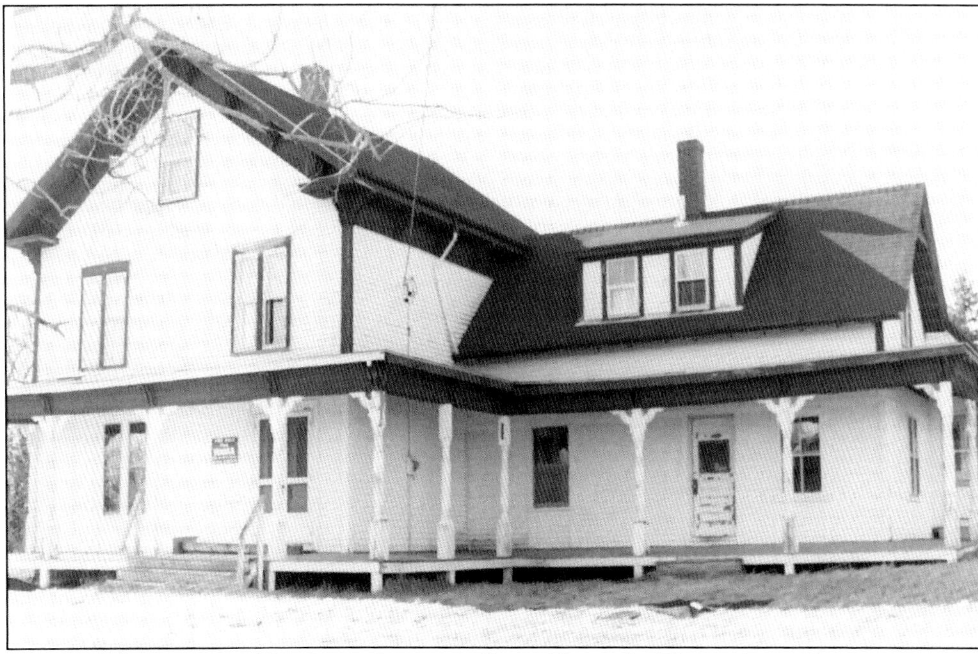

The Kelly home, owned by Capt. George Kelly and his wife, Elva, is located on Main Street near Sawyers Cove. The Kelly family had a farm and sold milk to the people of Jonesport in the 1920s.

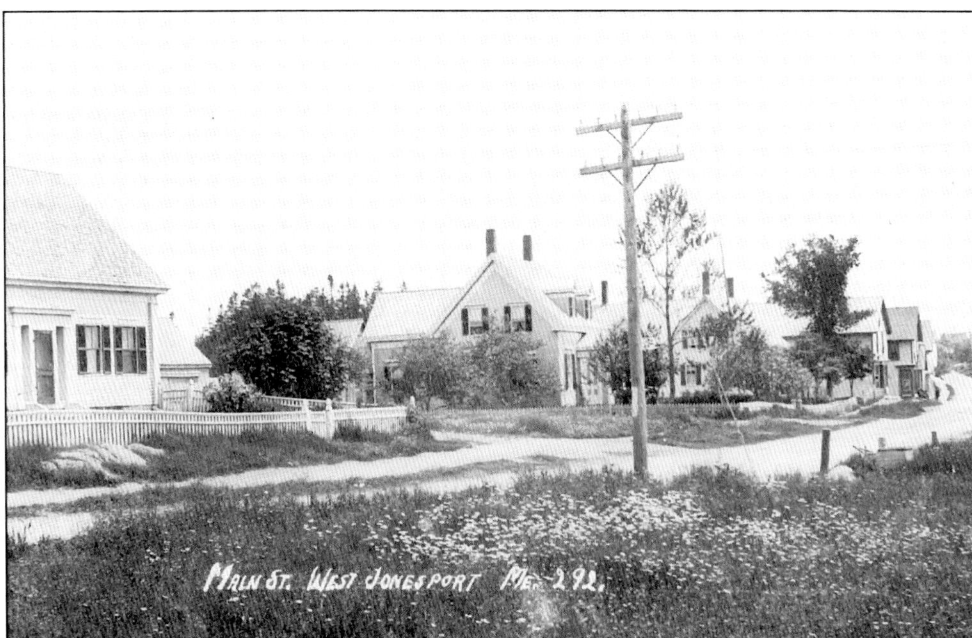

This 1931 view of West Jonesport was taken looking toward the town. Midway down on the left is the site of the present fire department and town hall.

Three

Churches, Factories, and Schools

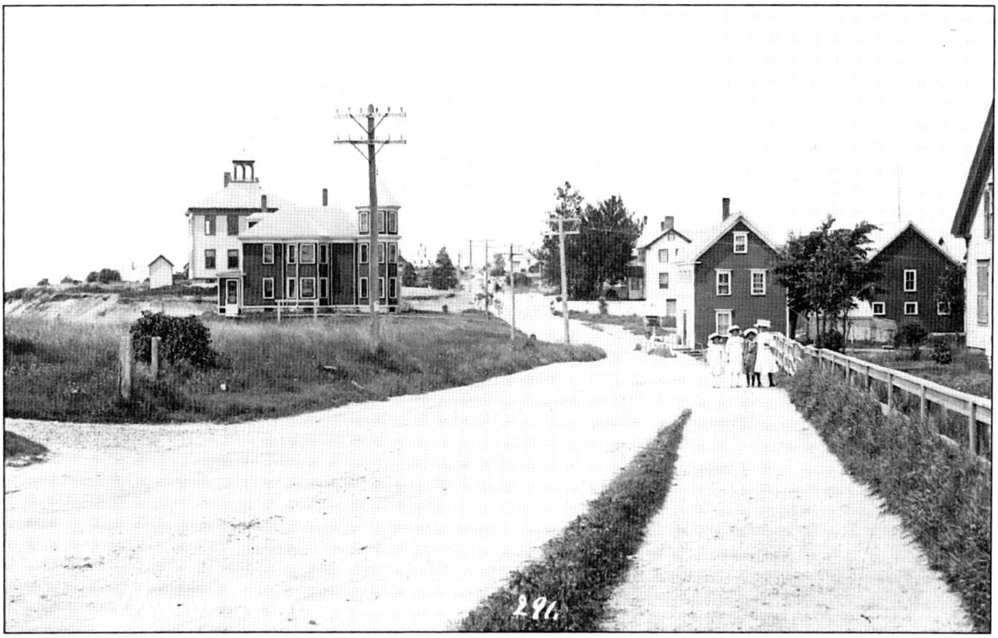

This picture was taken around the turn of the 20th century. On the left, in the distance, you can see the Lincoln School. The four girls are in front of Mr. and Mrs. P.R. Cummings' place of business. The couple carried on a general store that supplied the people of West Jonesport with staples, crockery, and glassware. Mrs. Cummings carried dry and fancy goods, ladies shoes, and specialty items for the lady folks in town.

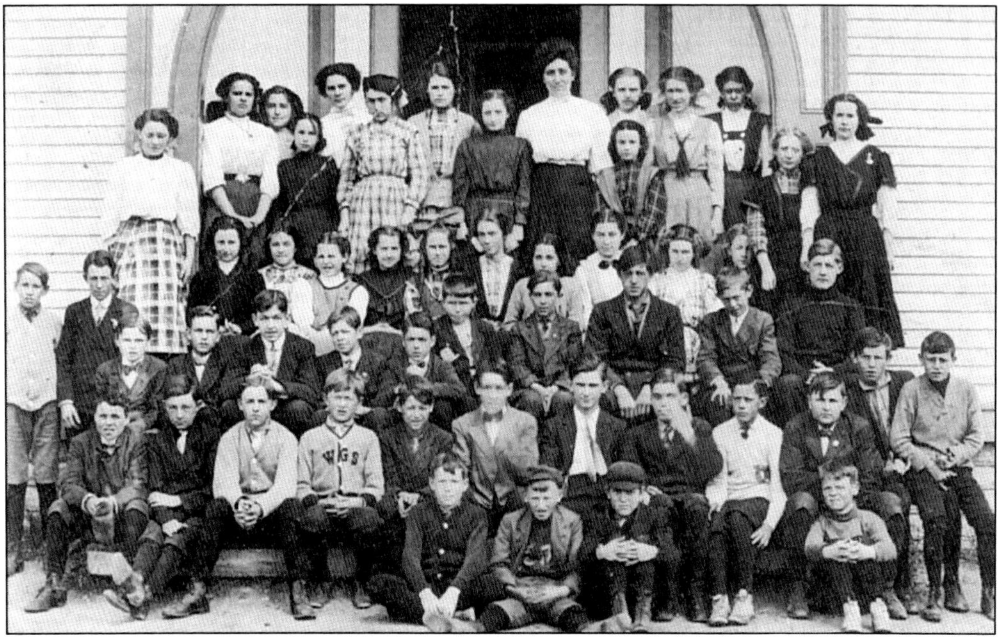

This Lincoln Grammar School class picture was taken *c*. 1910.

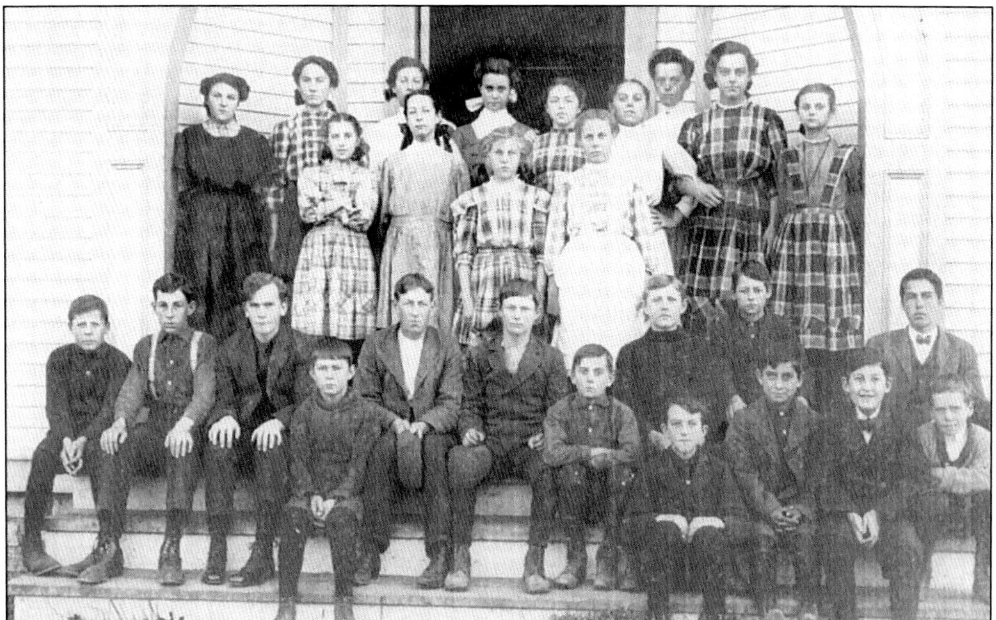

Seen in this Lincoln Grammar School class picture, from left to right, are as follows: (girl's front row) Lisa Atwater, Lizzie Sawyer, Gurtie Carver, and Phebe Norton; (girl's back row) Ida Worcester, Gladys Kelly, Annie Sawyer, Lois Alley, Algie Cummings, Helen Stede, teacher Lena Puney, Mildred Cummings, and Violo Lehman; (boy's front row) John Lamson, Danny Dobbins, Lawrence Norton, and Raymond Noyes; (boy's back row) Burton Faulkingham, Clinton Norton, Maenad Rumey, Will Wallace, Grover Worcester, Arthur Faulkingham, Neldor Joy, and Grin Cummings.

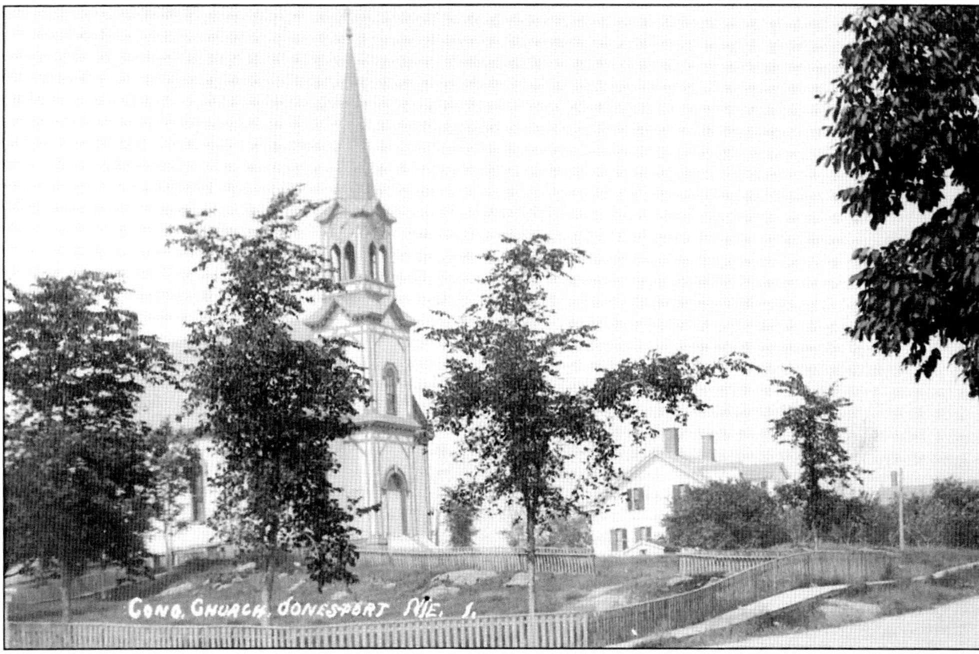

This view of the Congregational church in Sawyers Square was taken in 1913. The house on the left was the Mansfield Farm. The church was painted in contrasting colors to emphasize the architecture.

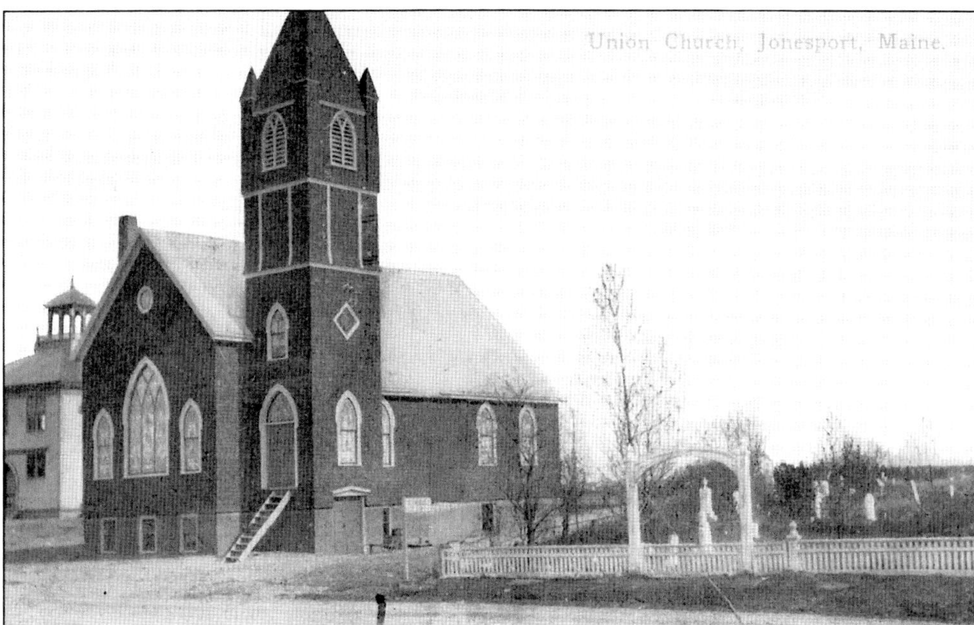

This 1914 picture shows the Union Church, located in West Jonesport at Cummins Corner. It is commonly known as the green church they painted white. Note that the front steps hadn't been built yet on the church when the image was taken. The Union Church sits right on the ocean looking over toward Beals Island.

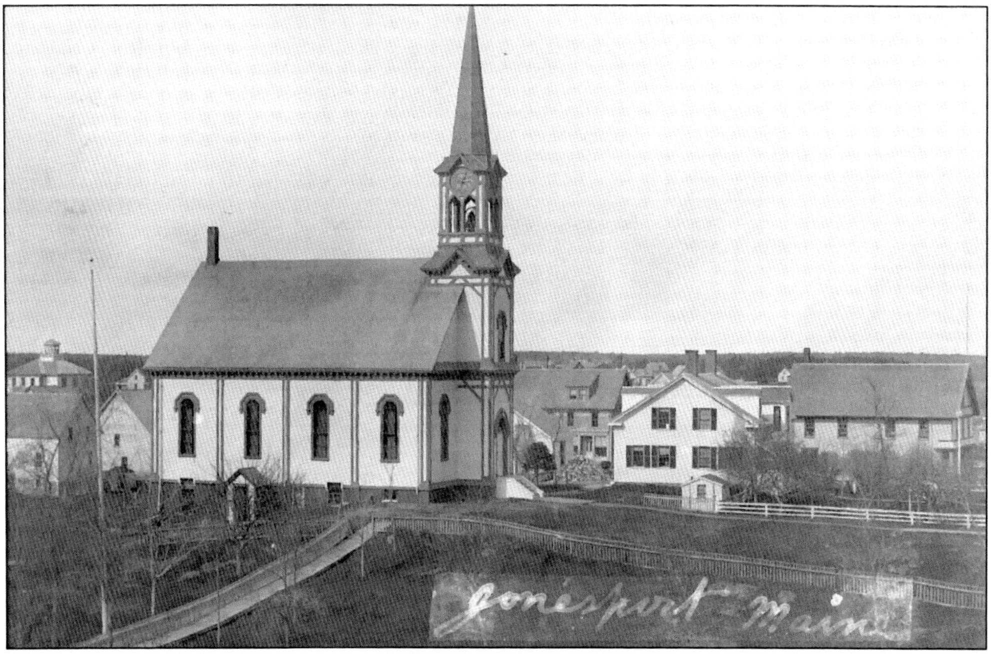

This is a view of the Congregational church in Sawyers Square in 1908. The Cove School is visible to the far left in the distance. From this angle, you can see just how many homes there were in the area; today it is less congested.

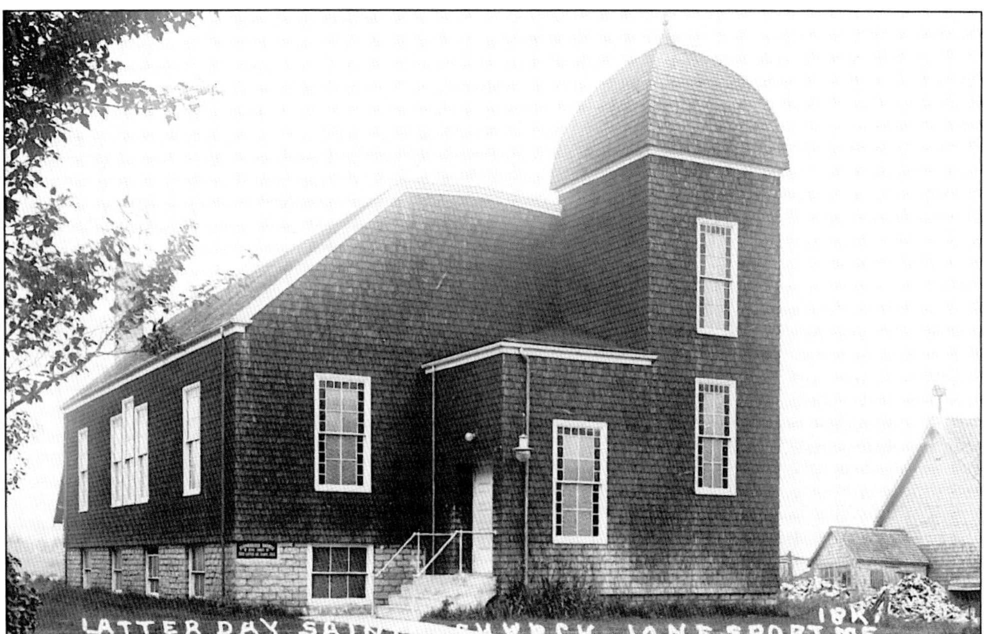

The Church of Latter Day Saints in the center of town burned down in 1996; a larger new church was built in its place.

The Sawyer Congregational Church in Sawyers Cove was built in 1857. Daniel Sawyer donated the money for the church and hired master builder and architect Charles Allen of Cherryfield to design and oversee the construction of the structure.

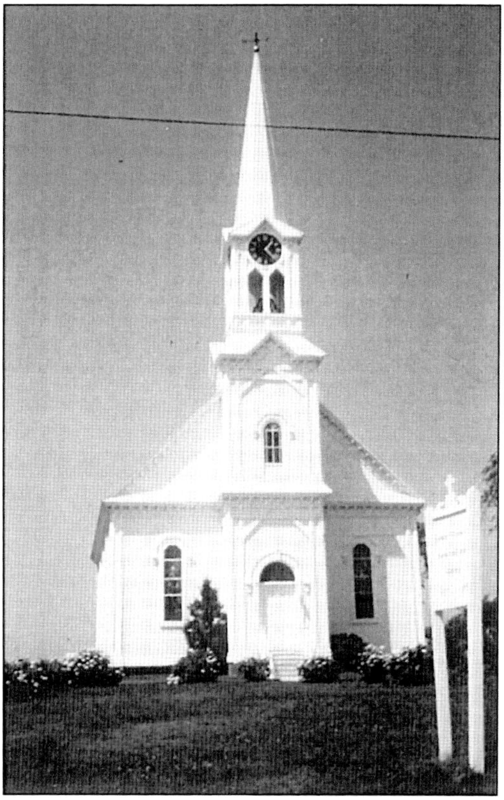

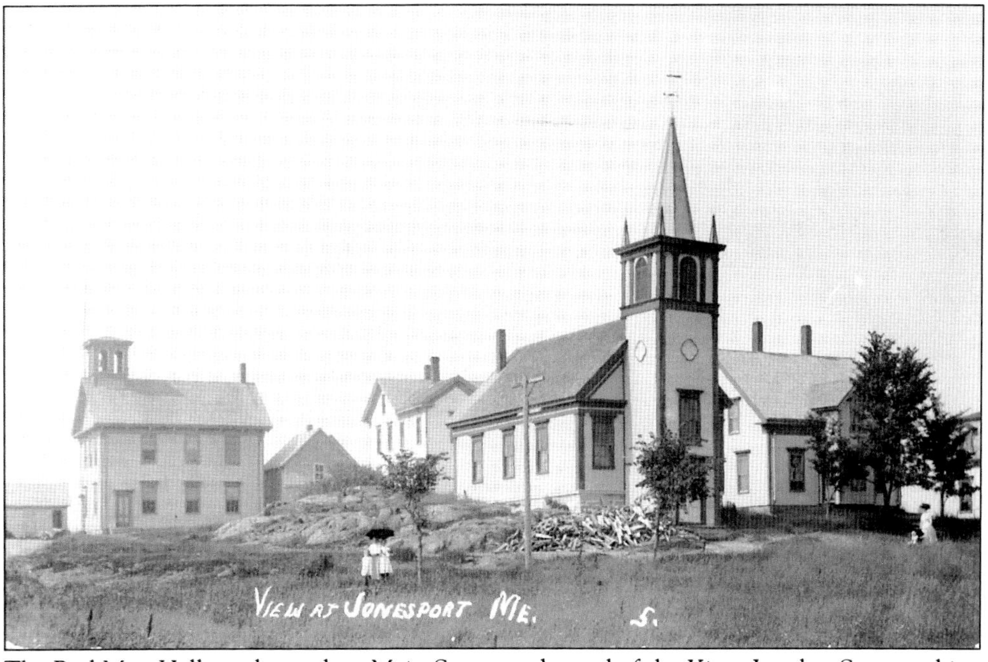

The Red Man Hall was located on Main Street at the end of the Kings Lumber Store parking lot. The school to the left of the picture is the Cove School. The house behind the church belonged to Will Crockes.

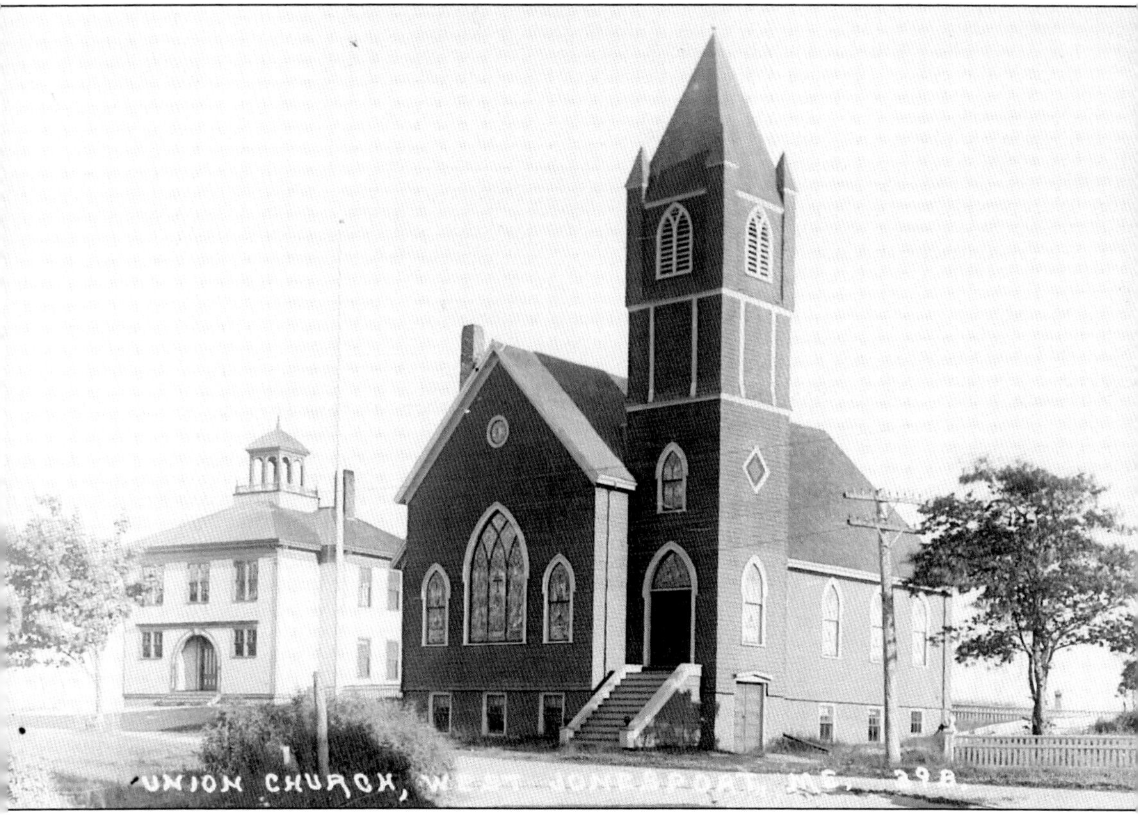

The West Jonesport School behind the Union Church in Cummings Square was called the Lincoln School. It sat on Moosabec Reach looking out to sea; I can image how much schoolwork I would have accomplished if I had that view to gaze at when I was a child. The school building burned in December of 1977, just after Christmas.

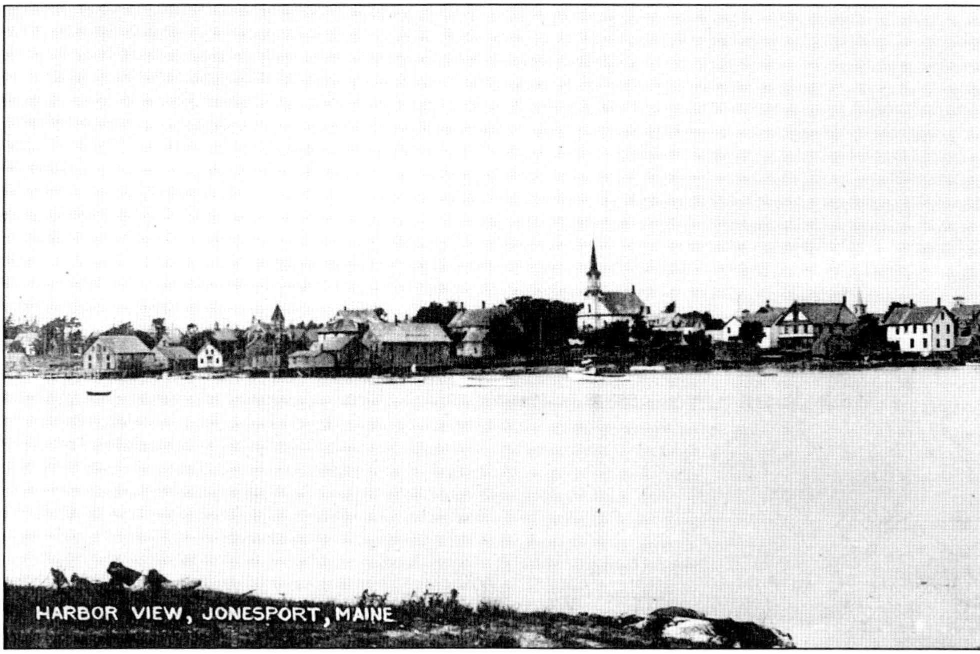

This harbor view of Jonesport was taken from Great Wass Island. The Mansfield Factory was located on the water edge in front of the Congressional church in the center. The Mansfield Factory was sold, dismantled, and taken to Portland, Maine, where it was reassembled.

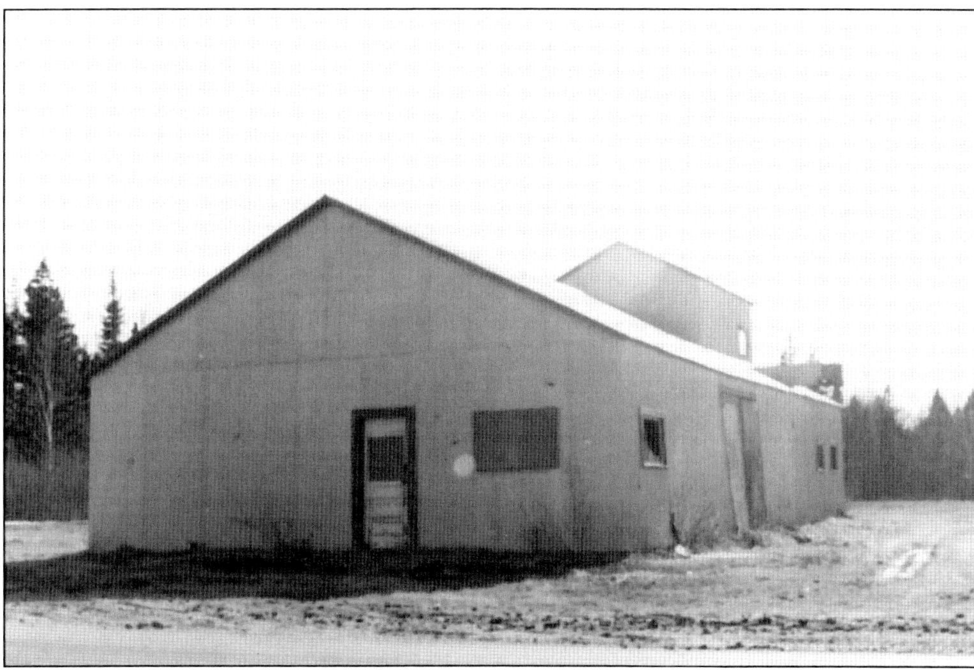

Peat was cut and processed for fuel at the peat bog factory, located just outside of the town limits of Jonesport. The factory, which was open for over 20 years, closed in the early 1970s.

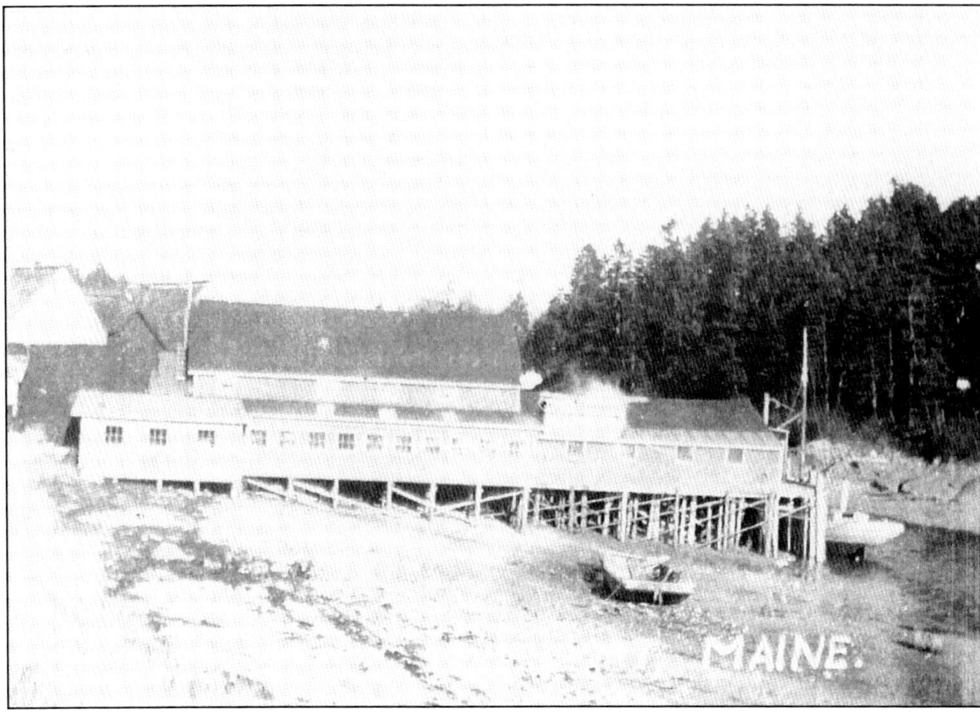

Fish were smoked and clams and lobsters were packed for market at the Charles Stevens Factory at Cross Cove.

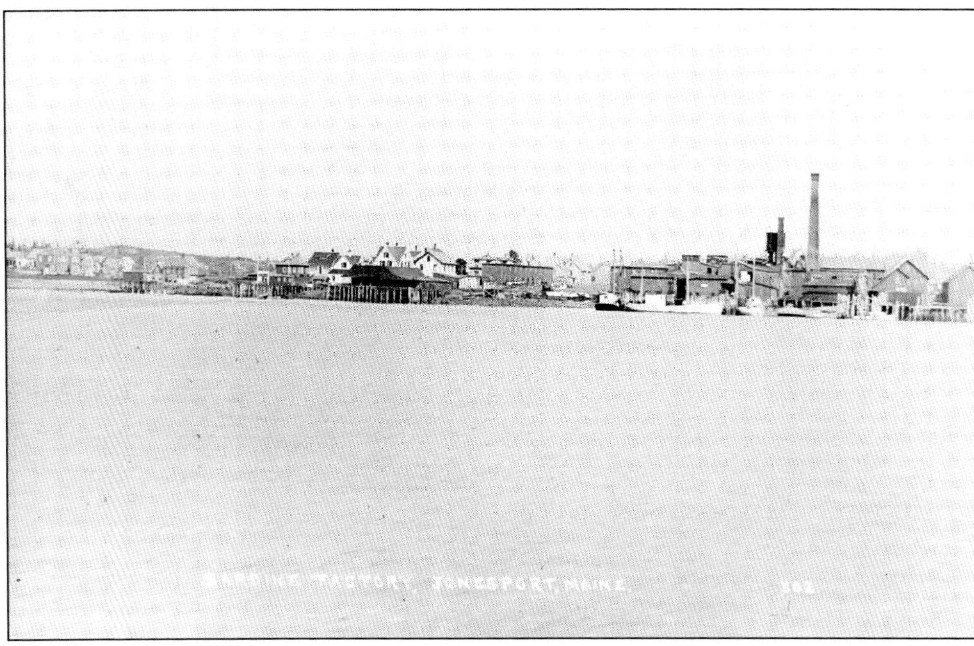

This is a view of one of the sardine factories in Jonesport. When the sardine factories first opened, people worked ten hours a day. Children also worked in the factories; the hourly wage was a dime.

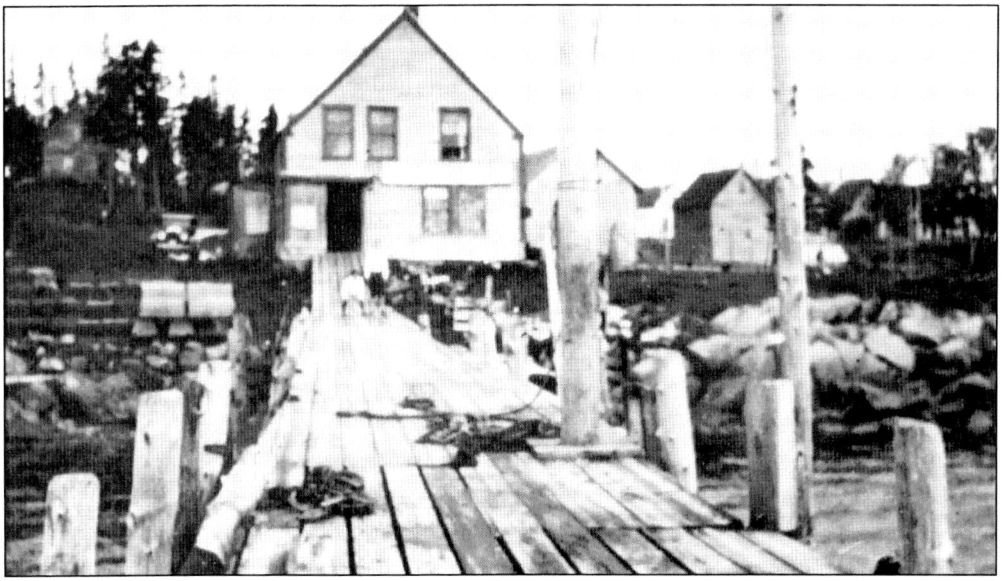

This is a picture of the Drisko Machine Shop on Sawyers Cove; the Drisko family lived on the second floor of the building.

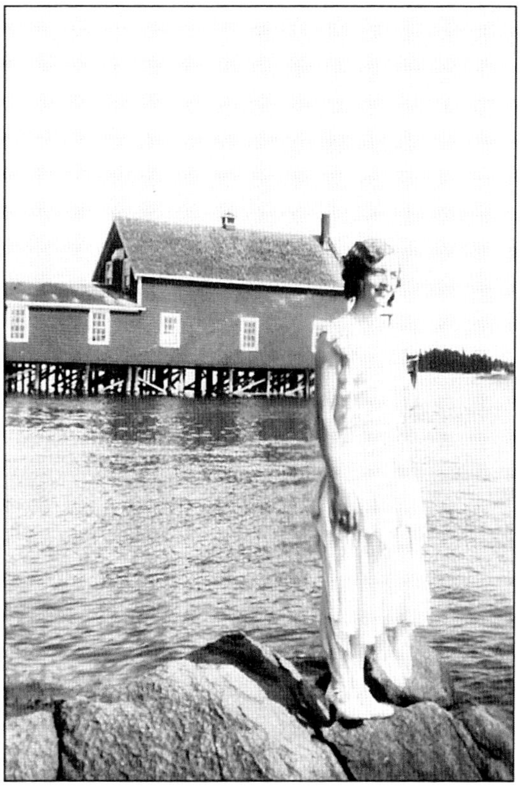

Cora Drisko, daughter of Merton and Addie Drisko, poses on the north side of the Drisko Machine Shop, down by the marina in Jonesport. The Bert Look waft is in the background.

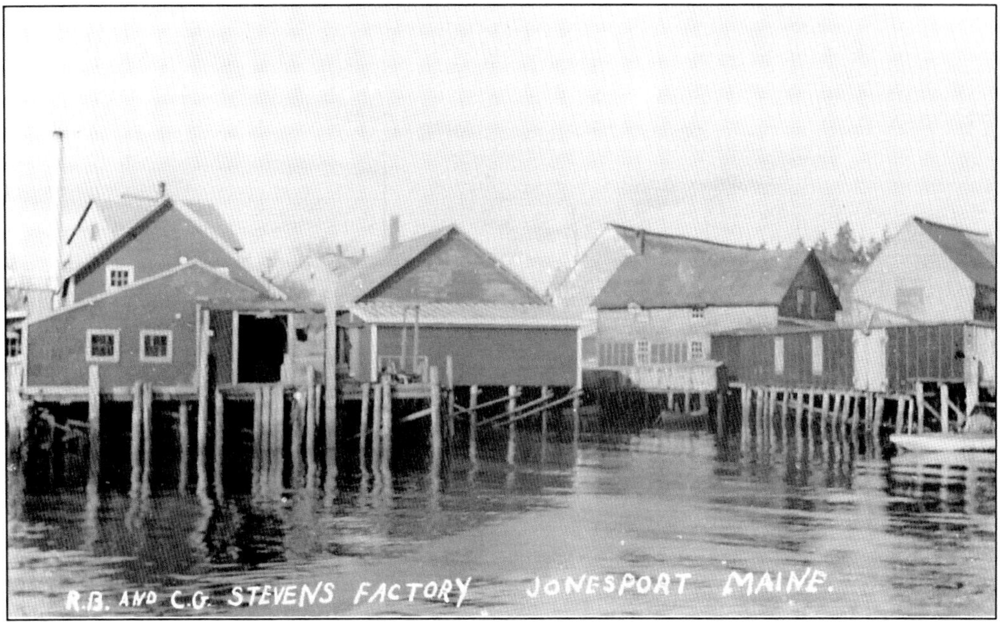

The Stevens Factory was a fish packing factory at Cross Cove. Mr. R.B. Stevens owned the smoked fish plant, which featured a 22-bay smokehouse. Mr. A.E. Drisco was an associate of Stevens; they were engaged in packing sardines and processing fish, and had a very modern plant for the times. The first level of the building was for processing fish and sardines, while the top level was devoted to packing their product and get it ready for market. They also had their own firm to manufacture cans so they could handle the process from beginning to end.

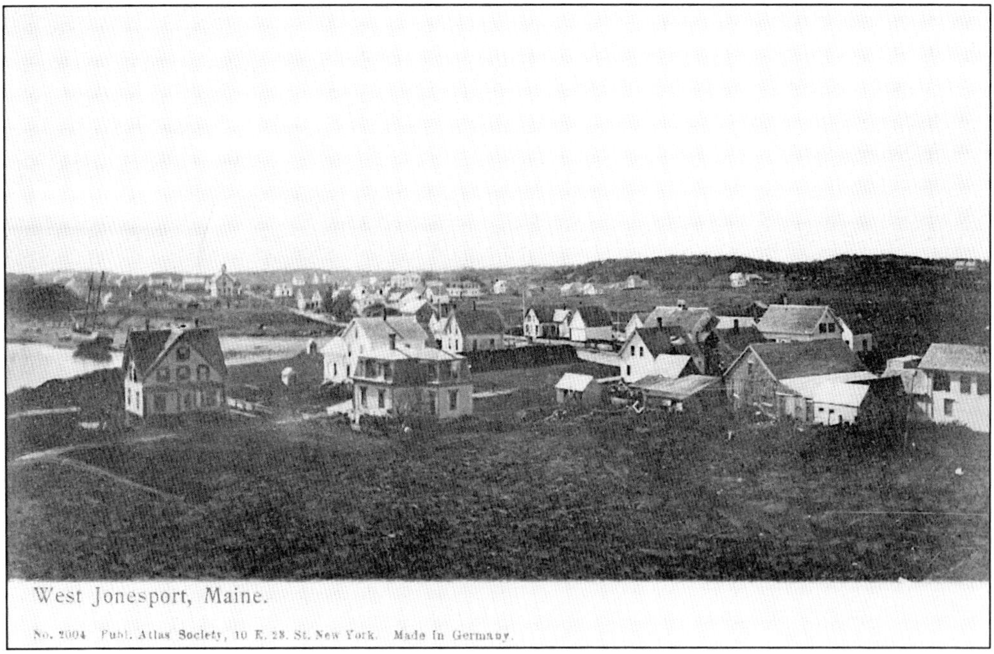

Mrs. C.A. Chandlers' dry goods store was located midway between Jonesport and West Jonesport. She sold ready-made cloths, boots, rubber shoes, and hundreds of other articles. This two-and-a-half-story building opened in 1867.

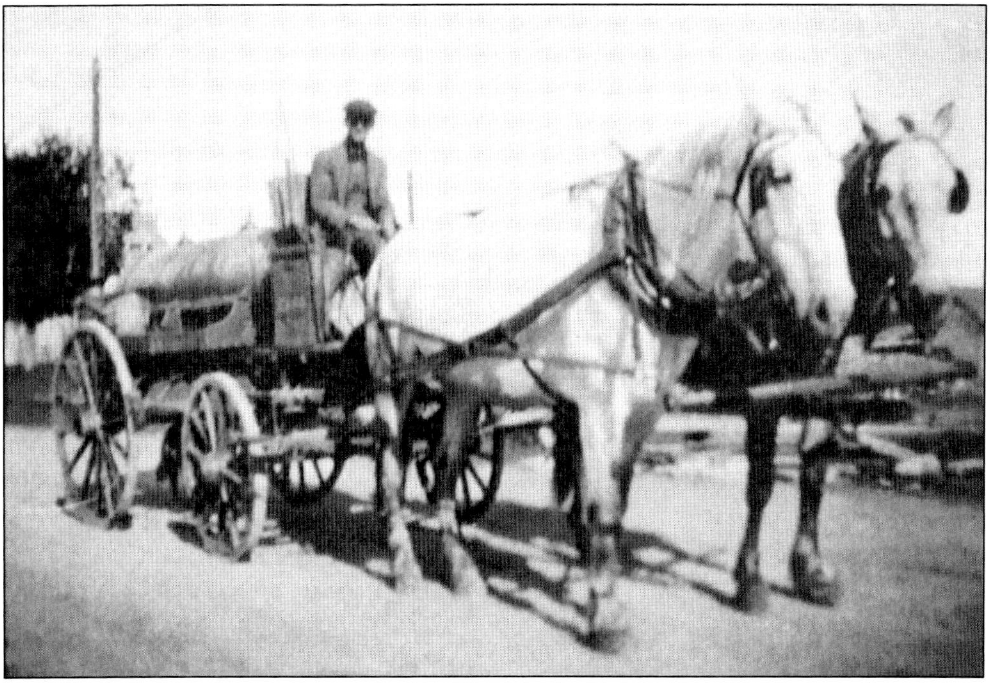

At the turn of the 20th century, the kerosene used to heat the homes and cook with was delivered door to door. This is a picture of Marcus Peterson; he had a delivery route in Jonesport and neighboring towns.

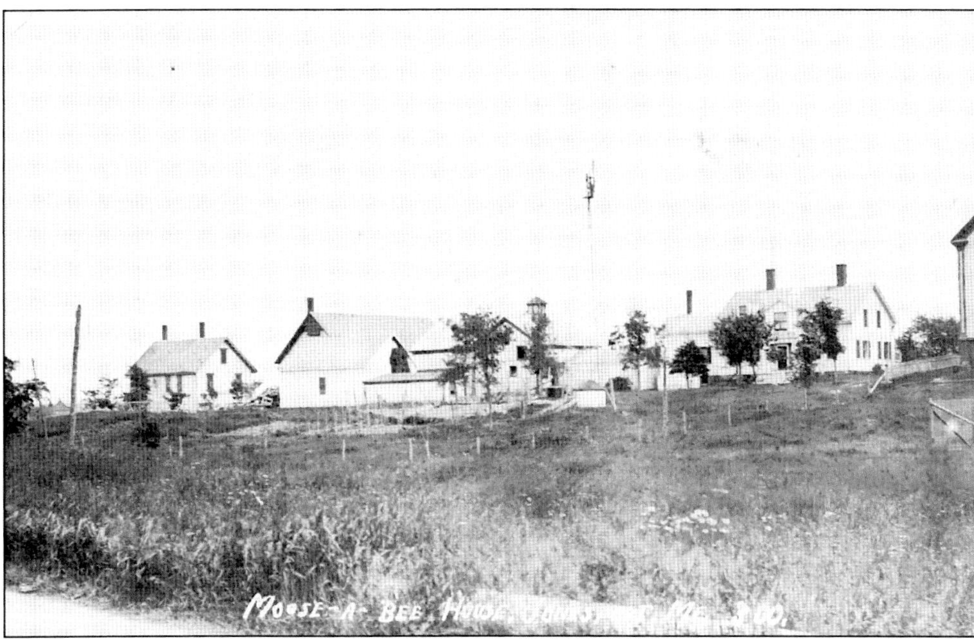

The Moosabec House was the first public tavern in Jonesport; this picture of it was taken in 1912. The owner and builder was Edward A. Mansfield. It was located at Mansfield Corner near the Congregational church.

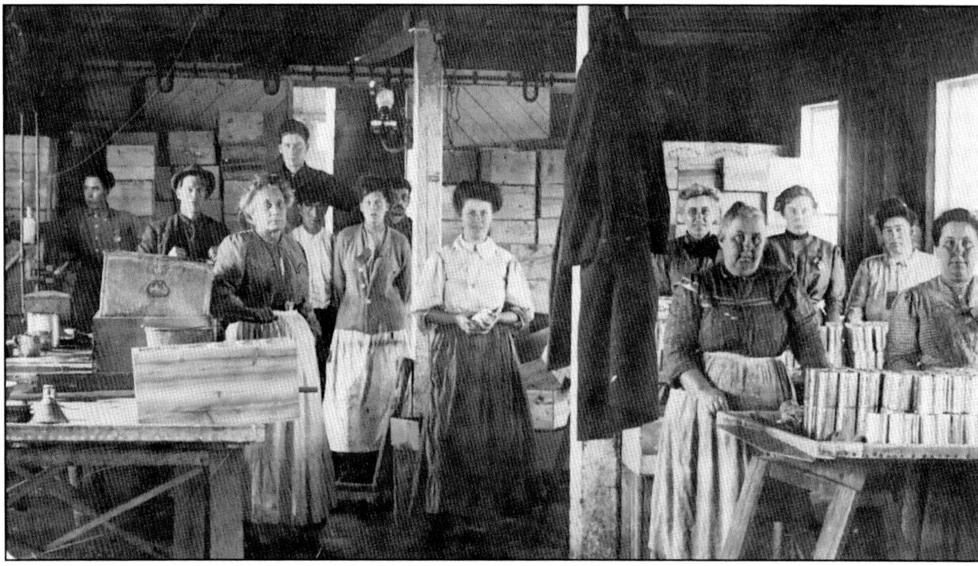

This is the interior of a typical clam factory. There were several clamming factories in Jonesport, including the Mansfield Clamming Factory in Sawyers Cove and the Mansfield's Factory on the site of the Maurice Grays Clam Shop. Most of the employees in the clamming factories were women.

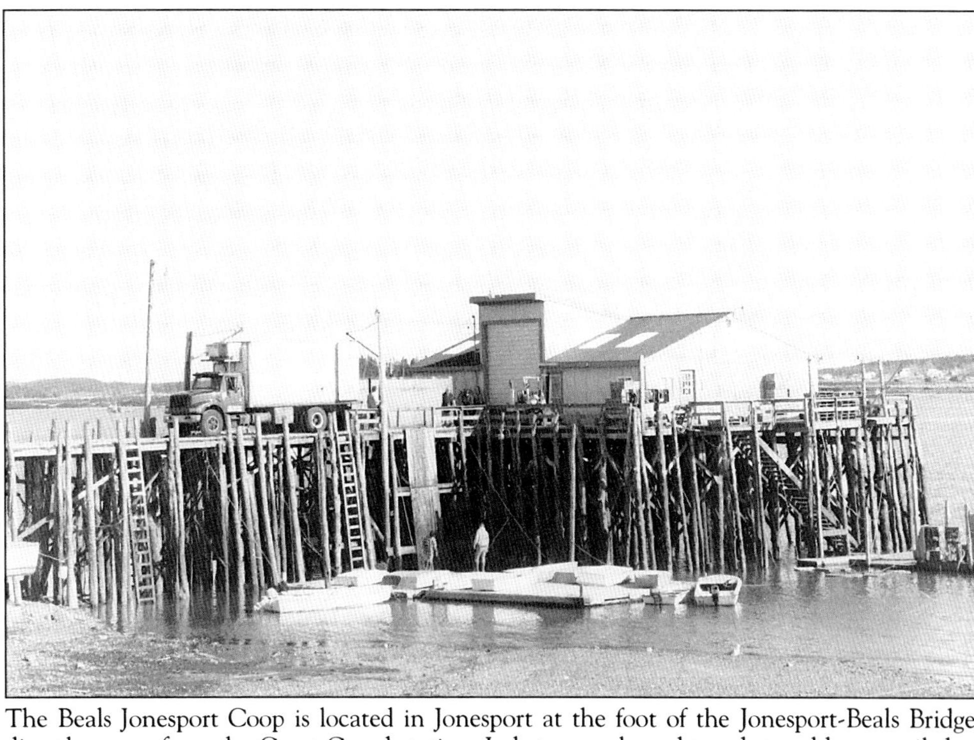

The Beals Jonesport Coop is located in Jonesport at the foot of the Jonesport-Beals Bridge, directly across from the Coast Guard station, Lobsters are brought and stored here until they can be shipped to market. At high tide, the water line is up to the top of the pier.

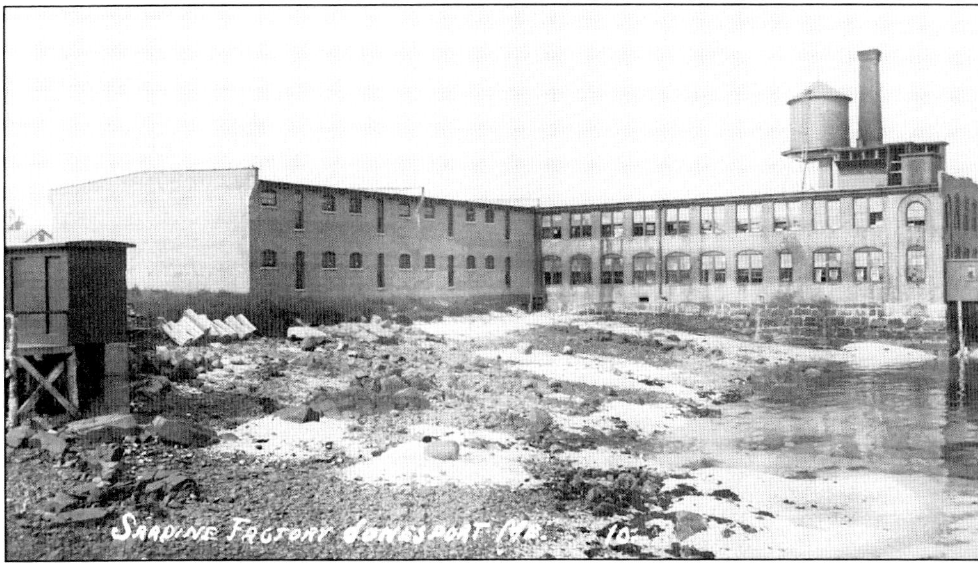

The William Underwood Sardine Factory was located to the right of the Jonesport-Beals Bridge, where the Coast Guard station is now operating. The original structure was built in the early 1800s. The factory packed sardines and clams for markets around the world, processing 600 to 700 bushels of clams a day. Many of the clams were cleaned in local homes and brought to the plant to be processed, diced for chowder, and packed. The plant had a sardine cutting machine invented by Arthur R. Roger of Jonesport; it was the only one of its kind in the country. The machine was a very important part of the process, as it cut the sardines all to the same length for packing. The sardines had to be packed by hand; an experienced packer could pack about 2,200 cans a day.

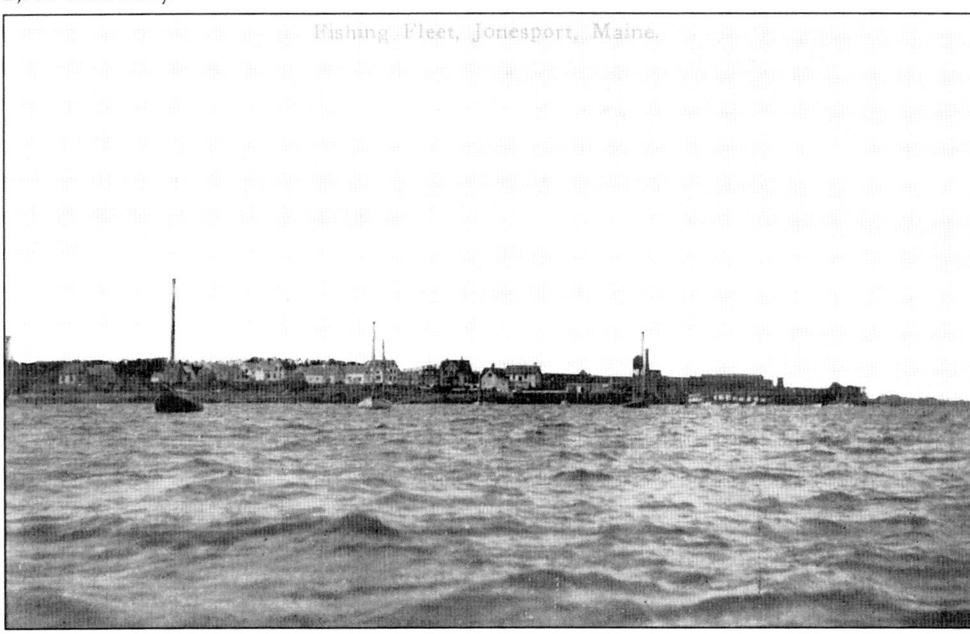

D.J. Sawyer built many three-mastered schooners from 1850 to 1890. He would stock the boats with merchandise from his general store for ports around the country. This is a harbor view of Sawyers Cove, where D.J. Sawyer's building was located.

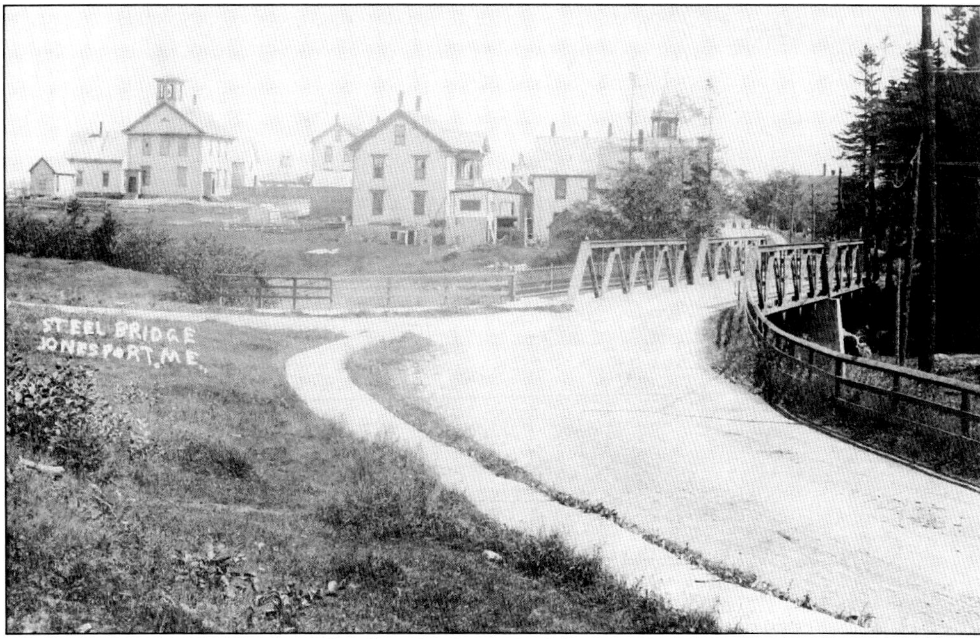

The Washington Grammar School is the large building to the left; in the foreground is the Sawyers Bridge. Directly over the bridge is the present home of Kings Lumberyard. The Washington Grammar School burnt down in the 1920s; the Cove School was built on its site.

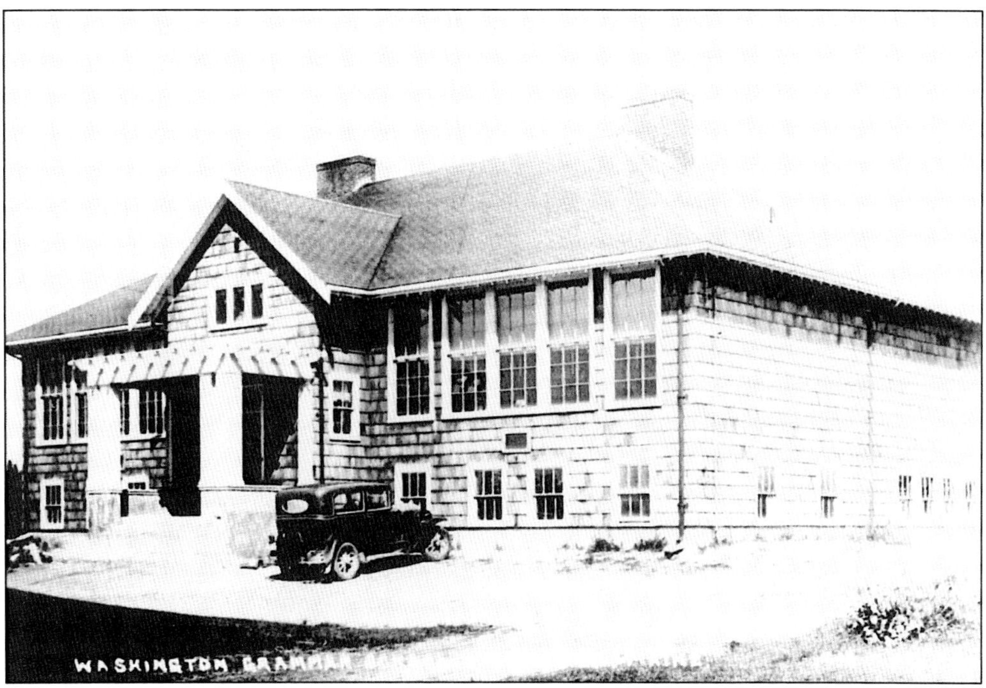

This picture of the Cove School was taken in the early 1930s. The Cove School is located behind Kings Lumberyard on Main Street, and is now the home of Nelsons Crafts.

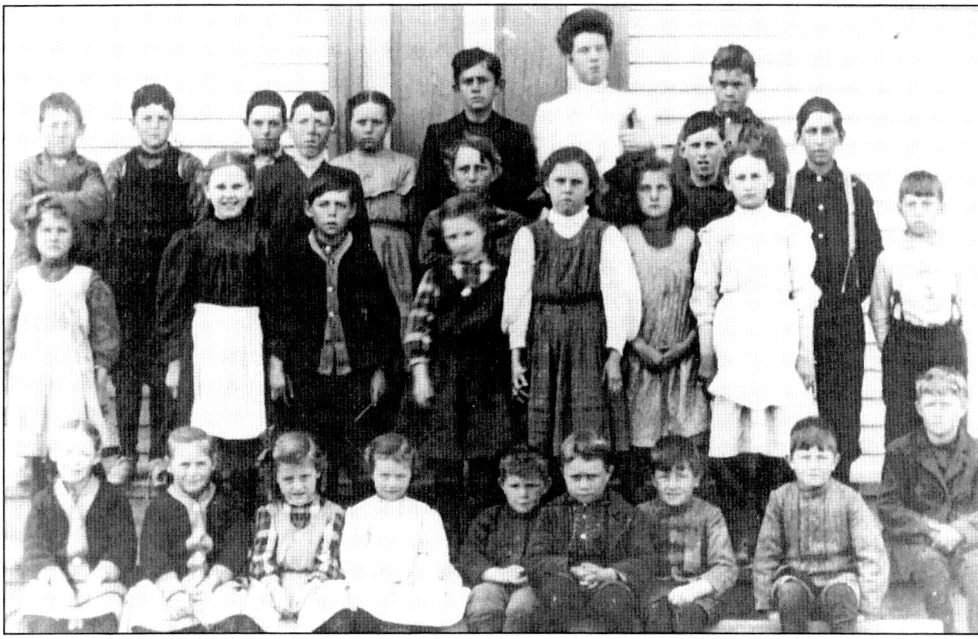

These 1908–10 Kelly Point Schoolchildren are, from left to right, as follows: (front row) Phyllis Smith, Alice Smith, Eleanor Donovan, Madeline Carver, Llewylln Kelly, Robert Church, Arthur Kelly, Cecil Kelly, and William Church; (middle row) Helen Kelly, Mini Kelly, Roland Smith, Verns Donavan, Floa Sawyer, Doris Kelly, and Irene Kelly; (back row) Lincoln Simmons, Allan Rogers, Frank Higgins, Howard Kelly, Velma Kent, Austin Beal, Morton Kelly, two unidentified adults (one apparently the teacher), Lewis Church, Merrill Kelly, and Byron Kelly. The schoolhouse is now the American Legion Hall on Kelly Point Road.

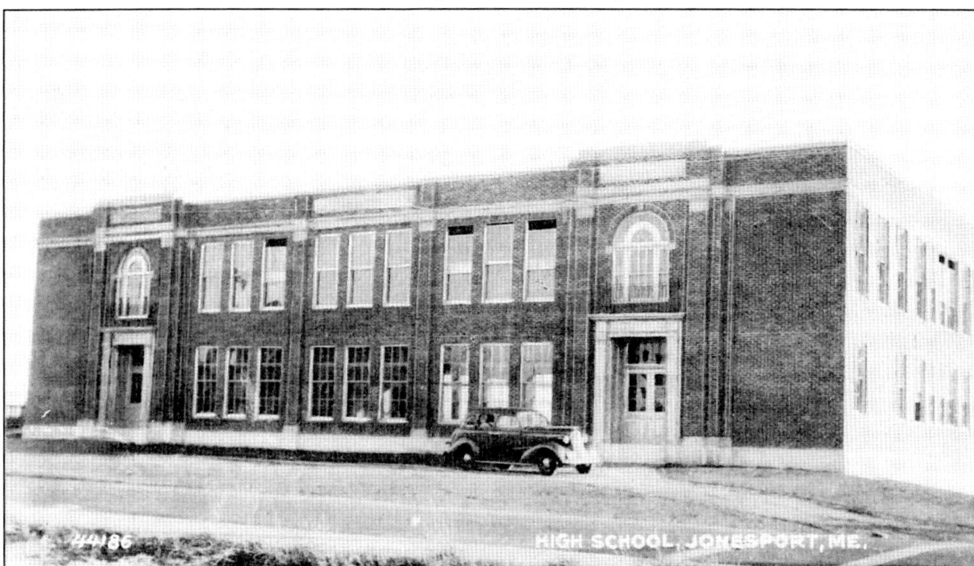

The second high school in Jonesport was located on Main Street. It was built and opened for classes in the fall of 1937. When it was opened, it had six classrooms and a science lab. In 1968, Beals' students joined the school and the name was changed to the Jonesport-Beals High School. The building has been remolded and is now an apartment building.

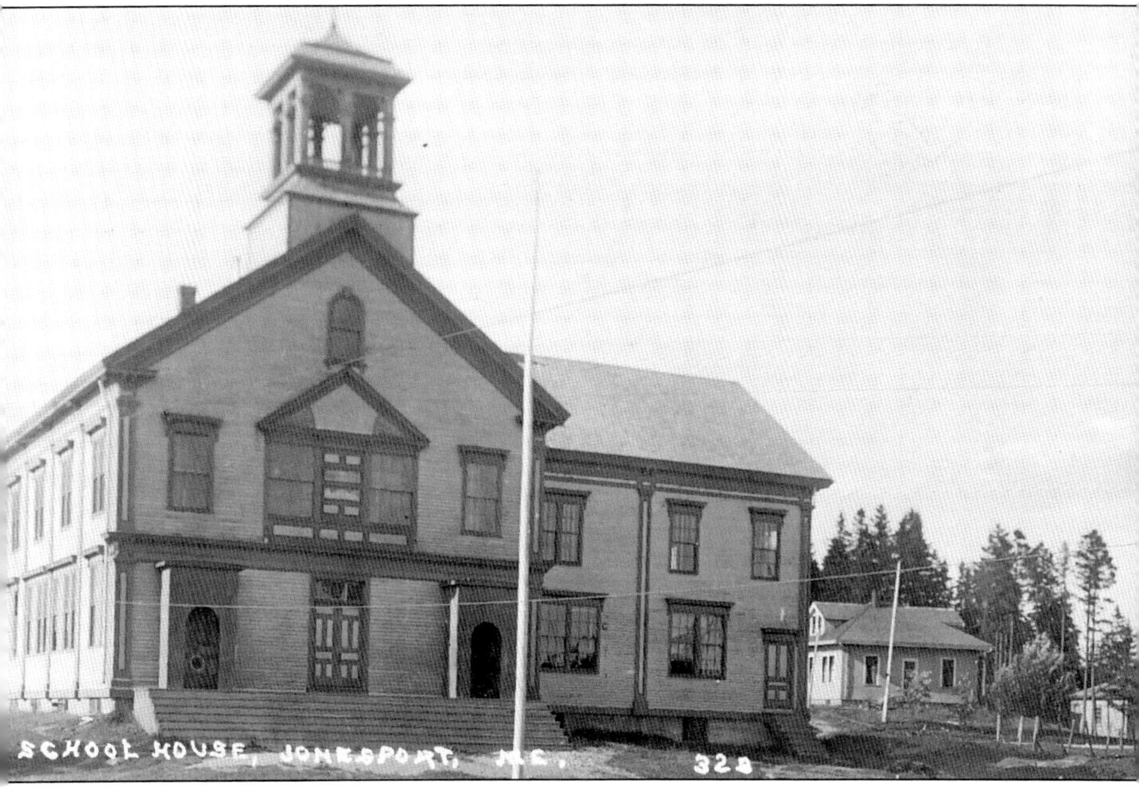

Jonesport High School was located on the vacant lot across from the present post office. The first floor of the school was classrooms; on the right of the second floor was the gym. The masons also held their meetings at the old high school. At one time, there was a stunt man in town who would climb the sides of buildings. He was called the human fly and he climbed the side of the high school to the belfry tower.

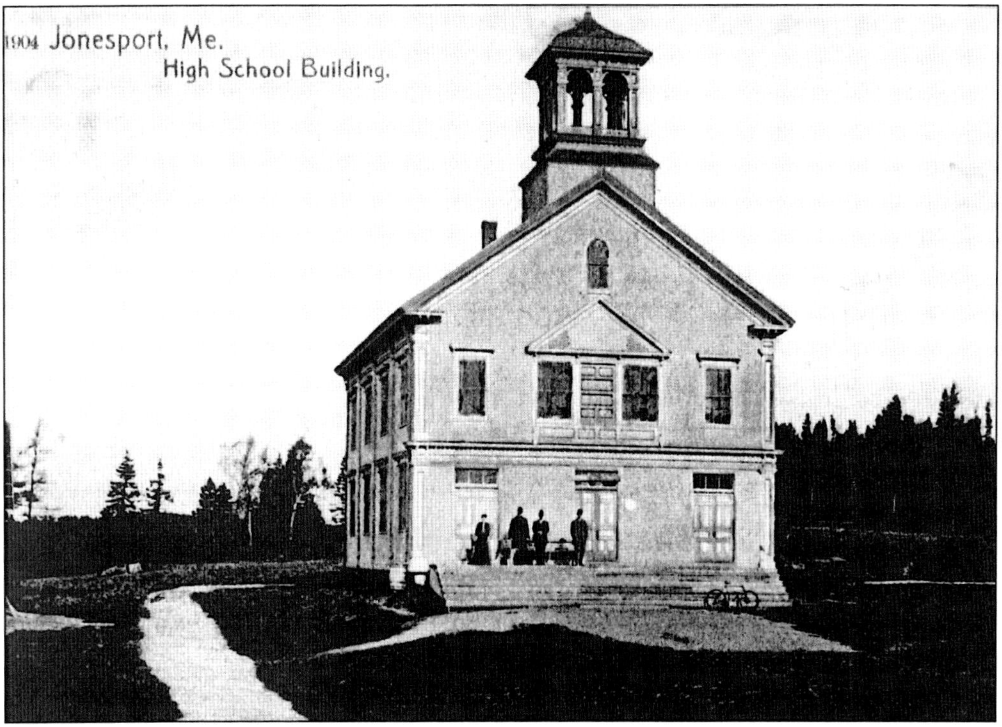

This is an early picture of the Jonesport High School before the ell was added. It was located across from the post office in town.

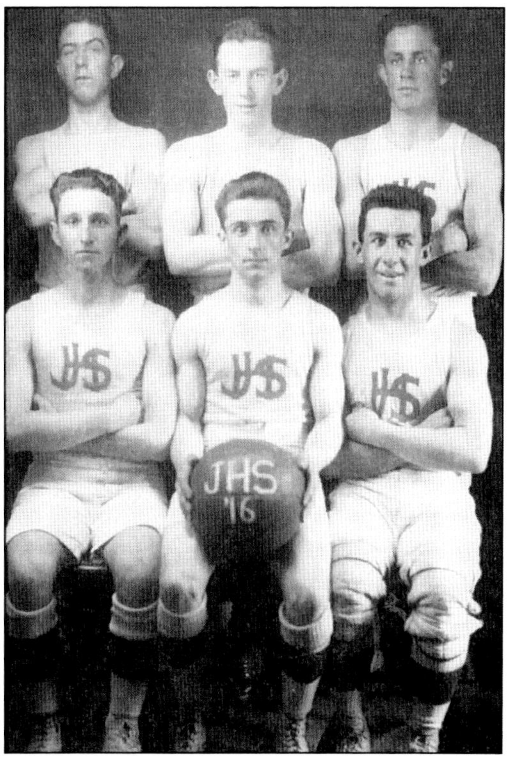

The Jonesport High basketball team of 1916 consisted of the following athletes, from left to right: (front row) Merton Kelly, Carl Davis, and William Norton; (back row) Harold Lamson, Ellison Drisko, and Austin Beal.

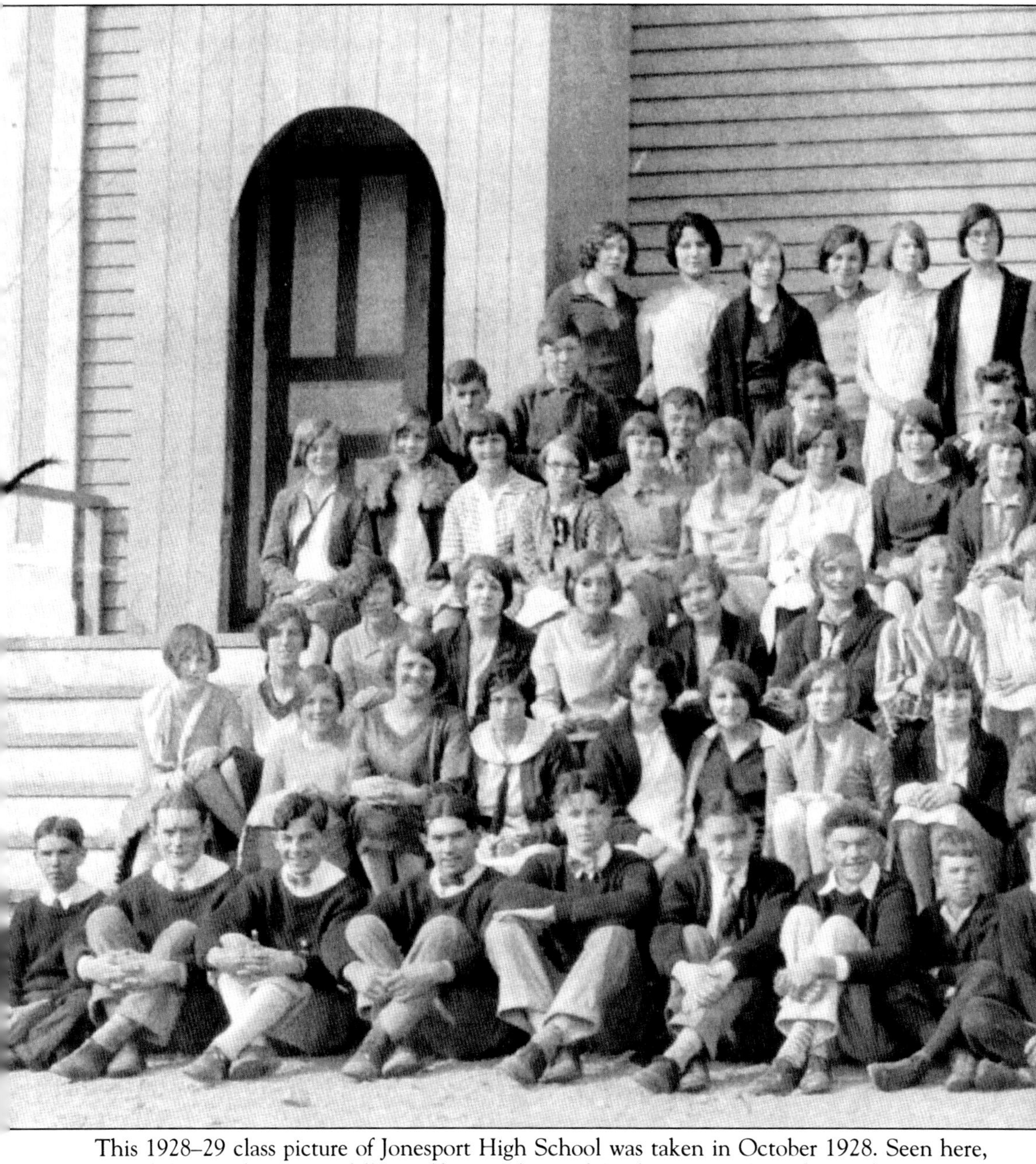

This 1928–29 class picture of Jonesport High School was taken in October 1928. Seen here, from left to right, are as follows: (first row) Virgil Bagley, Leroy Openshaw, Elma Sawyer, Charles Kilton, Bagley, Elery Mansfield, Edward Stevens, Warren Kelley, Royce Crowley, Douglas Hinkley, Gerald Frost, Lawrence Beal, Garfield, Hanland Knowles, Linwood Beal, and Carl Gray; (second row) Minesva Look, Ruth Noyce, Zelma Knowles, Ginevieve Carver, Helina Watt, Elna Kelley, Mildred, Gertrude Fross, Eula Crowley, Edna White, Vena Alley, Leonard Tibbetts, Ernest Smith, and Walter Wolfe; (third row) Violet Dawes, Marian Huntley, Blanche Beal, Veana Noyse, Gertrude Drisko, Lillian Kilton, Nola Lakeman, Gladys Beal, Marjorie Smith, Helen Cummings, Ruth Ginn, Pauline Wilson, Nataline Harman,Walter Church, Forrest Gray, Elwin Lamson, Earl Cofffin, and William Wilson; (fourth row) Cora

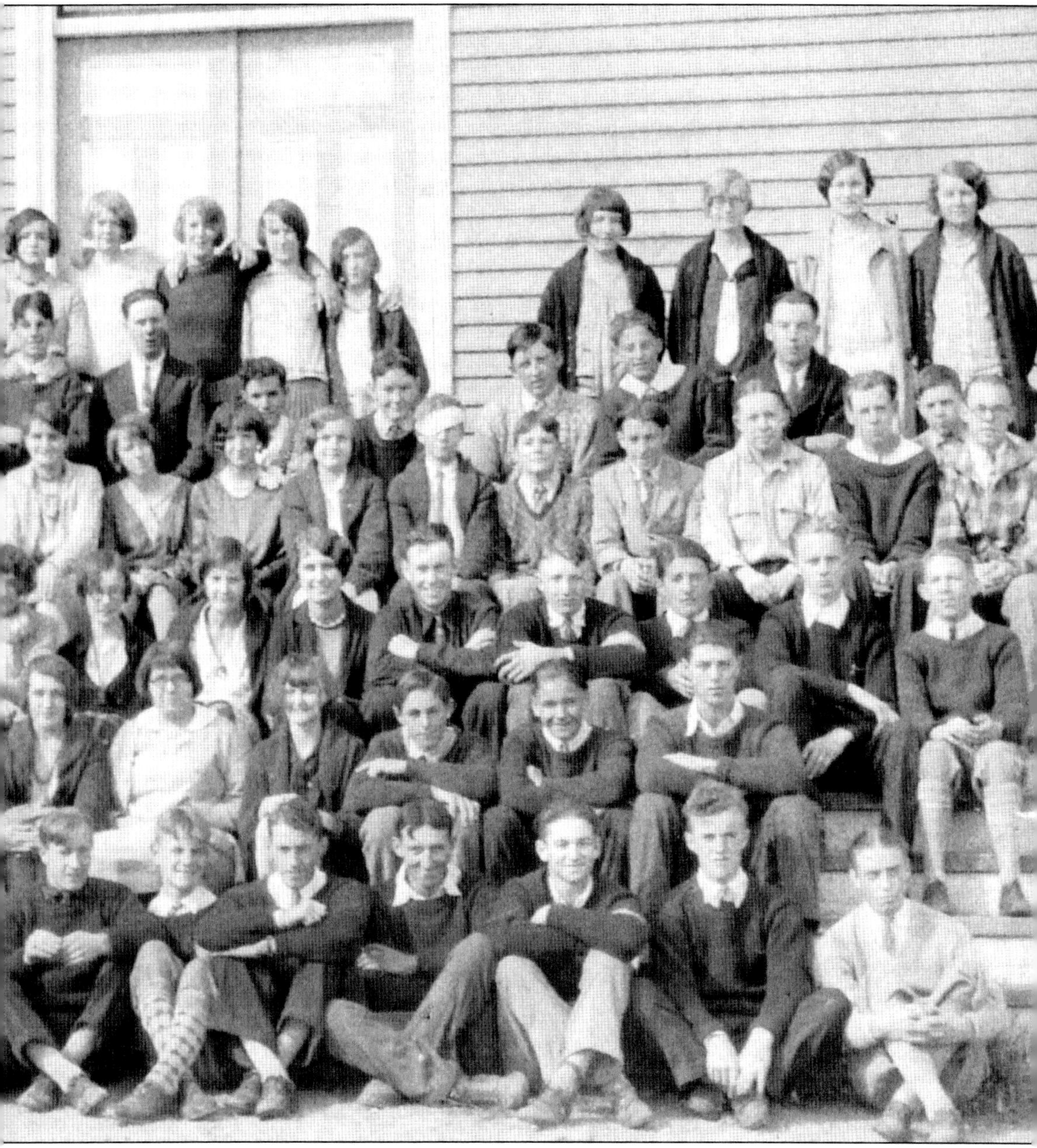

Drisko, Beverly Wilson, Bertha Beal, Zebra Hooper, Alice Norton, Edna, Gvetha White, Arlene Alley, Hilda Graves, Daisy Frost, Olive Blake, Thelma Garnett, Margaret Wilson, Robert Merchant, Frank McCallum, Fred Sawyer, Lester Woodward, Alton Kelley, and John Clark; (fifth row) Daniel Farnsworth, Eldan Beal, Charles Look, Frank Gray, Forrest Allen, Bubar, Hildred Tibbetts, Thurston Peabody, Marshal Kelley, Earlan Beal, Bertrum, Harold, Orel Noyar, and Raynard Calar; (sixth row) Sybil Norton, Evangeline Davis, Ella Drisko, Ida Beal, Elise White, Doris Farnsworth, Dorothy Carver, Sawyer, Evelyn Carver, Doris Leighton, Ruby Ginn, Virginia Carver, Hazel Smith, Mima Faulkingham, Eleanor Morris, and Marion Wilson; (teachers) Merrill Daisy (French and English), William Bailey (Science and Math), Phyllis Bowman (History and Latin), and Rose Drisko.

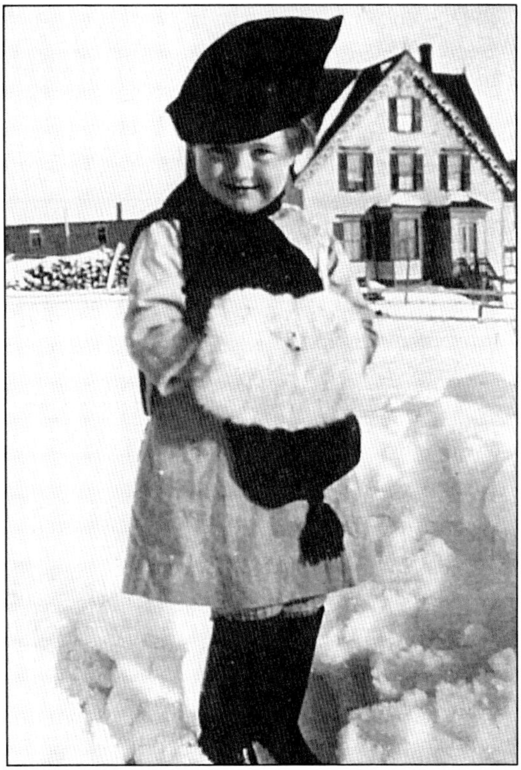

Irene Dobbins poses for a photograph with the Underwood Factory in Jonesport in the background. The picture was taken the winter of 1917; Irene was born in Jonesport and was the daughter of Austin and Eva (Faulkingham) Dobbins.

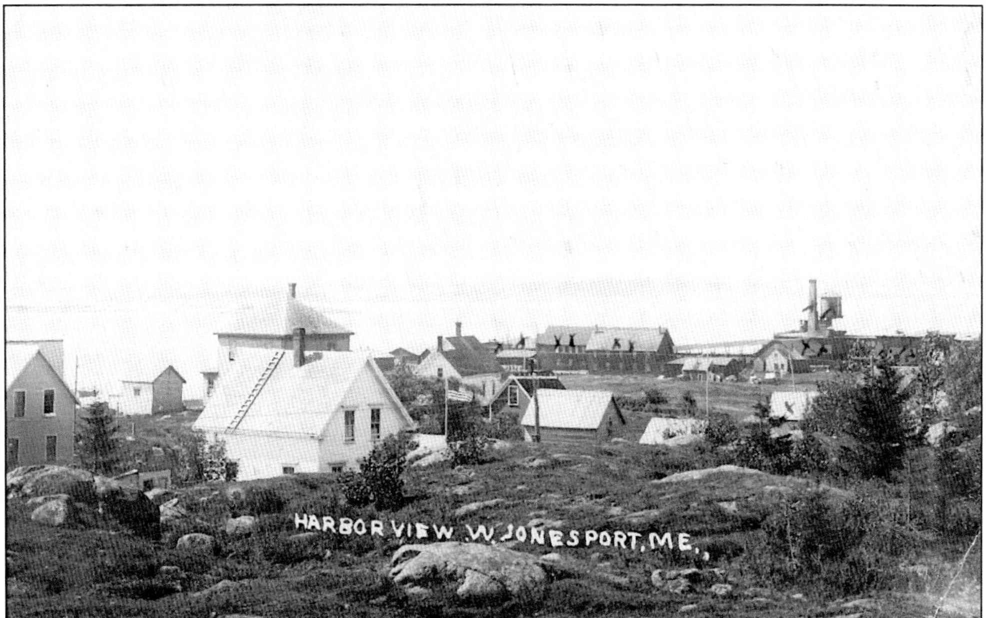

The building with the xx on the roof, the Underwood Factory, was located in Underwood Square near the Coast Guard station. Also located in Underwood Square were Cummings Hardware, F.l. McCollum Grocery, C.l. Jones Grocery, and D.N. Sawyers Dry Goods. It was a very busy part of town around the turn of the 20th century.

Four

Jonesport: Past and Present

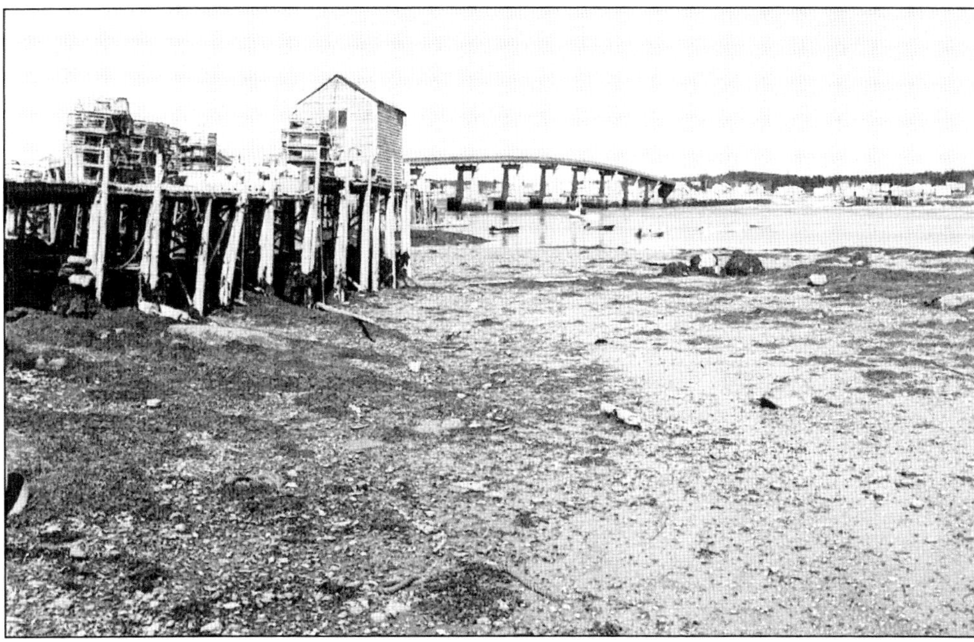

The piers in Jonesport are high due to the variation of tides. On the average day, they rise and fall about 18 feet every 6 hours. At certain times of the year, the tide fluctuates up to 28 feet every 6 hours, or close to an inch every minute.

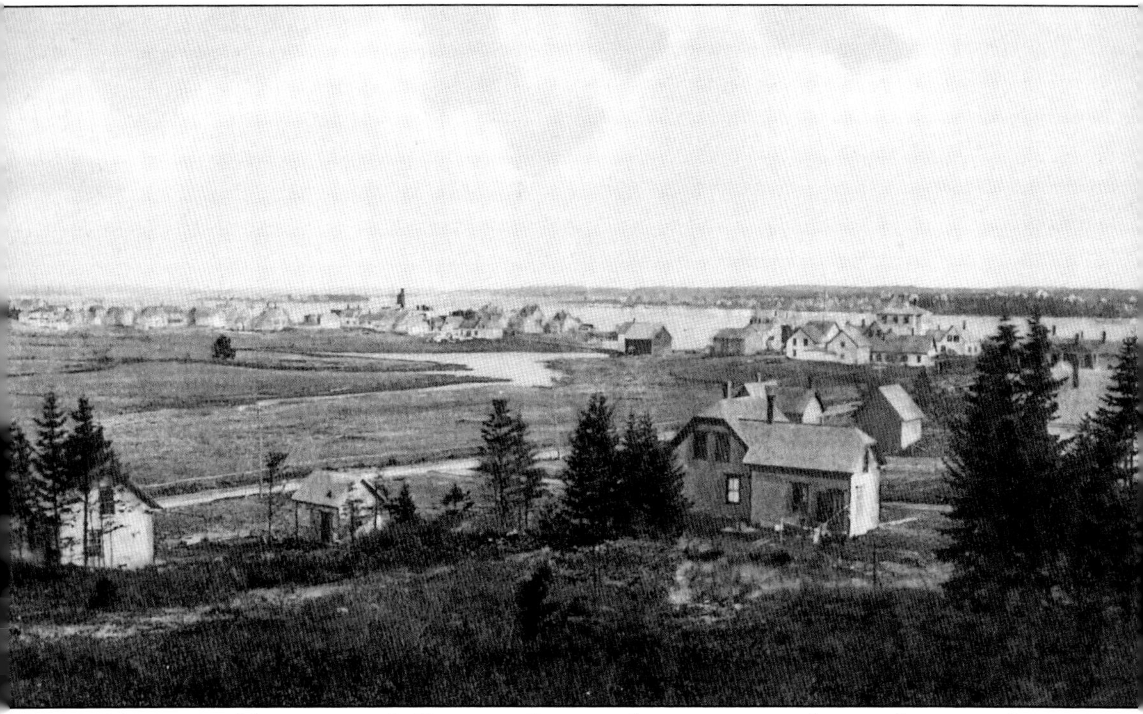

This view of Jonesport with Donovan Cove in the center reminds me of a poem that my Grandmother Davis wrote about the creek on Donovan's Cove. It's called the *Creek in the Summer*; every time I see a sunset no matter where I am I can see that creek in my mind.

THE CREEK IN THE SUMMER

There's a little creek in Jonesport;
That winds in through the land,
That every day the setting sun
Paints with a lavish hand.
There it loves to linger,
And with colors of red and gold;
Makes the creek a picture of beauty,
To behold.
The sun sinks low, the colors fade,
The evening breezes sigh;
The picture's changed! The creek reflects
The golden moon on high.
The sky above is studded
With diamonds in the blue,
Would that I were an artist
To paint this scene for you.
Many pretty scenes I've viewed,
As miles I've chanced to roam;
But never one as lovely as,
The little creek back home.

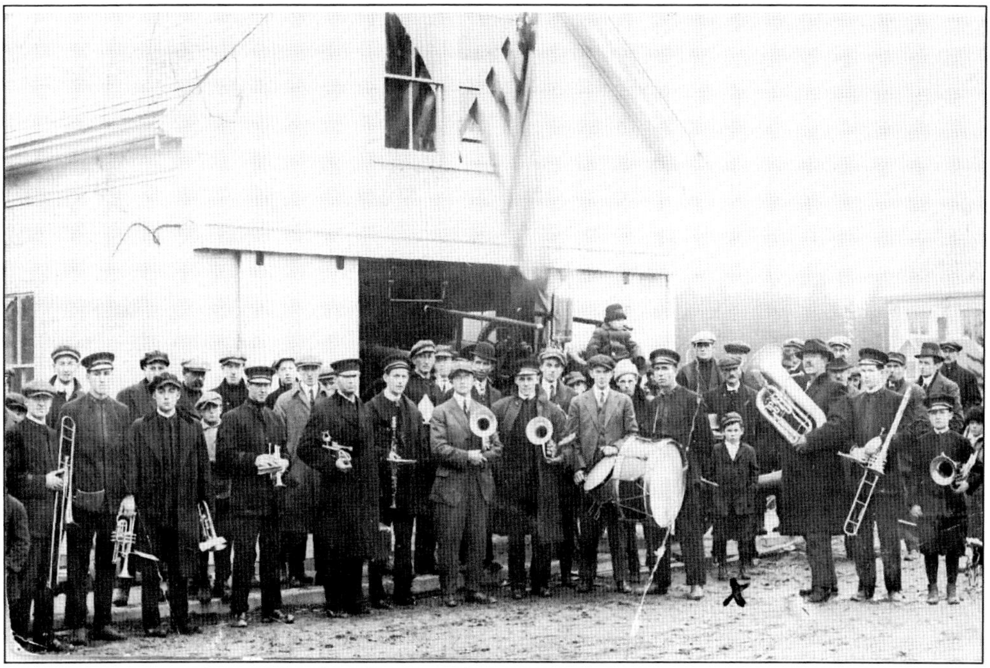

The Jonesport Band posed for this photograph on July 1, 1916. the little boy at right in the front is George Carver.

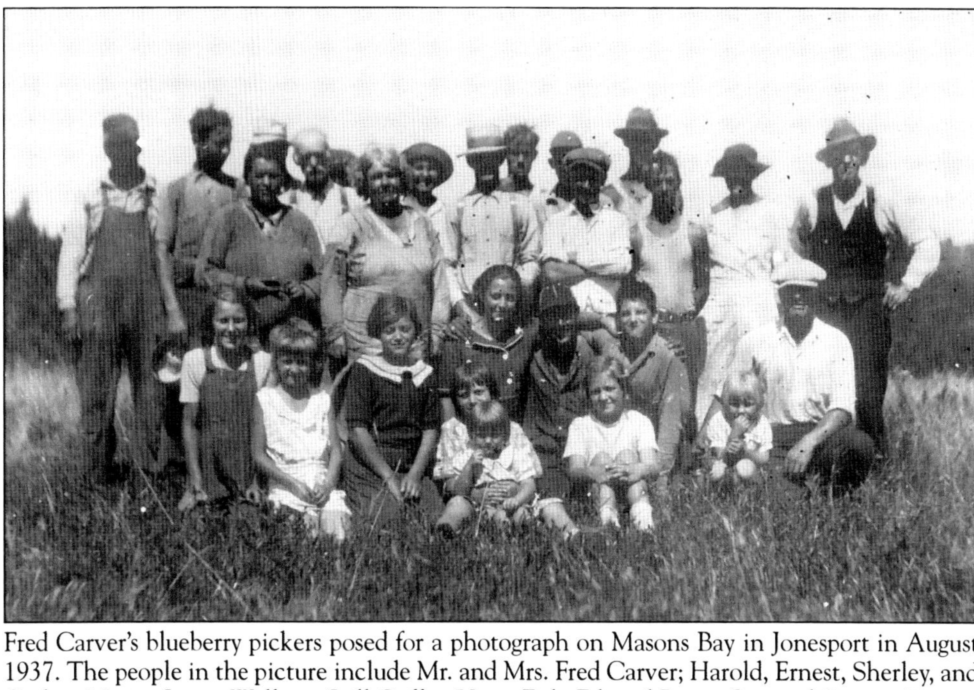

Fred Carver's blueberry pickers posed for a photograph on Masons Bay in Jonesport in August 1937. The people in the picture include Mr. and Mrs. Fred Carver; Harold, Ernest, Sherley, and Qudrey Meritt; James Wallace; Still Coffin; Harry Fisk; Edward Berry; Osmand Graves; Vinton Smith; Henry Smith; Vincent Church; Laura, Pauline and Elizabeth Myrna; and Mr. and Mrs. George Reed and family.

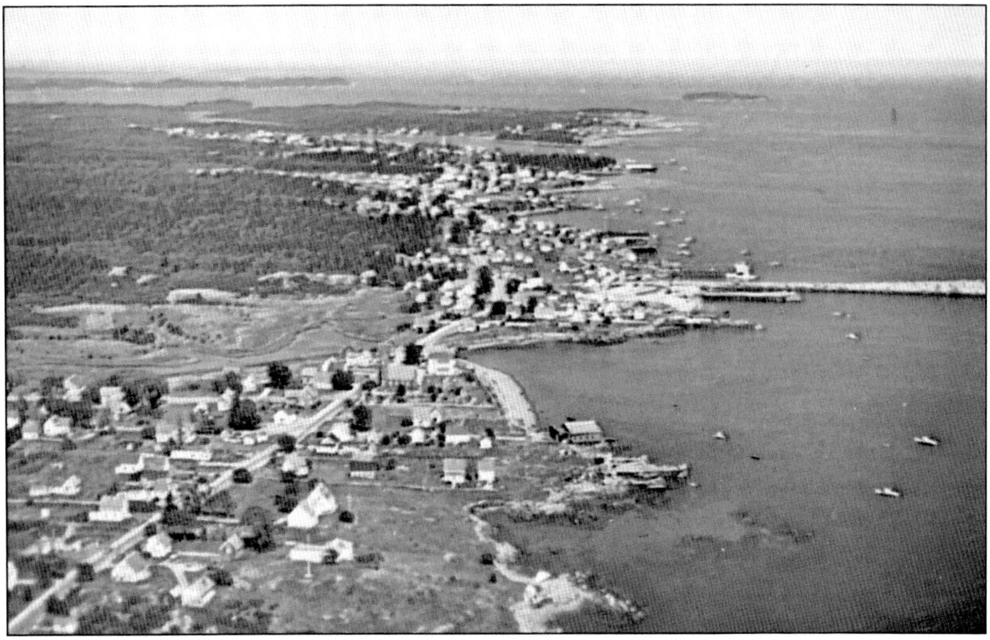

This aerial view of Jonesport shows the coastline from West Jonesport in the foreground all the way down Moosabec Reach. In the center is Donavan Creek; the building with the xx on the roof, at the edge of the water, is the Smith Wharf. The Jonesport-Beals Bridge is now located in the center of the photograph.

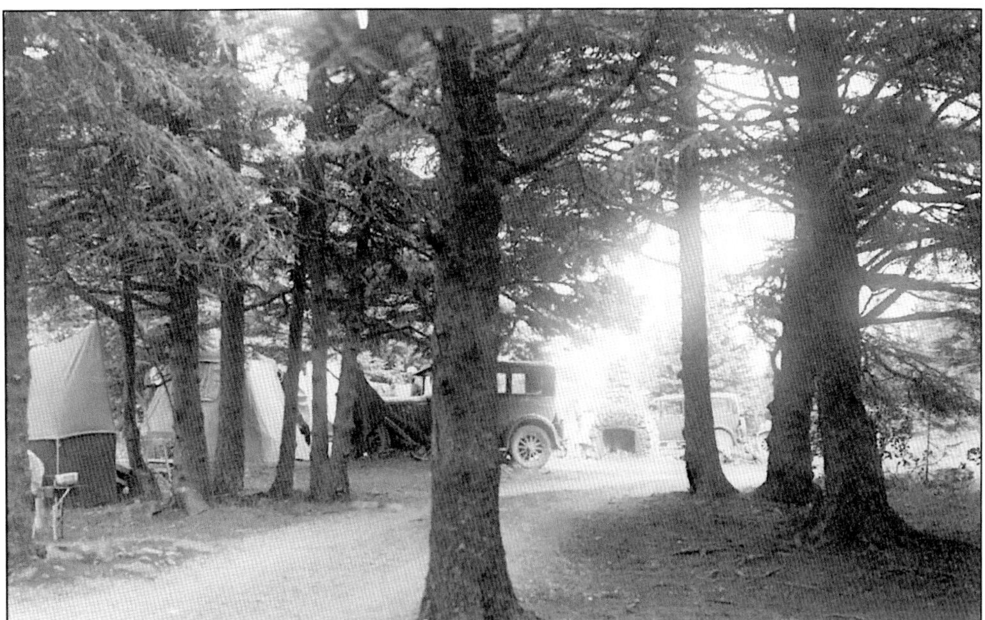

People have been camping on Henry Point at the campground for many years. In early times the Passamaquoddy Indians would come to the area and camp by the shore. They would pick sweet grass, hunt seals, and fish here. The campground looks over Sawyers Cove and the neighboring islands.

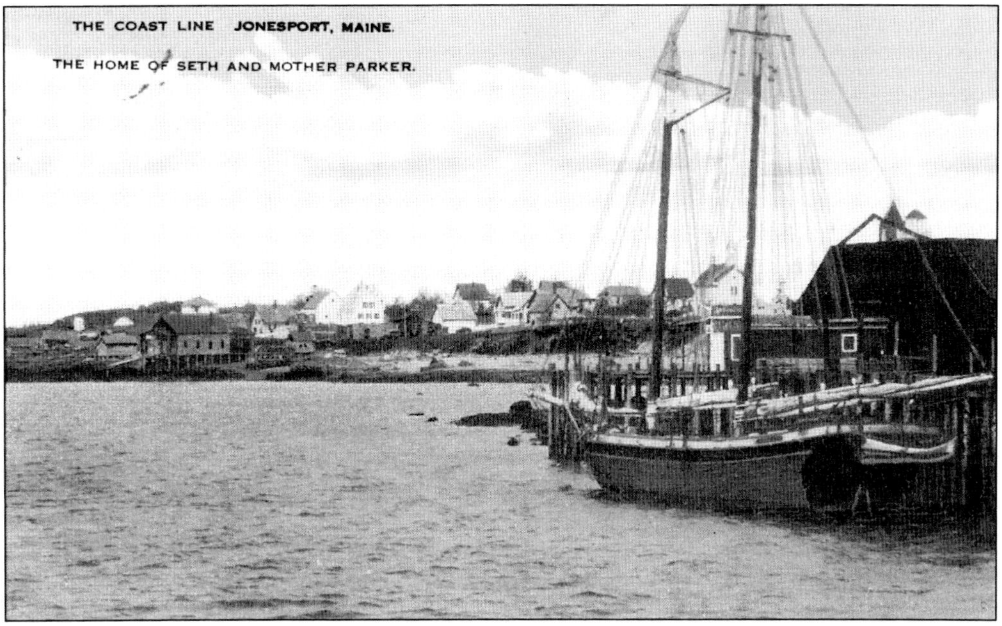

Two- and four-masted schooners were a prime example of the ships that went into port in Jonesport in the 1800s.

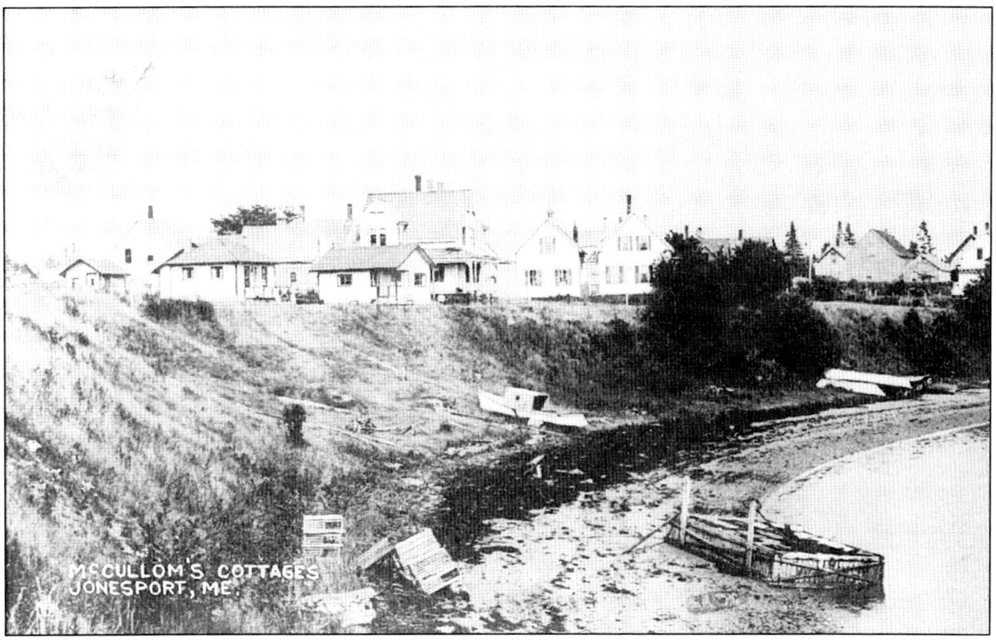

The McCullom's Cottages are located on the shore of Moosabec Reach just past the IGA Supermarket. The Cummings home is to the right of the cottages.

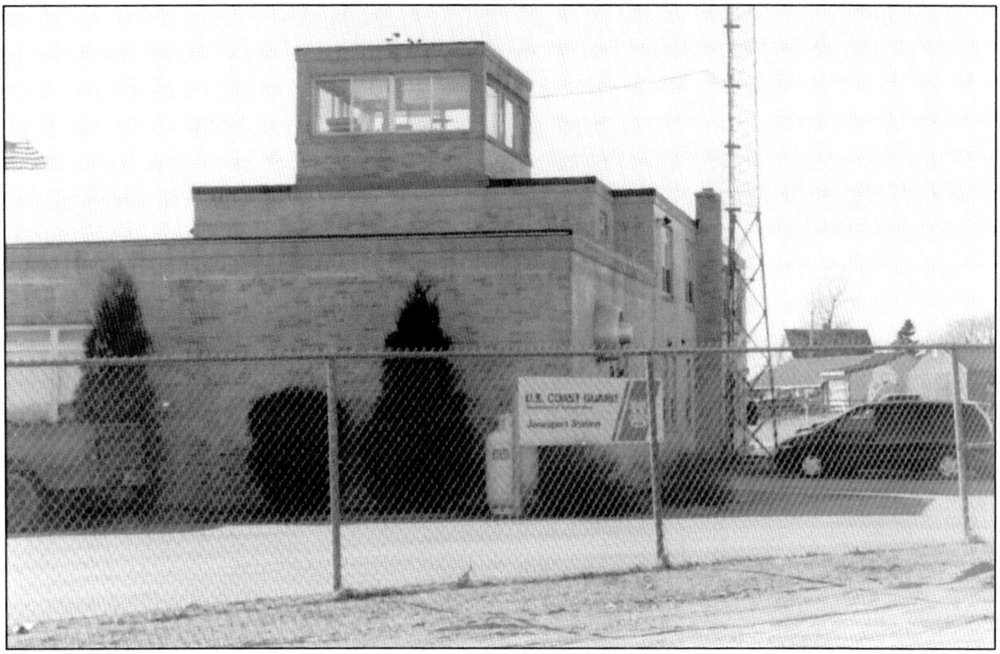

The Coast Guard station was built in June of 1969. It is located at the foot of the Jonesport-Beals Bridge.

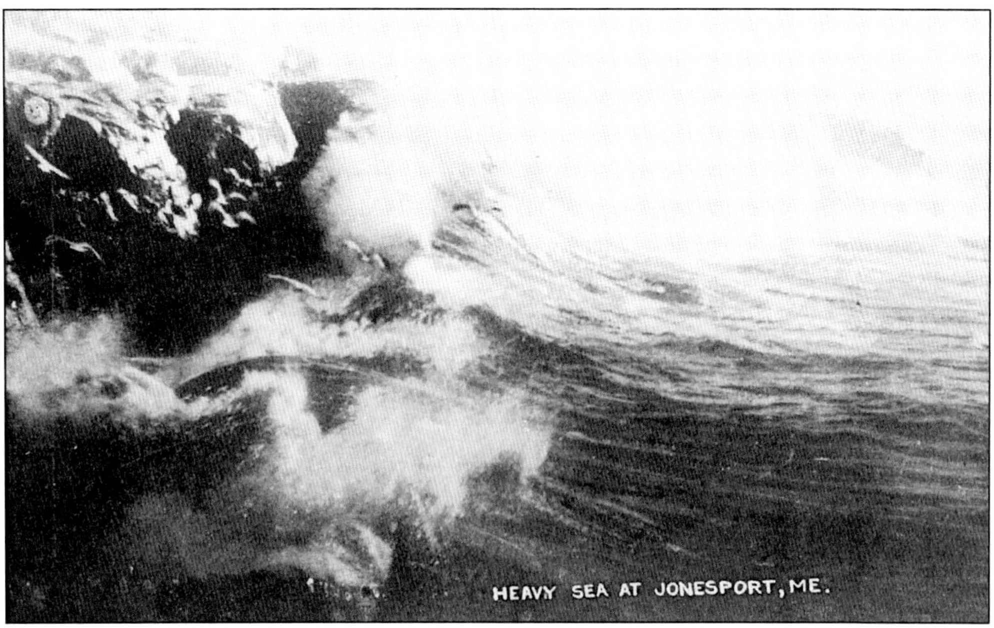

When there are heavy seas in Jonesport, the ocean goes right up over the rock and onto the road at Wash Out Point or crashes into the homes between Wash Out Point and Sandy River Beach.

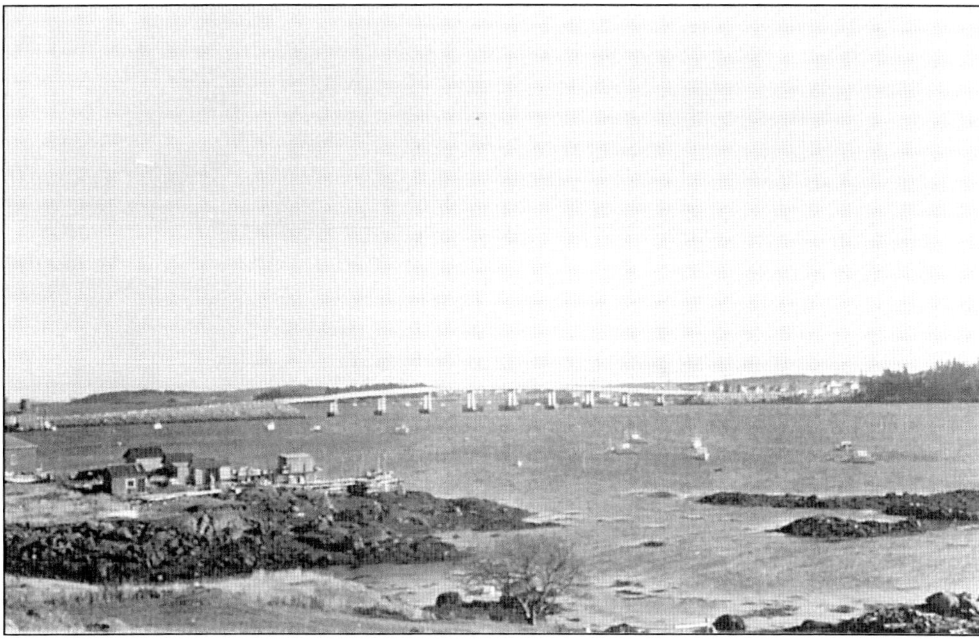

This panoramic picture was taken from West Jonesport. The Jonesport-Beals Bridge in the distance was built in 1957. At the time of its construction, it was one of the largest bridges to link an offshore island with the mainland.

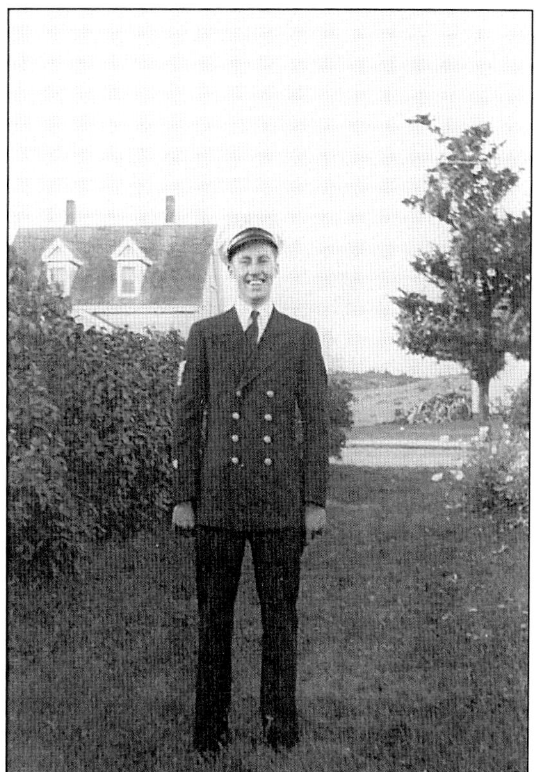

Capt. Barna Norton poses in front of the family home in Jonesport across from the present fire department. The captain ran a charter boat and would take tourists to see the puffins at Machias Seal Island.

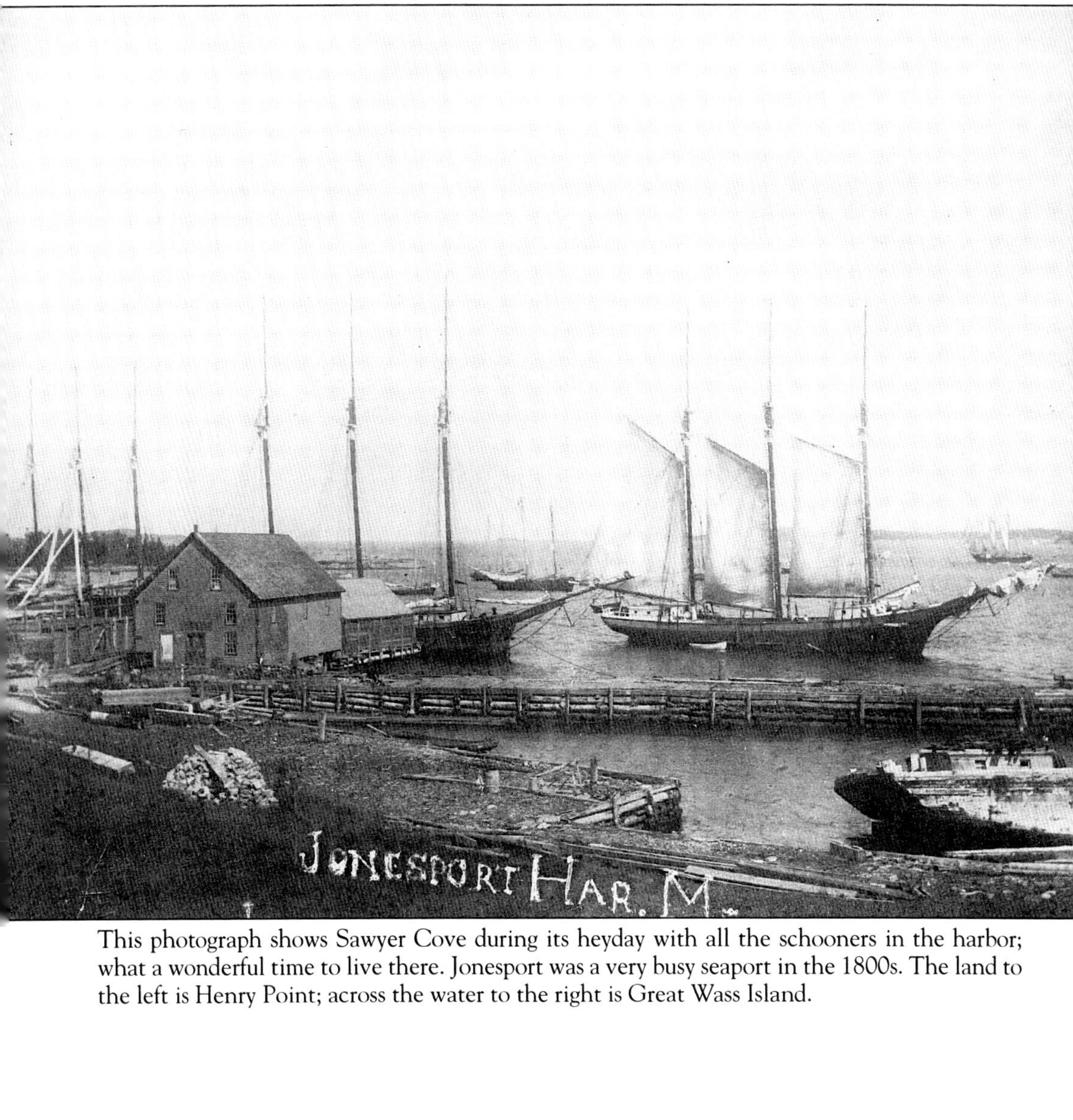

This photograph shows Sawyer Cove during its heyday with all the schooners in the harbor; what a wonderful time to live there. Jonesport was a very busy seaport in the 1800s. The land to the left is Henry Point; across the water to the right is Great Wass Island.

Clyde Lamson stands on the Smith Wharf looking over toward Beals Island, c. 1945.

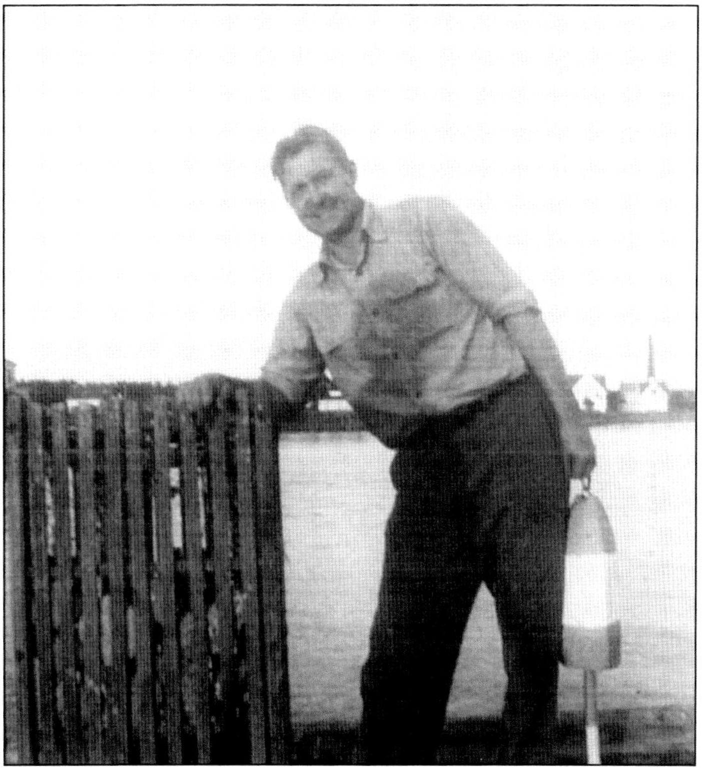

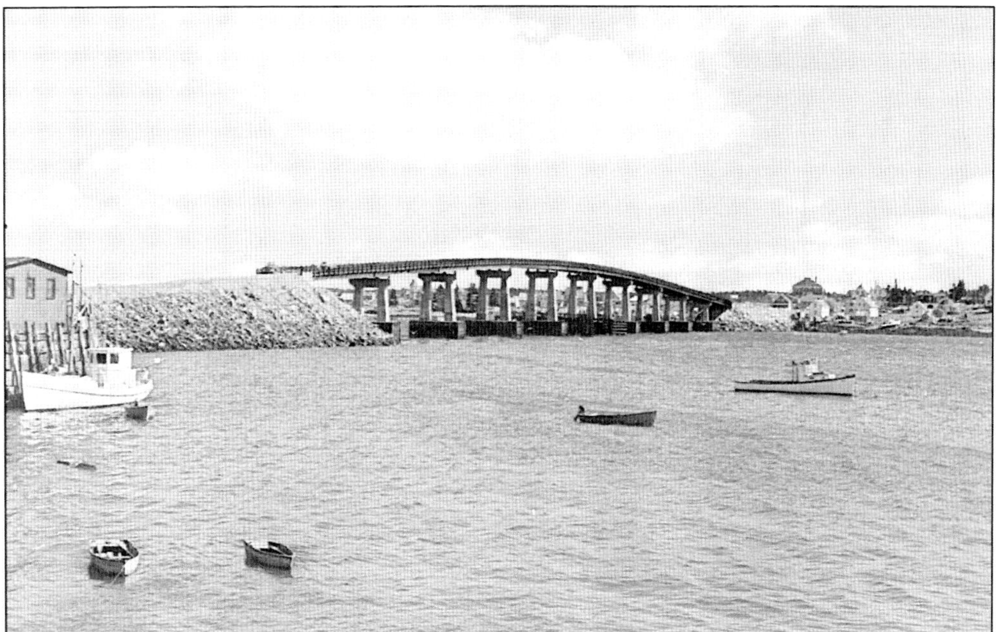

The Jonesport-Beals Bridge was built in 1958. Before the bridge was built, this site was the location of the steamboat dock. It was also where the ferry that brought people from the island to the main land docked.

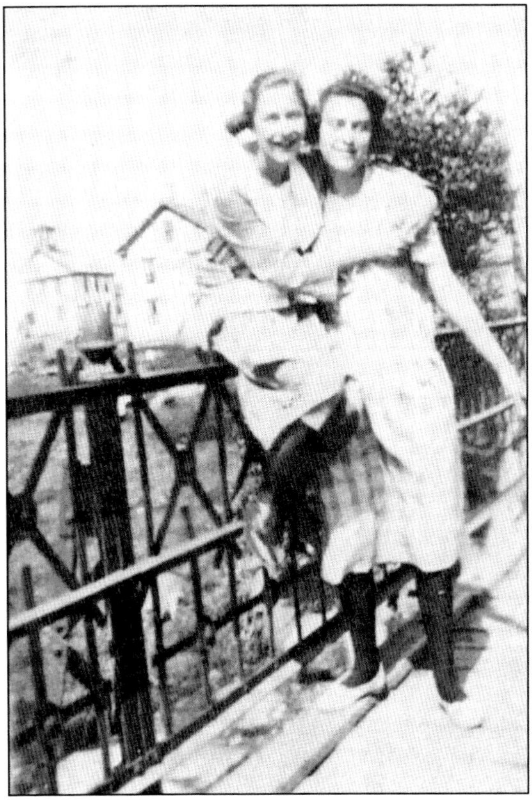

Lula Davis and Cora Watson pose on the Cross Cove Bridge in Jonesport; you can see the Washington School in the distance.

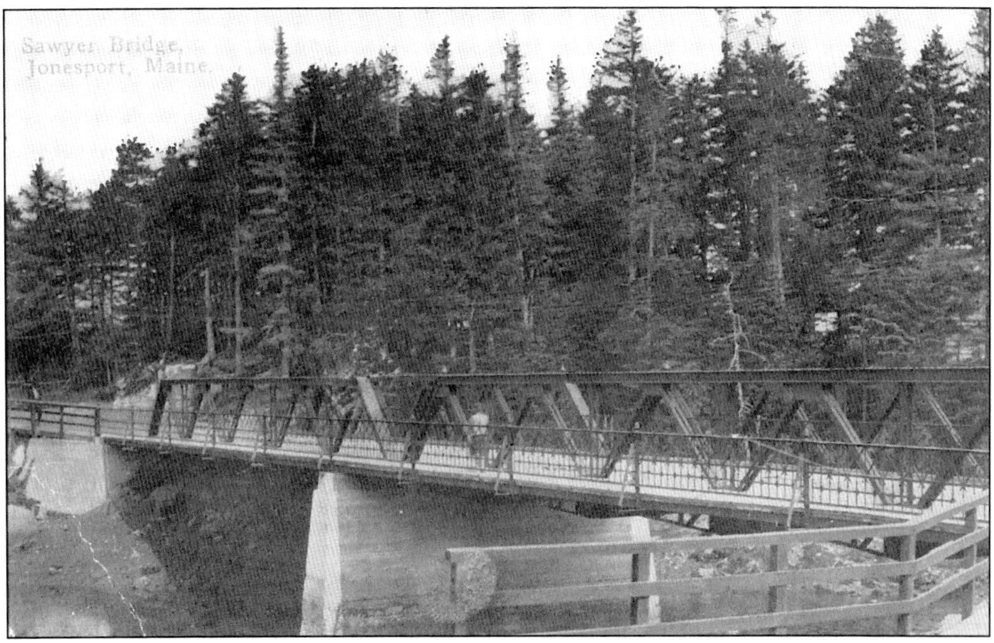

The Cross Cove Bridge was built in the summer of 1935. Arletta Faulkingham rented out her home to the men that were constructing it and went to Aroostook County to stay with friends for the summer.

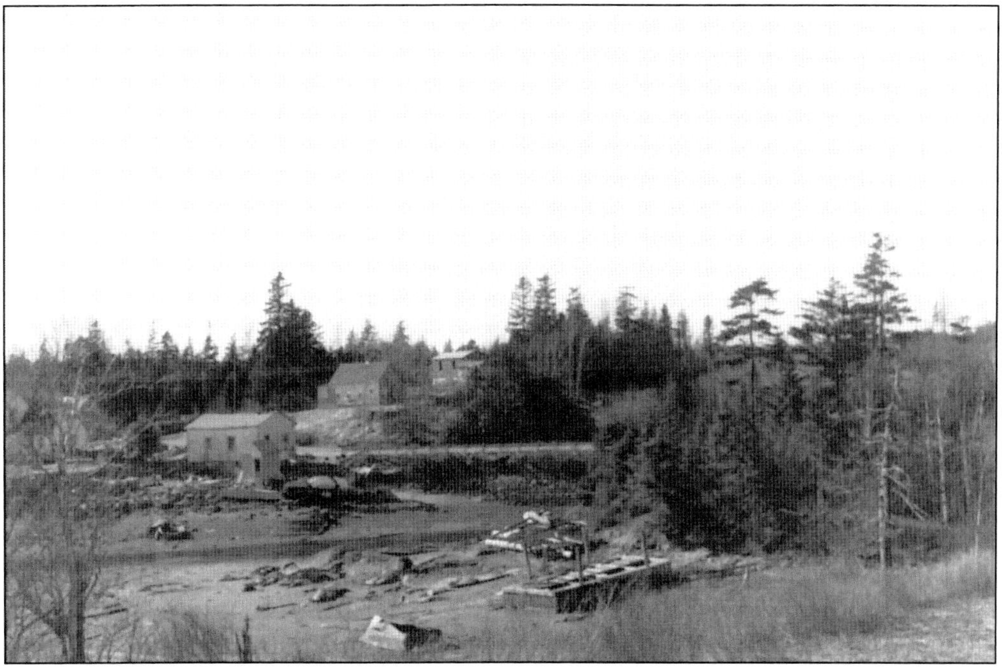

This is a view of Cross Cove during low tide looking across to Main Street in Jonesport.

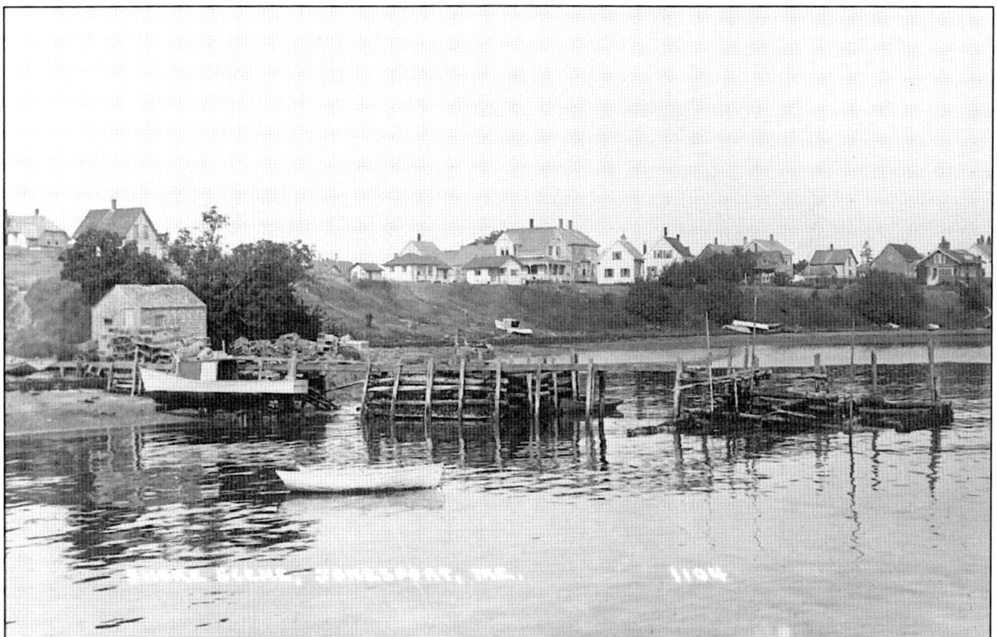

The Stevens Factory was one of the best-equipped plants for smoking fish and was located at Cross Cove. The factory employed from 75 to 100 people. It also produced about 70,000 boxes of smoked fish per season.

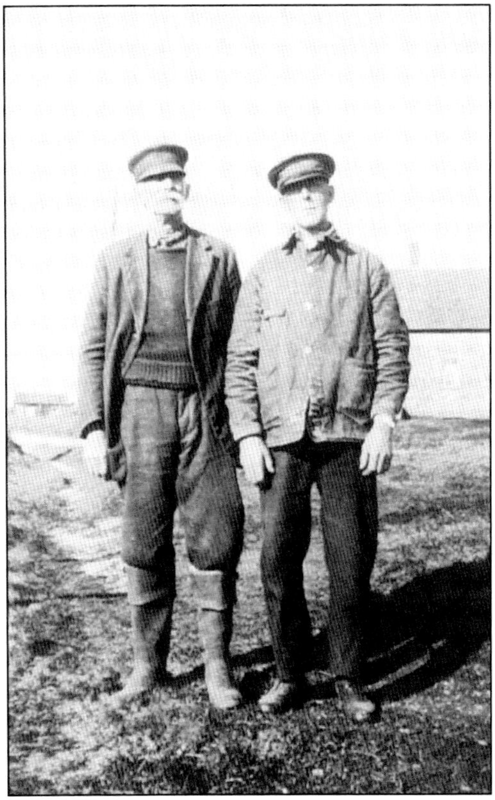

Fred Dobbins and Andrew Peabody stand on the road to Hopkins Point in West Jonesport, c. 1915.

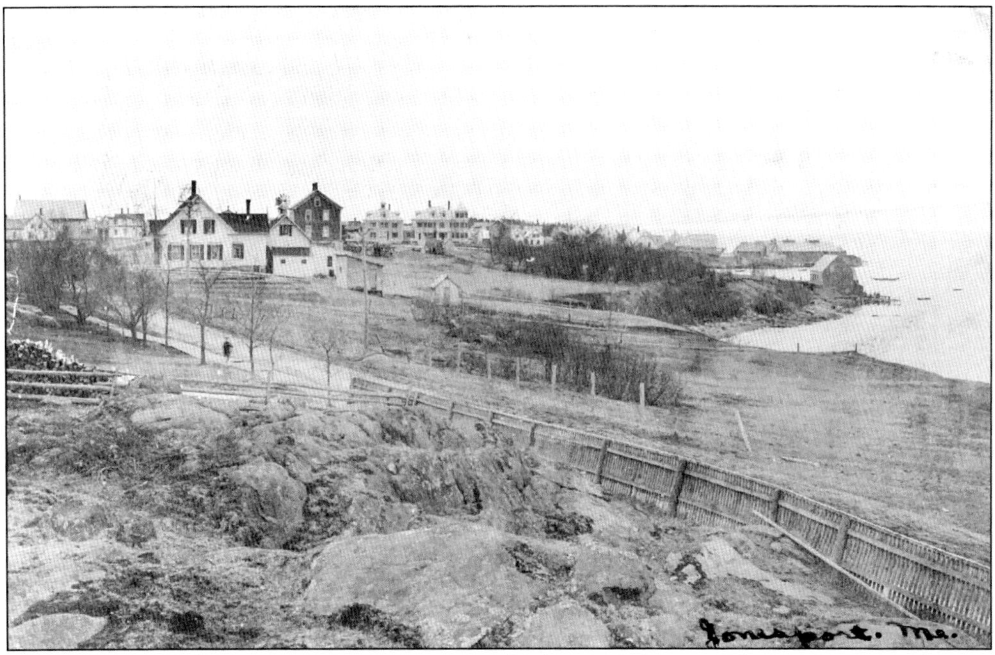

This view of Hopkins Point in West Jonesport looks toward town. The picture was taken in 1906; there weren't many homes in the area at that time.

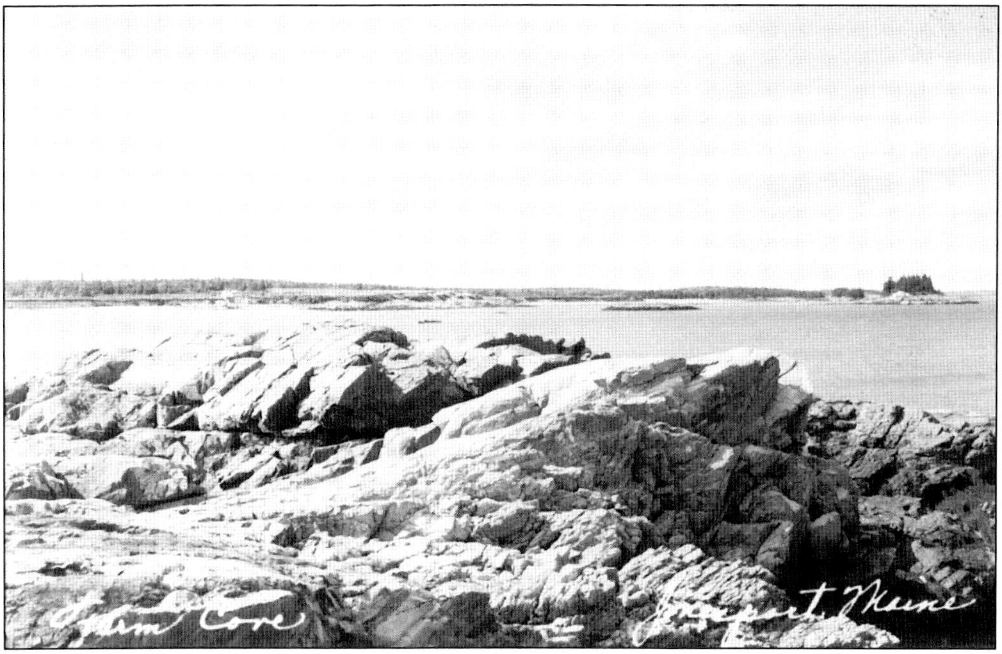

Farm Cove on Chandler Bay is shown here in a view looking across at Roque Island.

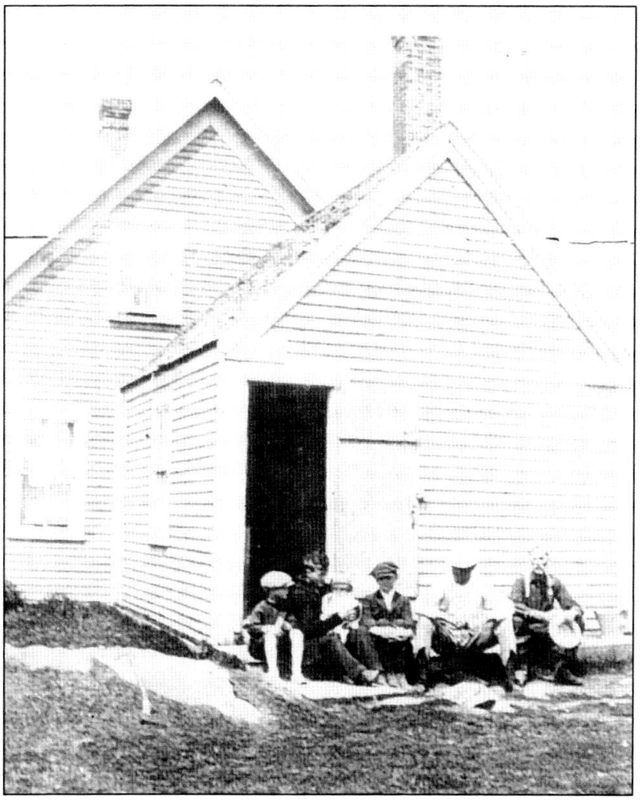

This picture was taken in 1915 at the Peabody home in West Jonesport. Seen here, from left to right, are an unidentified boy, Austin Dobbins (holding his daughter Irene), another unidentified boy, Irving Dobbins, and Fred Dobbins.

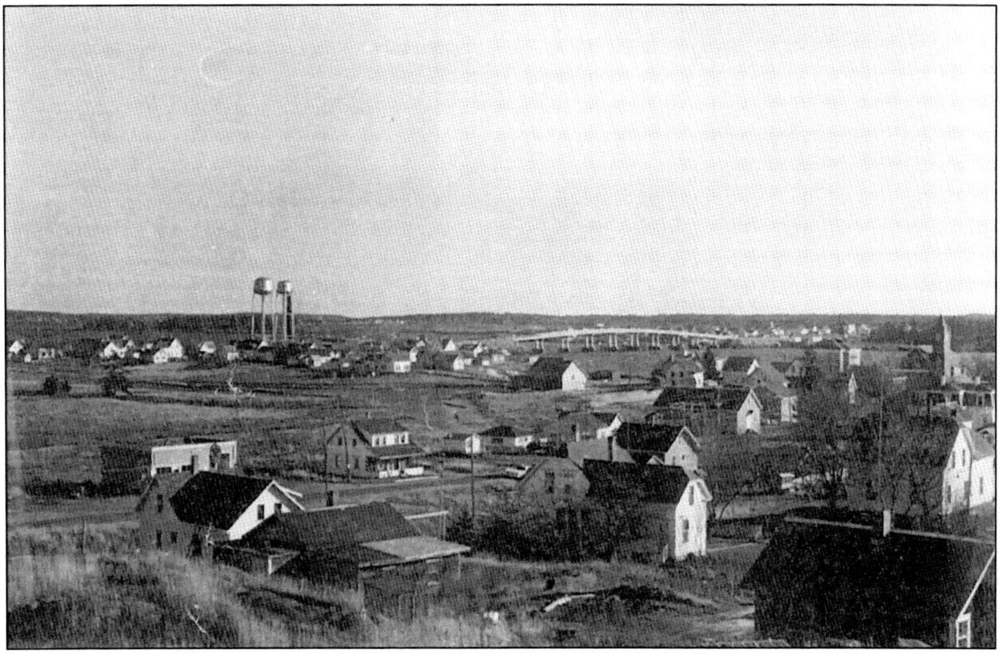

This is a view of Route 187 going into Jonesport. In the distance, you can see the water towers at the Underwood Factory at the foot of the Jonesport-Beals Bridge.

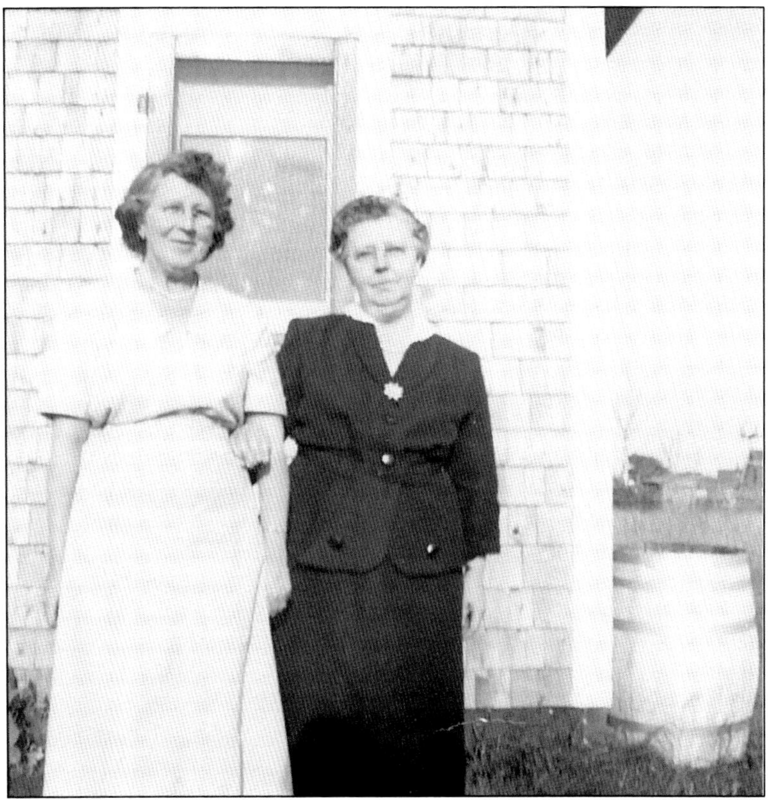

Sister's Elva and Eva Faulkingham are standing in front of the home their brother Philip in West Jonesport. The water towers from the Underwood Factory are in the background to the right.

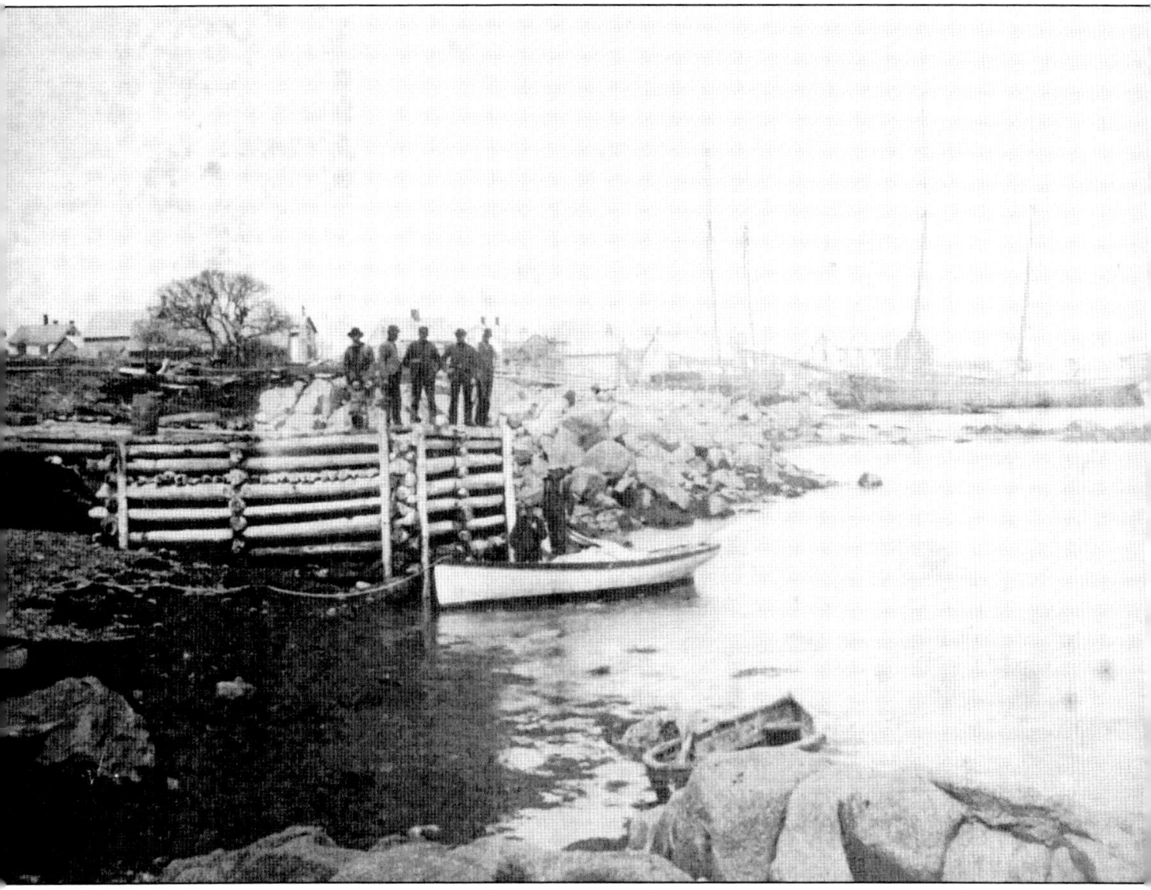

This is an early view of the Jonesport fishing village with the schooners and sardine factory in the background. In the 1880s, the sardine factories were called middle factories.

This photograph of Loon Point was taken in the 1930s. The islands in the distance are Little Spruce and Roque Islands. Some of the early settlers of Loon Point were Thomas Cromwell and his family.

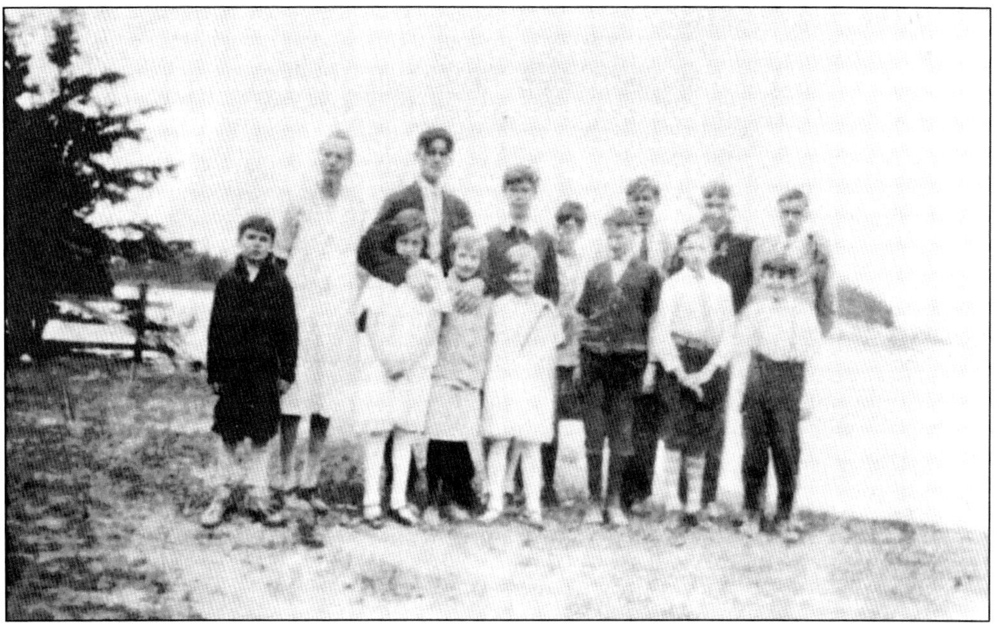

The Class of 1928 at the Indian River School held their outing at Loon Point. Seen here, from left to right, are as follows: (front row) Joe Emerson, Florence Gray, Hazel Gray, Elisabeth Gray, Billy Bradford, Reg Gray, and Arnald Emerson; (back row) Helen Small, teacher Arnold Davis, Blanch Seavey, Jennie Wass, Leland Davis, Maurice Gray, and Phillip Gray.

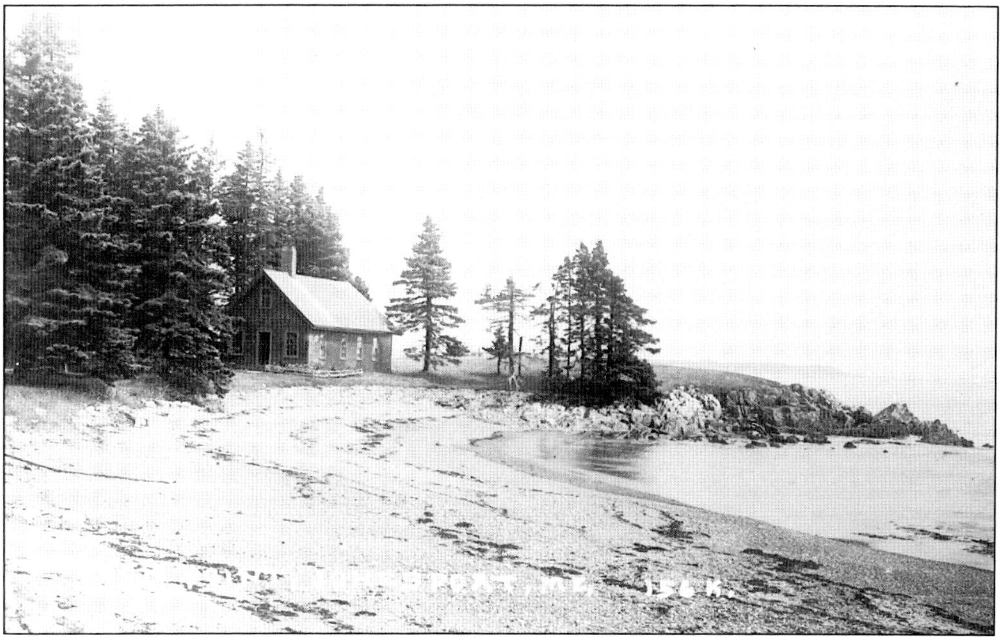

Loon Point was a frequent camping ground of local Native Americans, who were probably part of the Passamaquoddy Tribe.

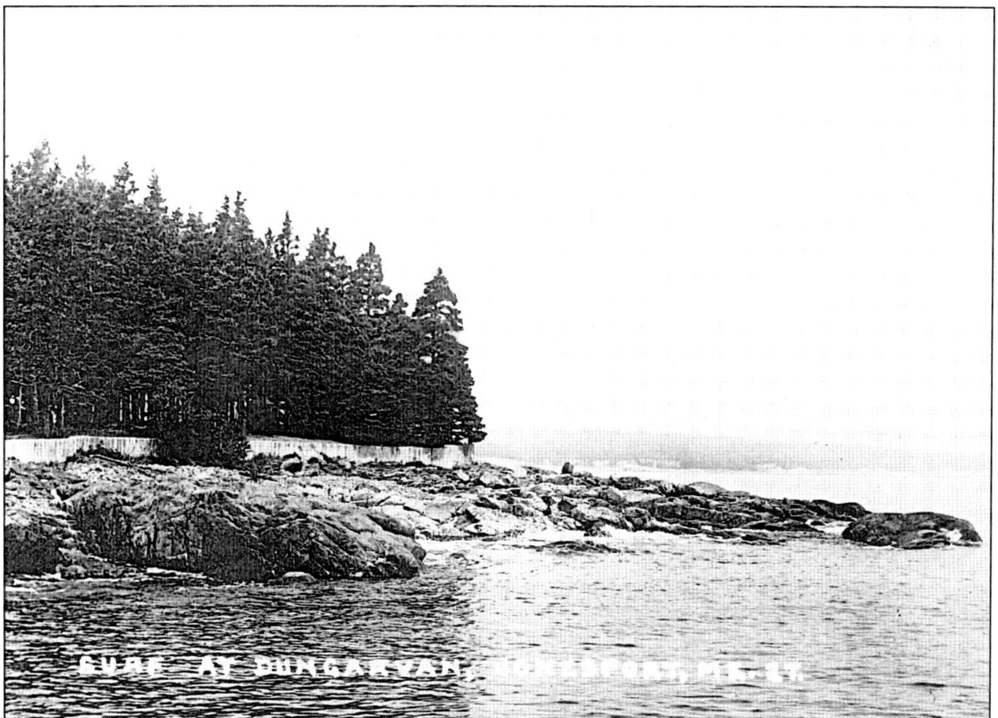

Dungarvan is located between the Loon Point and the Wash Out. When you leave Jonesport, heading down Route 187 toward Masons Bay, you go by Greenwood Cemetery. The old net and twine building is on the right; the entrance to Dungarvan is right after the building.

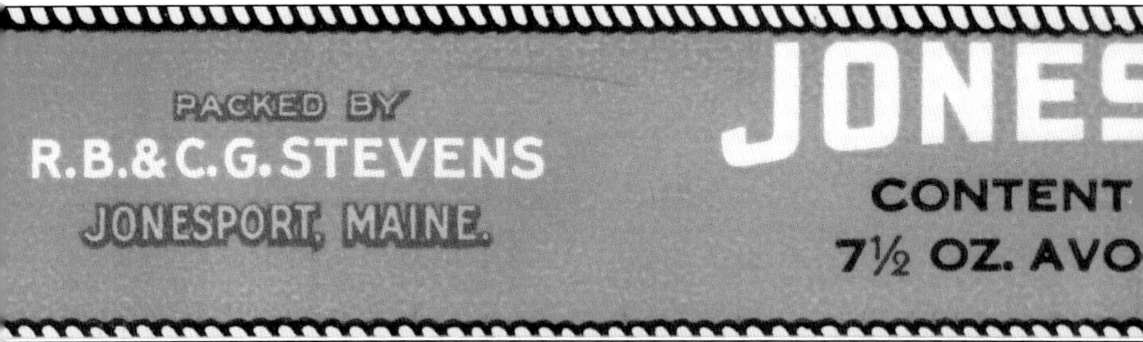

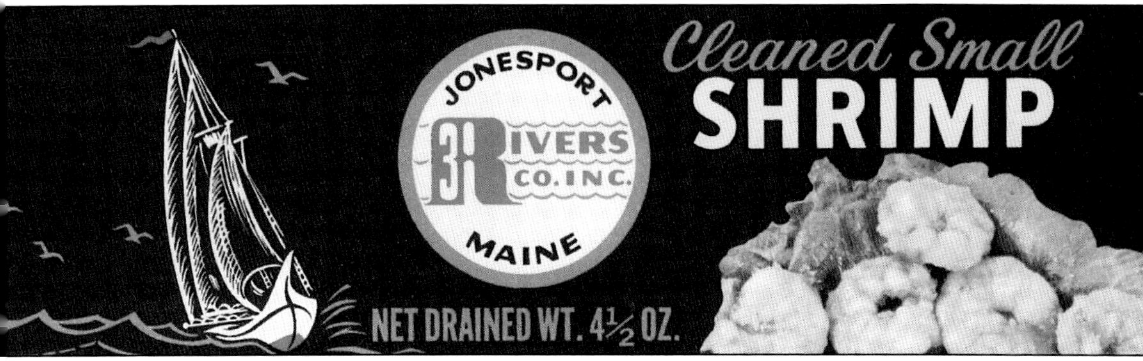

Here are a few of the labels from

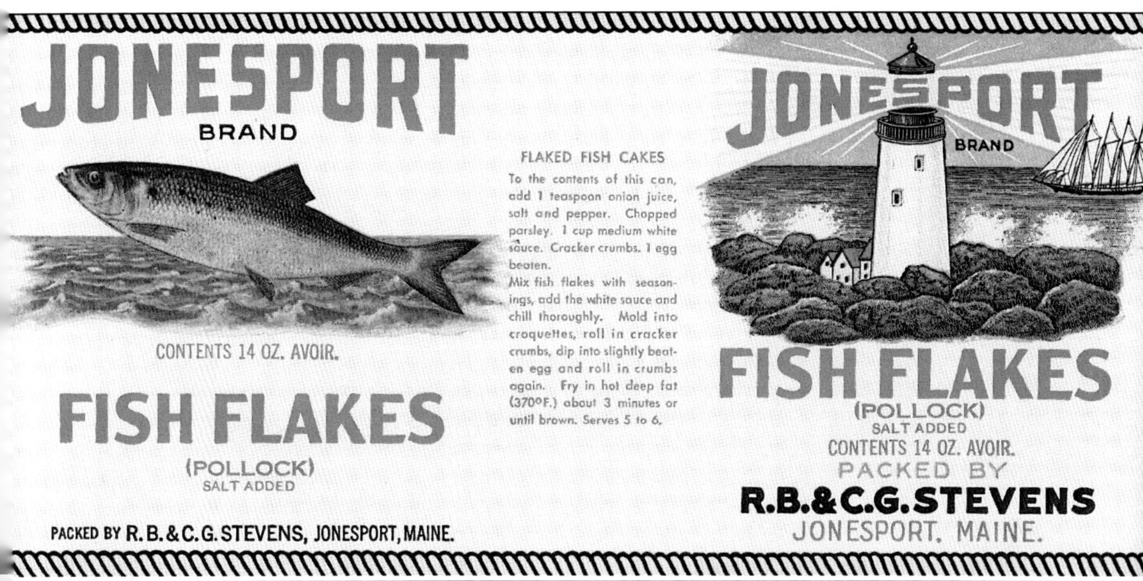

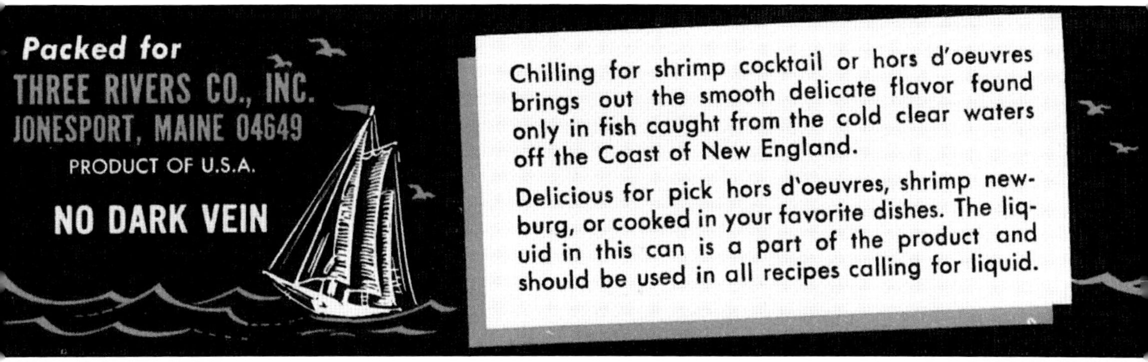

the factories of Jonesport.

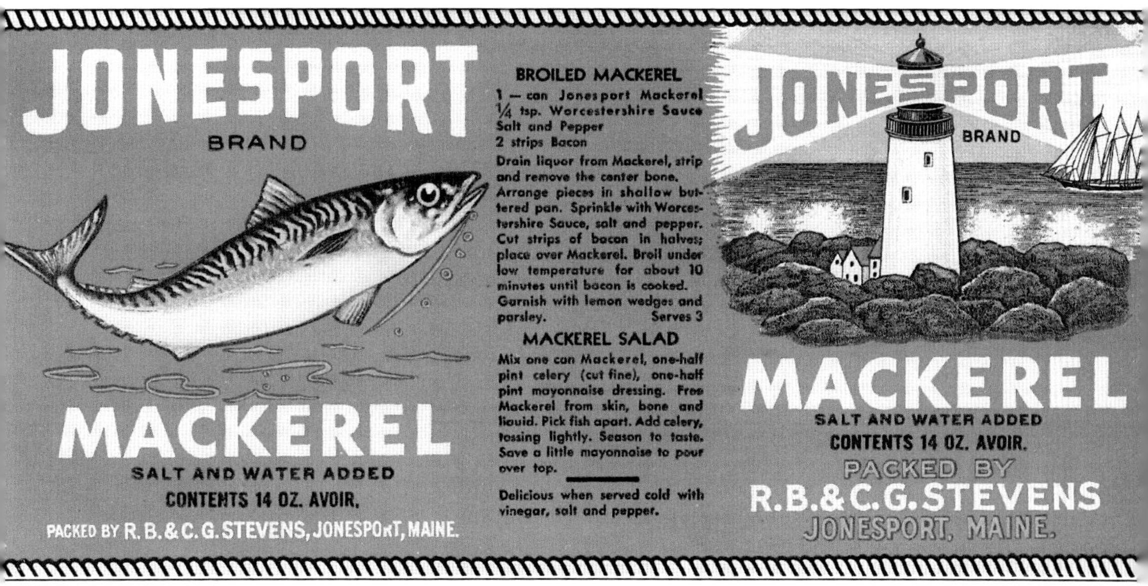

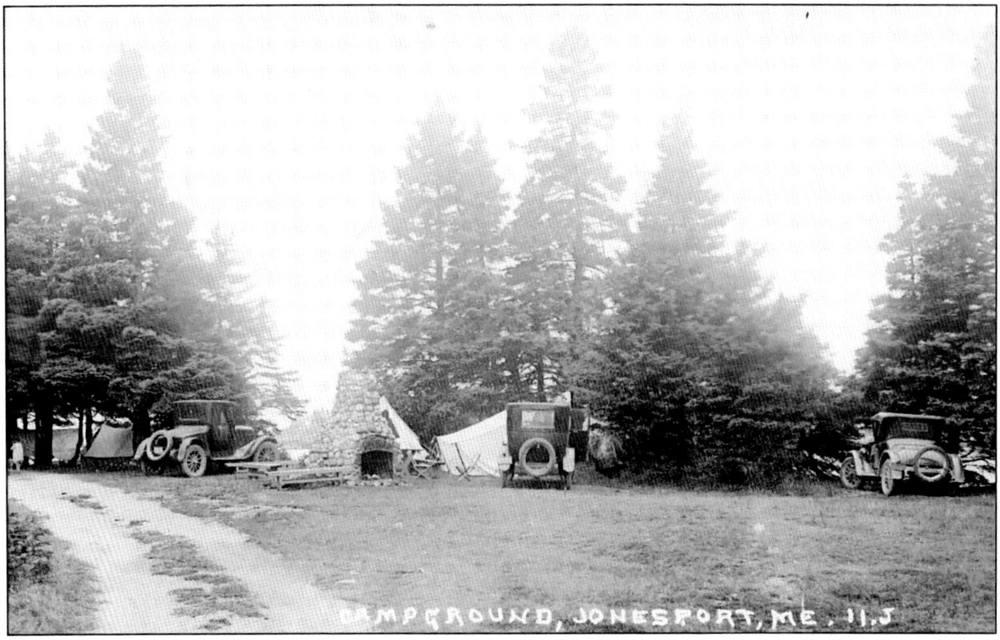

Henry Point Camp Ground was a popular place in the 1930s. The early cars can attest to that. The outhouse at the campground was a two-holer. Imagine sharing a bathroom with someone you didn't know.

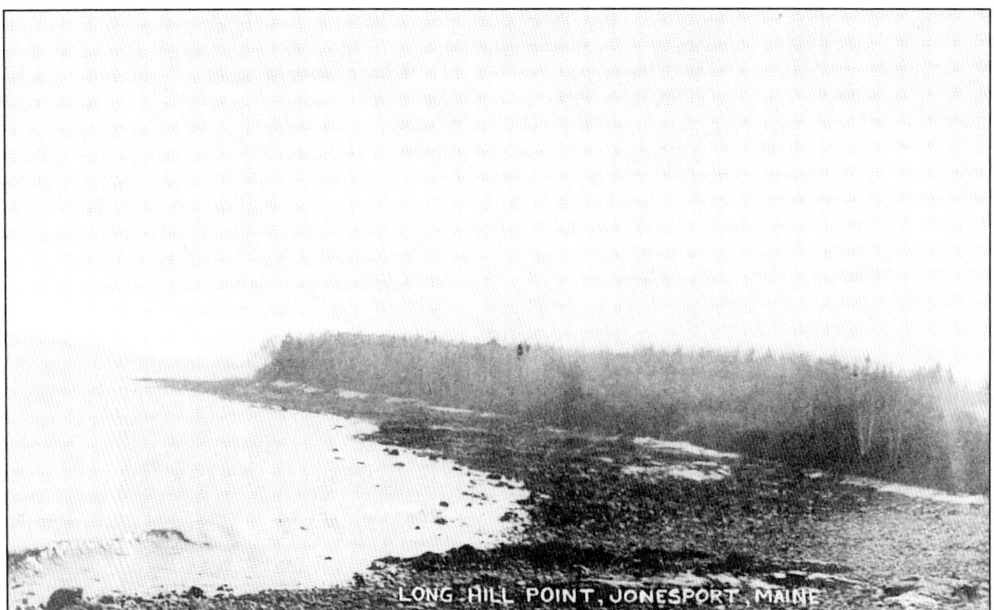

Long Hill Point is located half way between Masons Bay and the Wash Out. It's a beautiful rocky beach that looks across toward Roque Island.

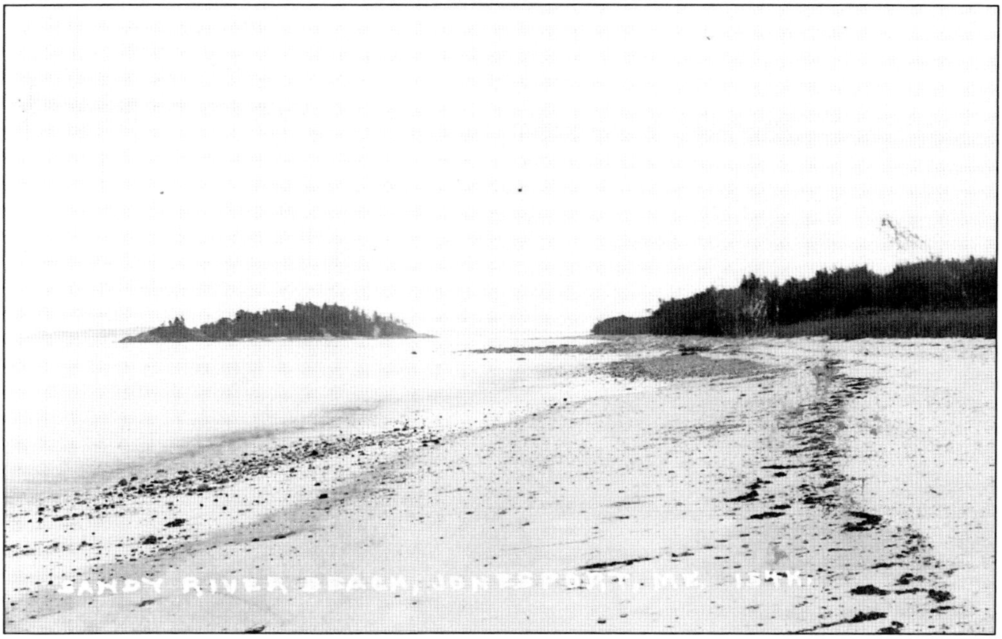

There are several small and large islands that shelter Sandy River Beach from devastating seas. The small island off the shore of Sandy River Beach, Mink Island, is accessible by foot during low tide. Sandy River Beach is located between Wash Out Point and Hall's Dike Marsh.

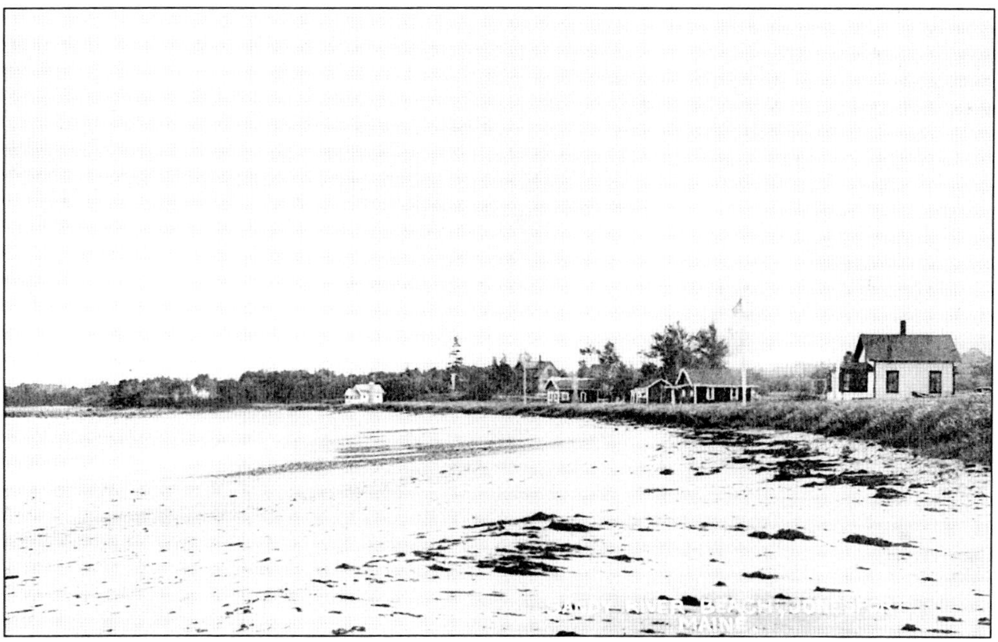

Sandy River Beach is about 3 miles north of town. It's on the Chandler Bay side of Jonesport. The sandy beach is a rare half-mile seashore dotted with cottages in Jonesport.

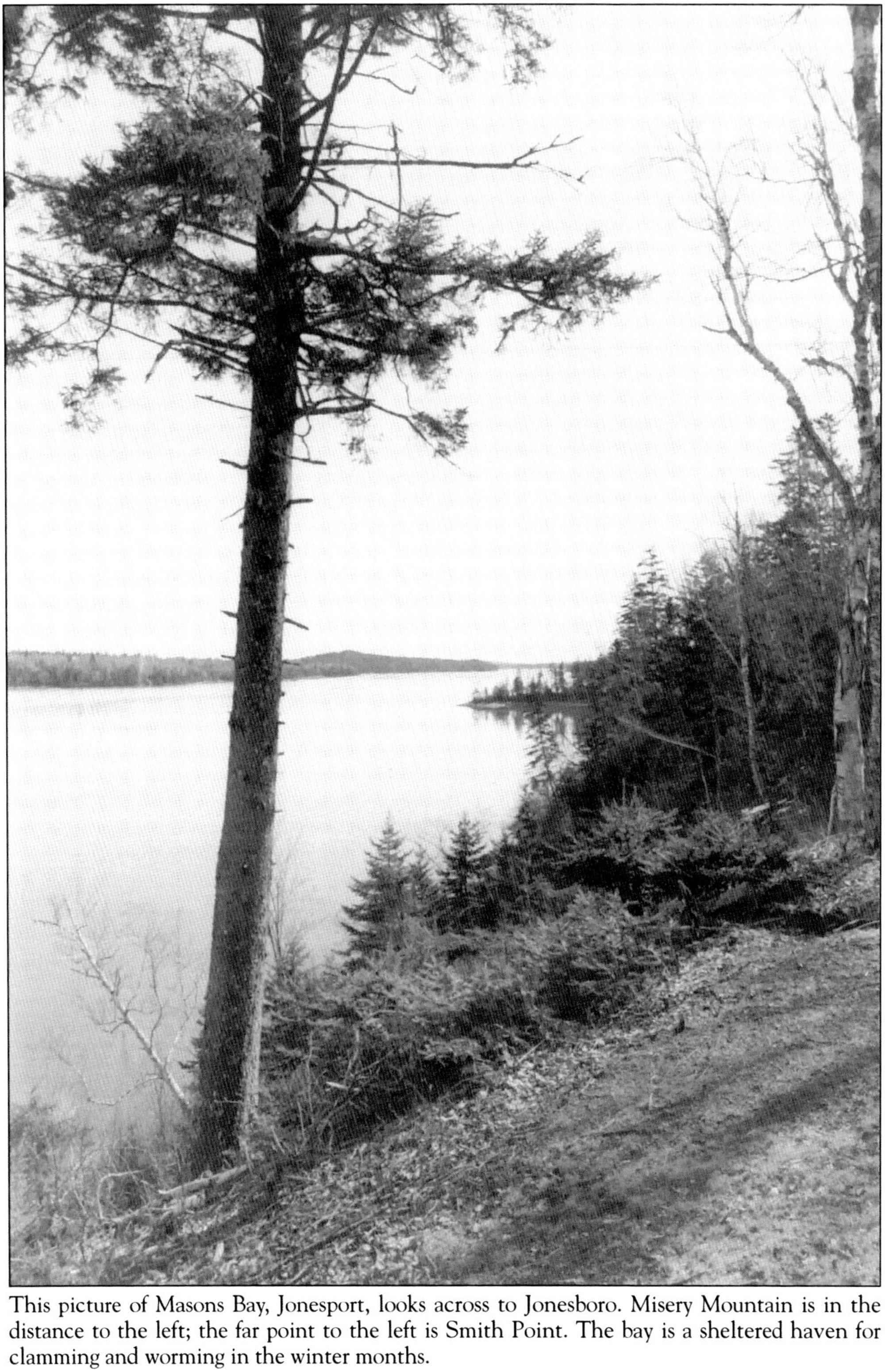

This picture of Masons Bay, Jonesport, looks across to Jonesboro. Misery Mountain is in the distance to the left; the far point to the left is Smith Point. The bay is a sheltered haven for clamming and worming in the winter months.

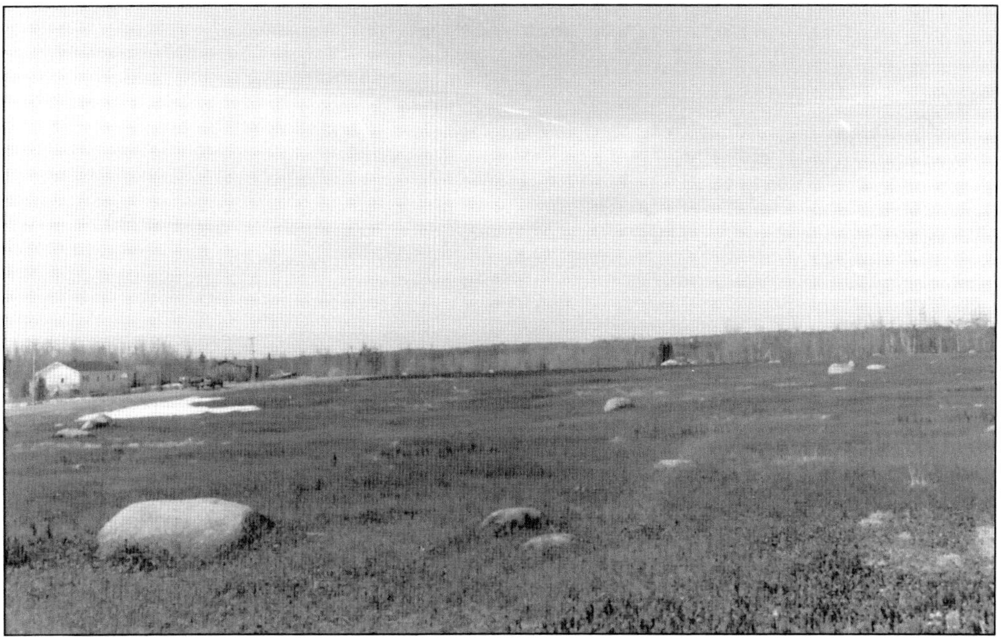

The blueberry barrens on Masons Bay in Jonesport are a beautiful shade of crimson in the winter and gorgeous shades of blue in the late summer. The glaciers formed the barrens millions of years ago. The sandy soil the glaciers produced provides the perfect condition for growing low bush blueberries. The large boulders are a reminder of what Nature's furies can do. Washington County produces about 90 percent of the nation's blueberries.

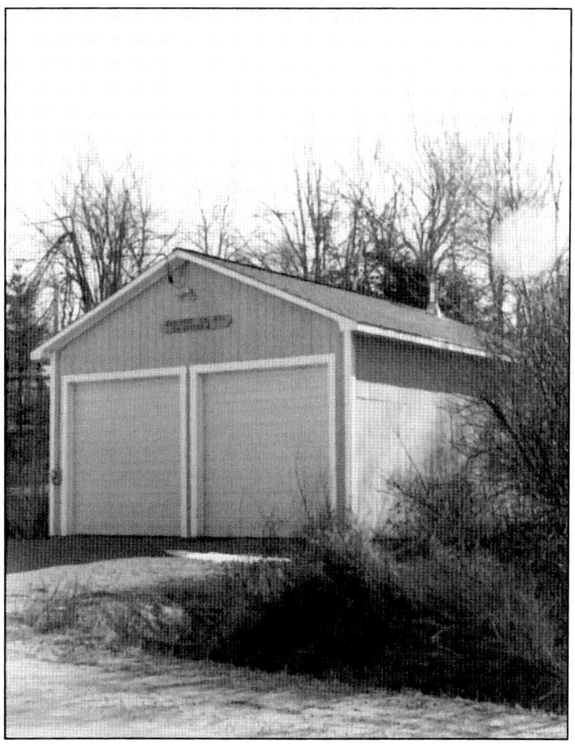

This fire station is located on Masons Bay in Jonesport. The substation is located about 7 miles from the center of town.

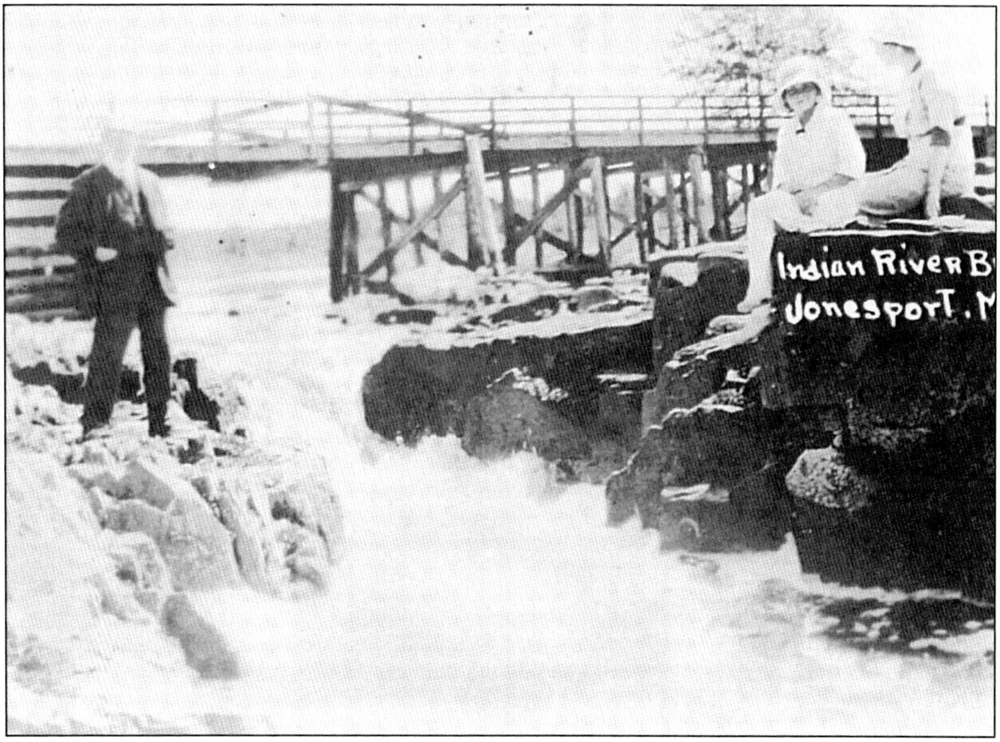

The Indian River Bridge connecting Jonesport to Addison was made out of wood. Both pictures were taken in the 1920s. The land behind the bridge is Crowley Island.

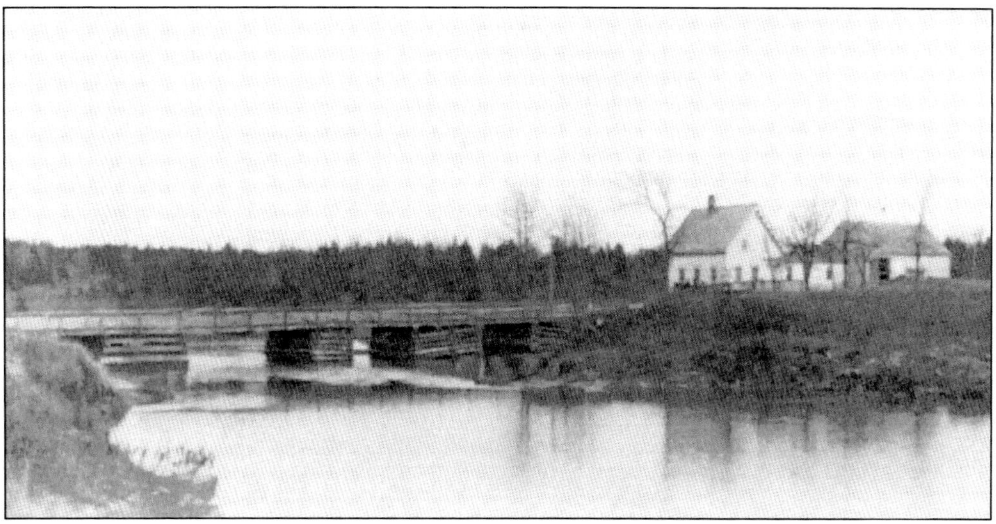

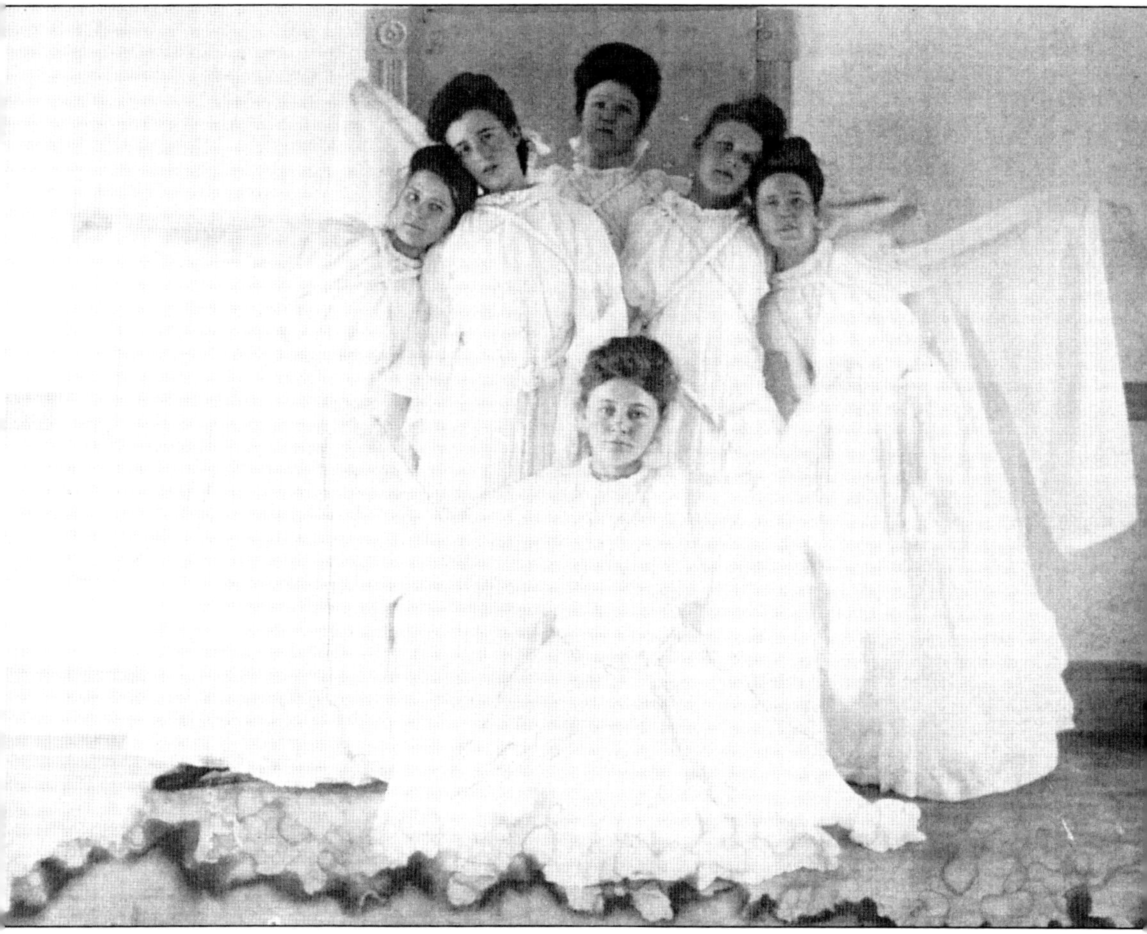

From left to right, Lena Tibbetts, Addie (Emerson) Drisko, Elmira (Leighton) Prebble, Winifred Wass (sitting), Lula (White) Morse, and Pattie Foss perform at the Grange Hall on Indian River.

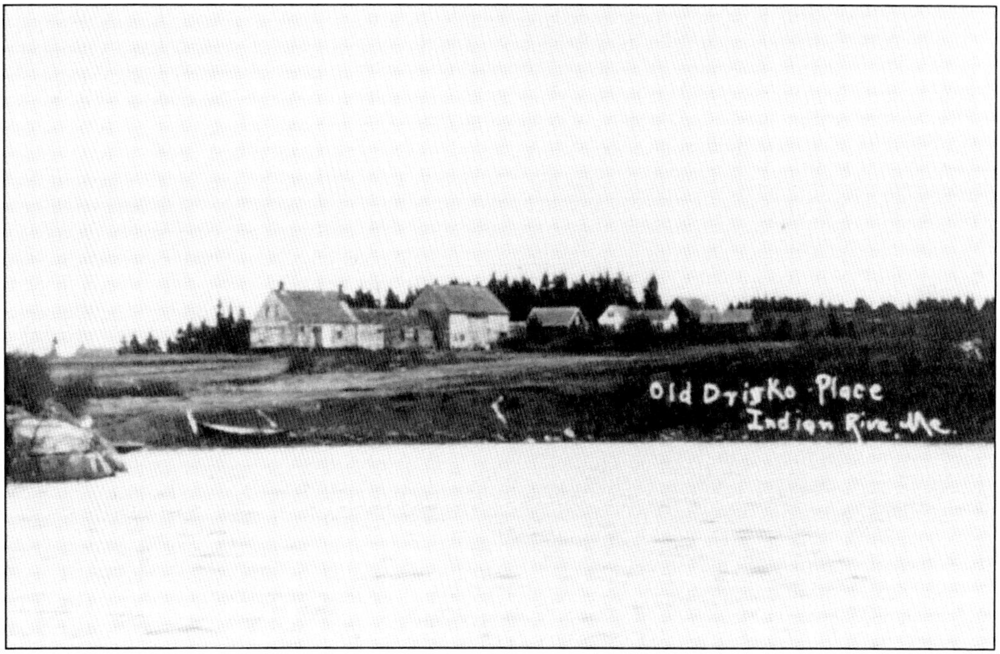

Patten Dorr Cove on Indian River is shown here on the Jonesport side. The houses in the picture belonged to Patten Dorr; you can also see the old Drisko Place.

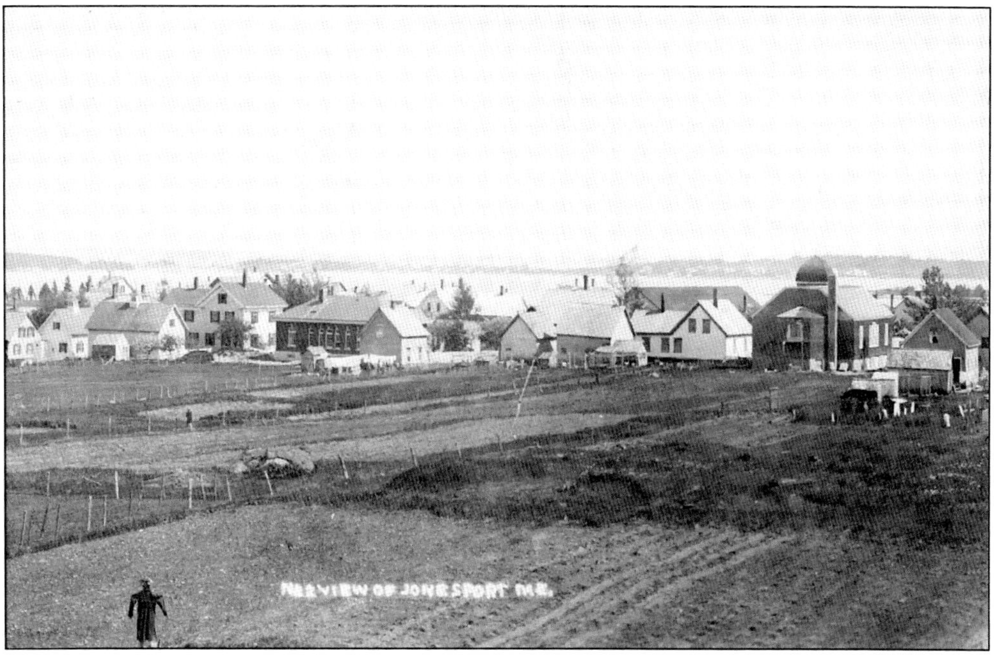

This view of Jonesport in 1910 shows the backside of the Church of the Latter Day Saints. Looking across the water, Beals Island can also be seen.

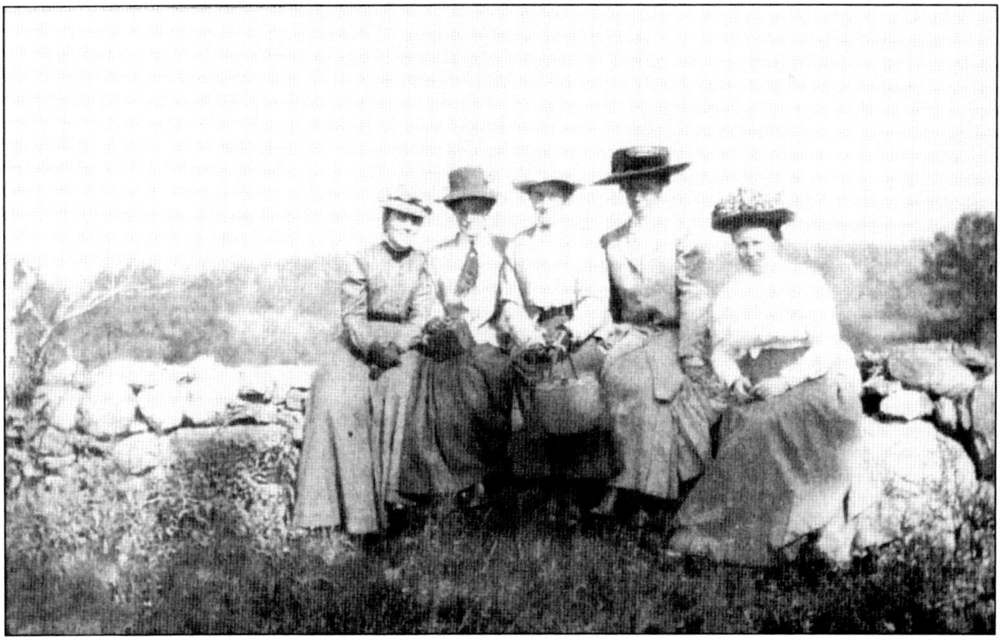

Ladies of Jonesport pose for a picture. From left to right are Annie (Charles) Mansfield, Josie (Bowles) Sawyer, Annie (Morrison) Sawyer, Myra Sawyer, and Mrs. Edgar Brown.

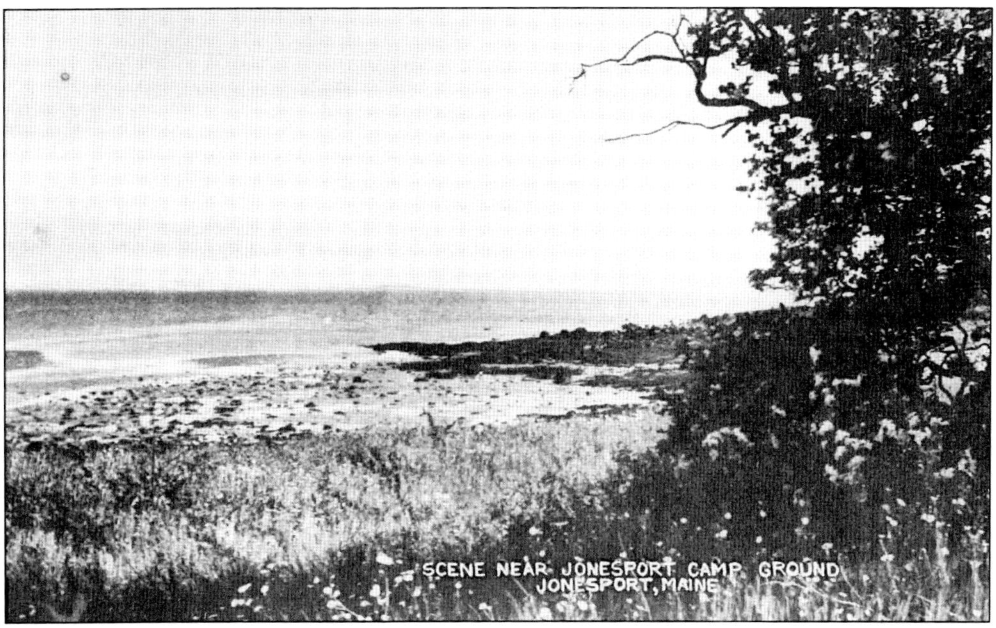

This photograph of the campground on Henry Point was taken looking out to sea. Pig Island is in the distance off the coast of Jonesport.

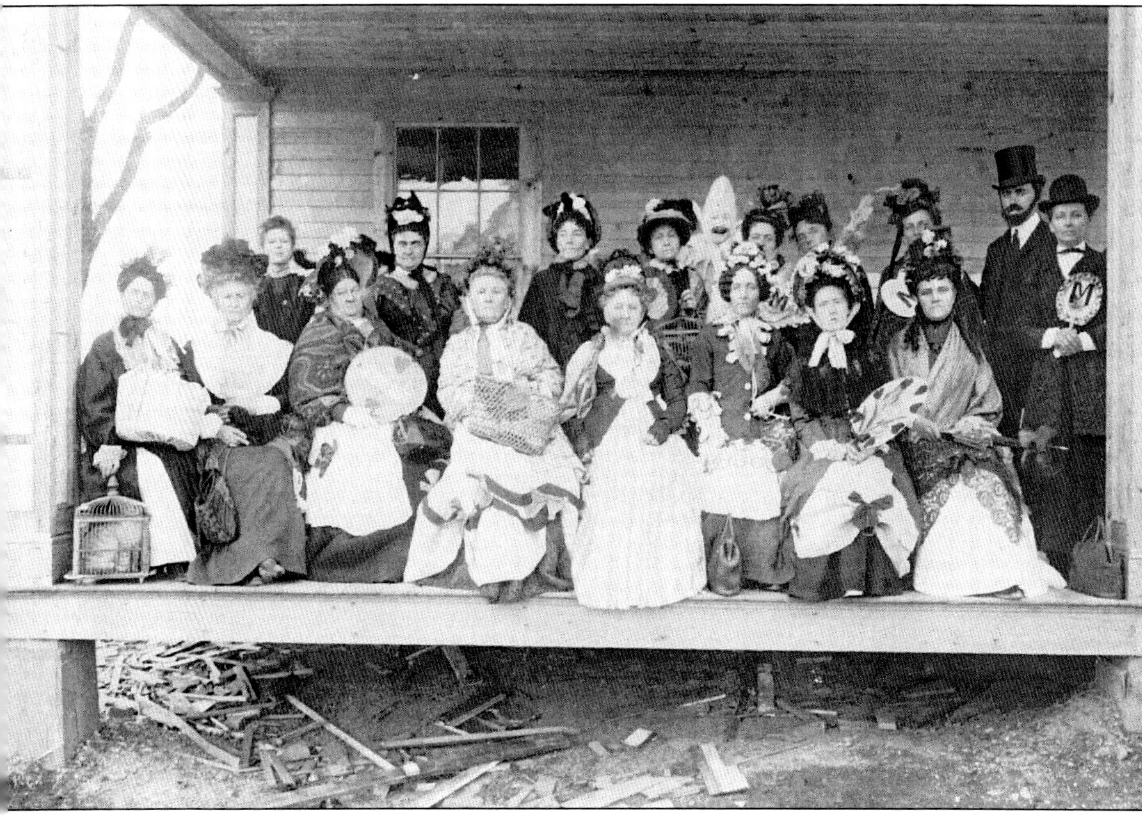

The names are lost, but the picture is priceless. The group put on a play at the Indian River Grange *c*. 1906–1907.

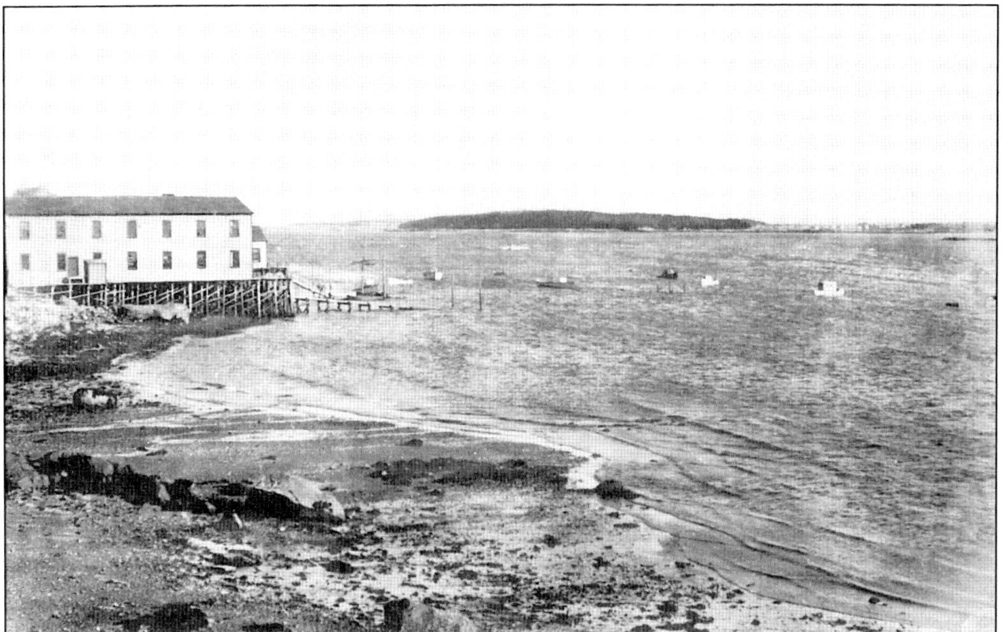

Jonesport - by - the - Sea, the Home of Seth and Mother Parker, way down on the coast of Maine.

The Jonesport Boat Building is the large structure on the shore; note the ramp in front of it used to lower boats into the water. It is located in Jonesport near the IGA Supermarket. Beals Lobster Pound is located on the other side of the building.

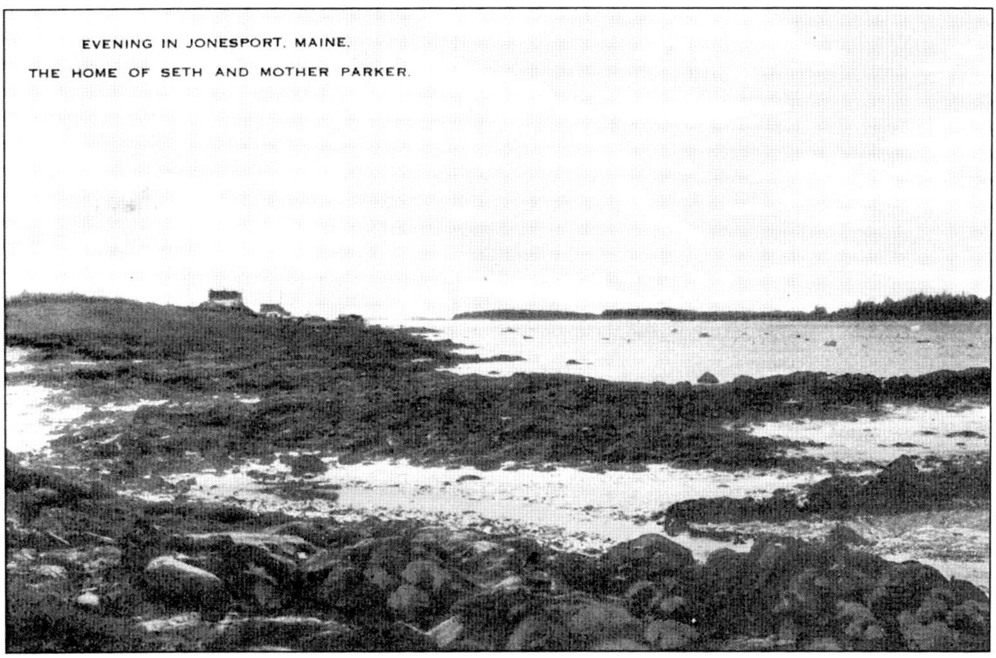

The *Nellie Chapin* sailed on August 11, 1866, from Jonesport to Jaffa, Israel. A lot of families from Jonesport were on board. They left their lives behind dreaming of a new life in Jaffa, but most returned after they realized that life there wasn't what they dreamed it would be like.

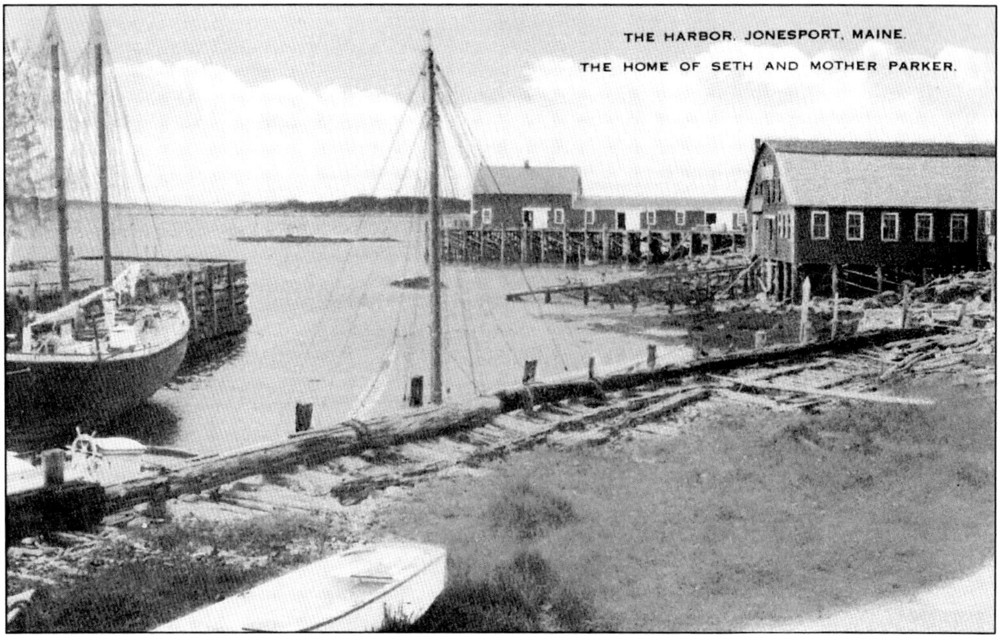

The seafaring village of Jonesport has had its share of tragic storms, and through the years many fishing boats have sought refuge in Cross Cove.

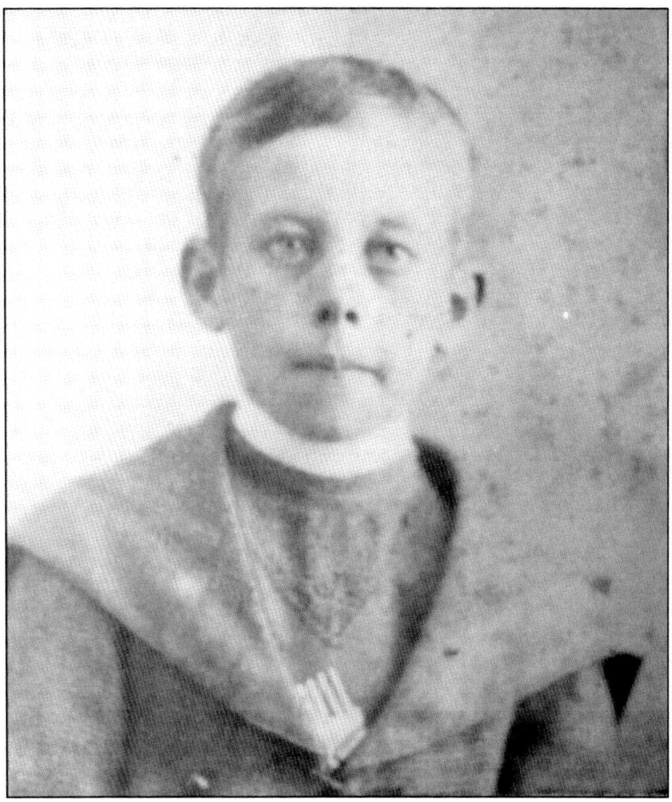

Austin Dobbins posed for a photograph around the turn of the 20th century.

Eva (Wallis) Dobbins stands in front of her home in West Jonesport.

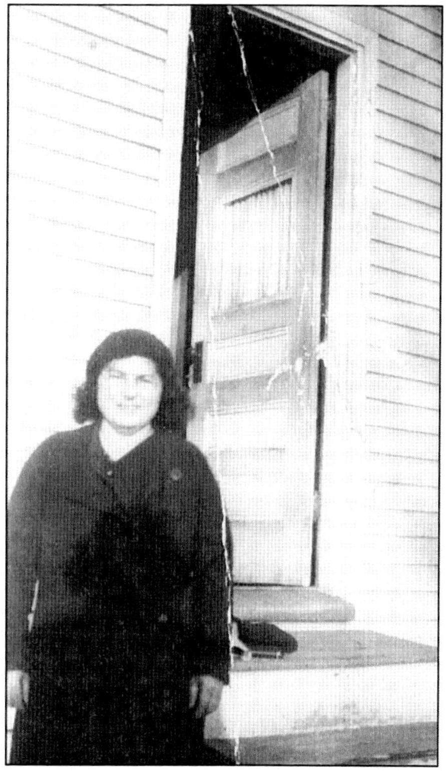

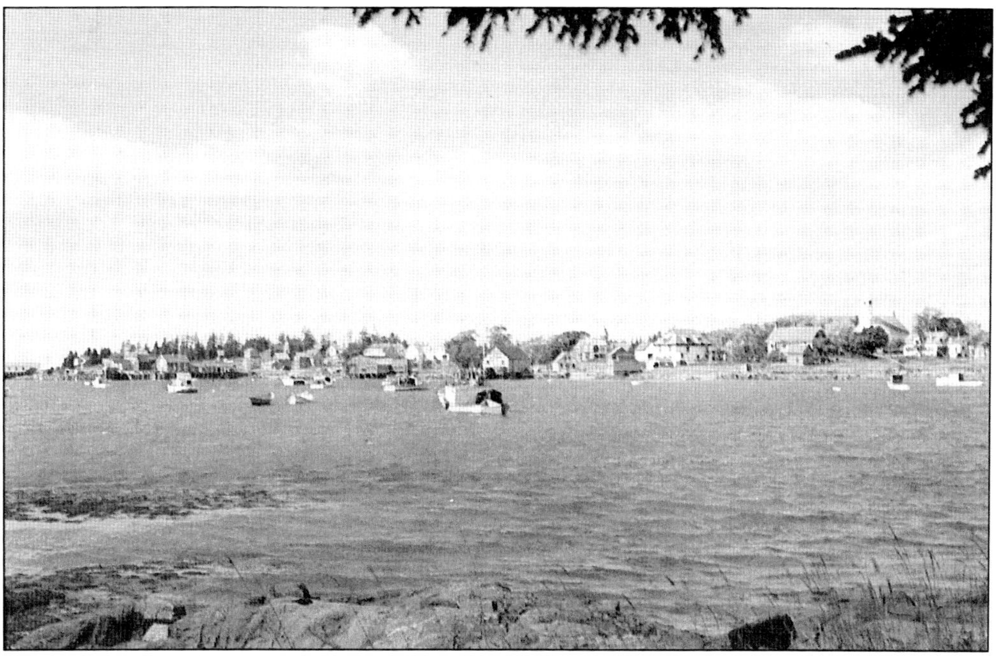

The Lobster Boat Race has been held every Fourth of July for over 100 years on Moosabec Reach. The boats race in pairs up and down the reach and under the Jonesport-Beals Bridge. People travel for hundreds of miles to see the competition. Back in the 1800s, they would race dories by rowing in pairs up the reach.

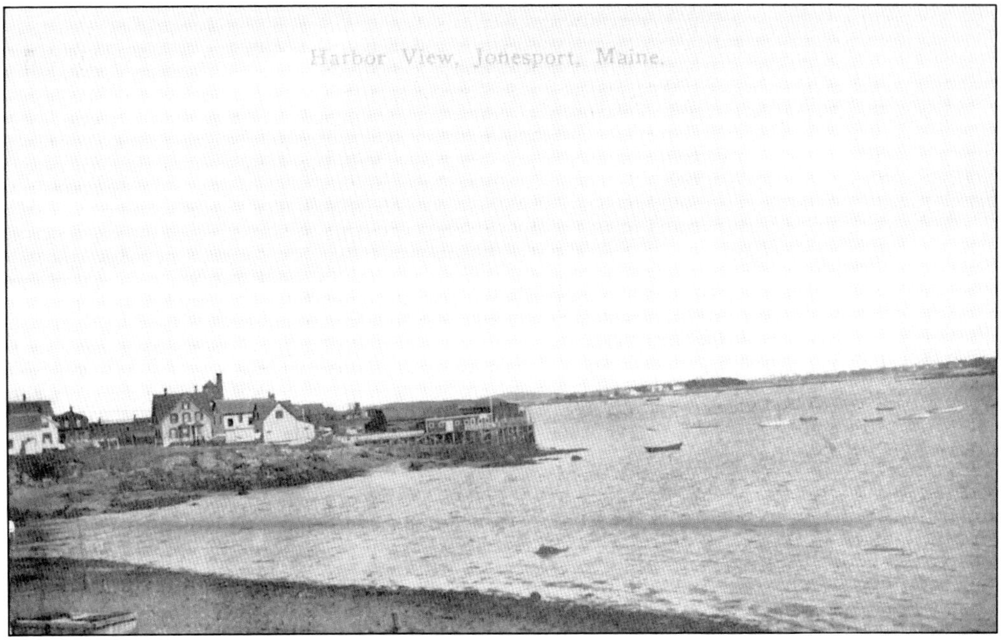

This harbor view is near the present site of the Coast Guard station at the foot of the Jonesport- Beals Bridge. It was also the site of the first factory erected in Jonesport by William Rumery in 1859.

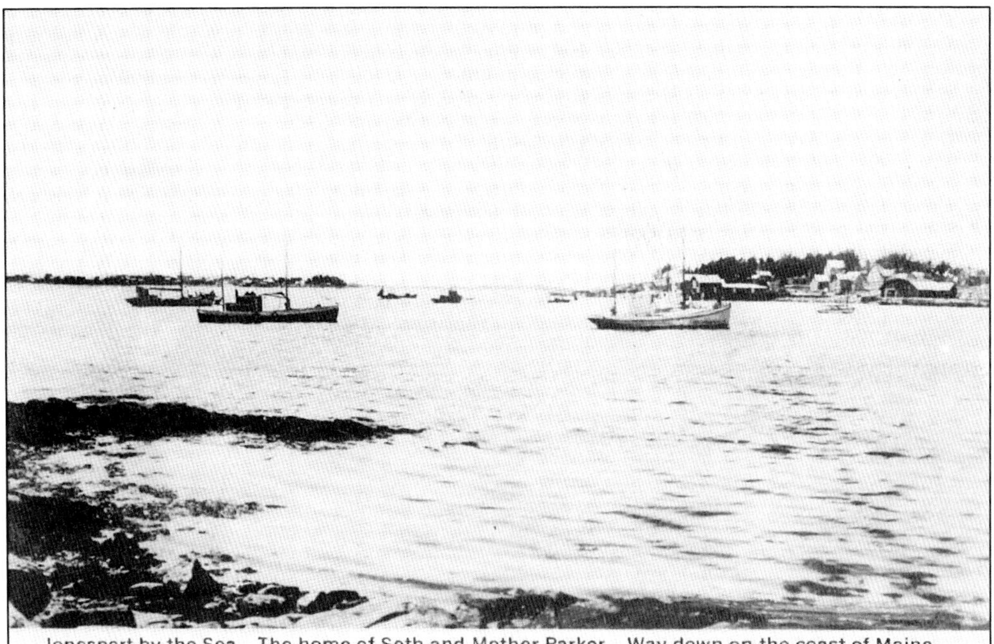

Jonesport-by-the Sea, The home of Seth and Mother Parker. Way down on the coast of Maine.

Jonesport Harbor is shown here in 1946. The land to the upper left is Beals Island before the bridge was built connecting the island to Jonesport.

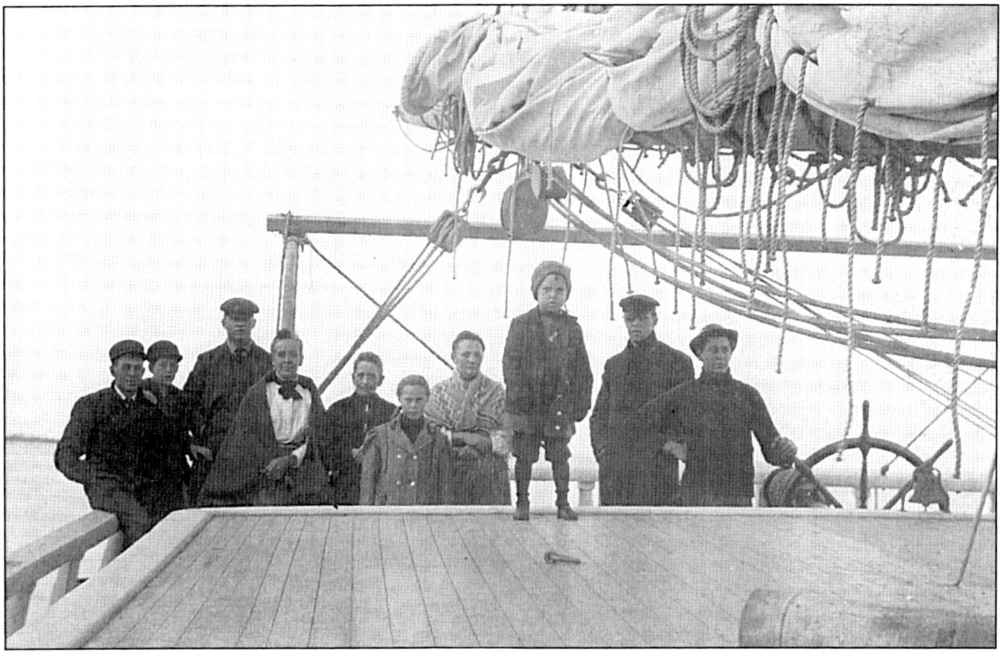

Posing on a sailing vessel at the turn of the 20th century are, from left to right, Rollins Dobbins, Wellington Sawyer, Carl Atwater, Ada Dobbins, Sophronia Leighton, Phebe Norton, Bessie Norton, Lester Dobbins, Will Atwater, and Willard Dobbins.

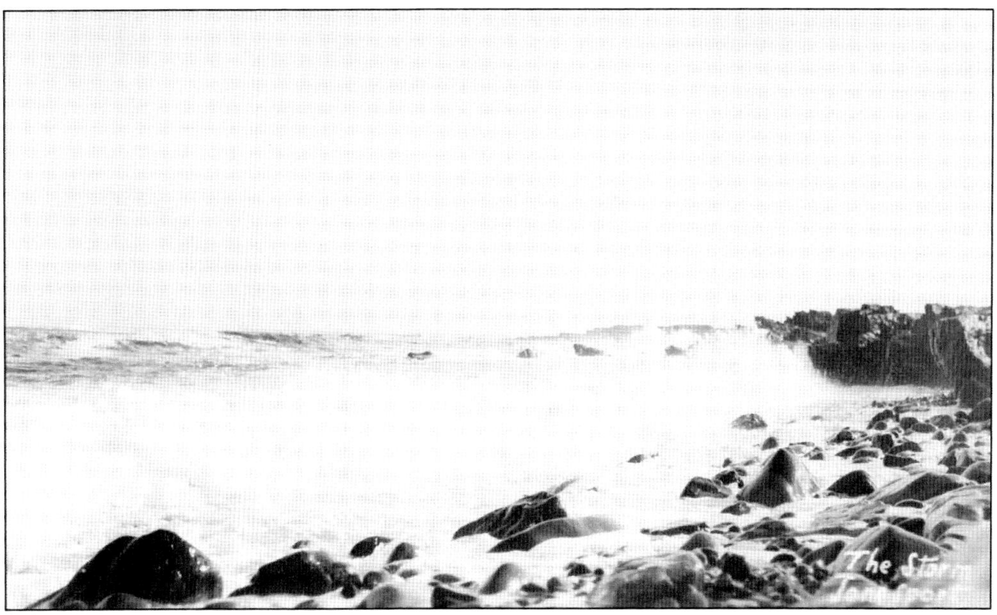

Many islands shelter the main land of Jonesport; this heavy surf is unusual. But when a storm does hit, the seas can be treacherous. The fishermen usually bring their boats into the sheltered harbors and bays for protection during storms.

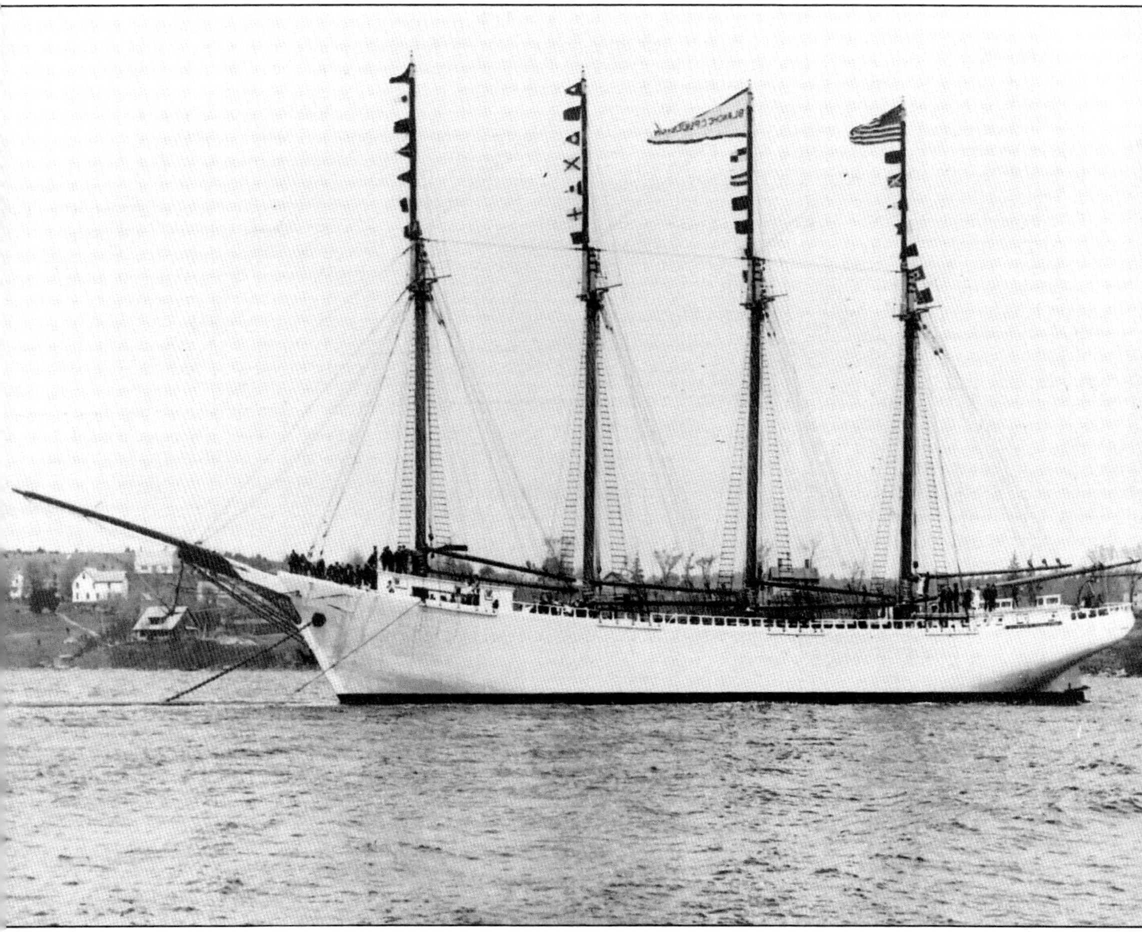

This sailing ship anchored in Jonesport Harbor around the turn of the century.

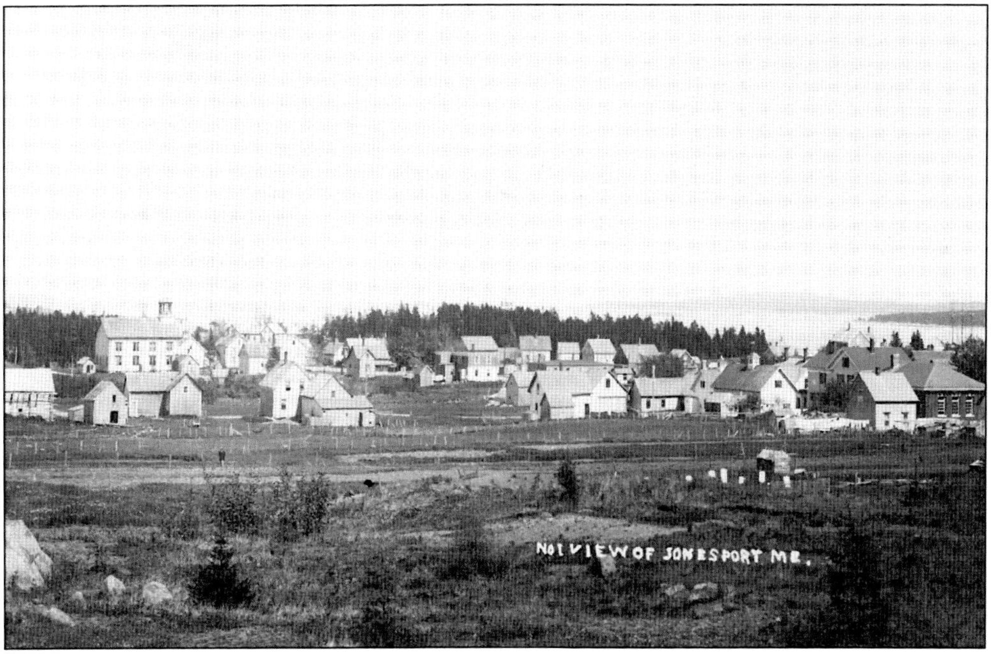

During the Civil War, 100 men enlisted from Jonesport. The town paid citizens $200 for enlisting in the Union Army during the war.

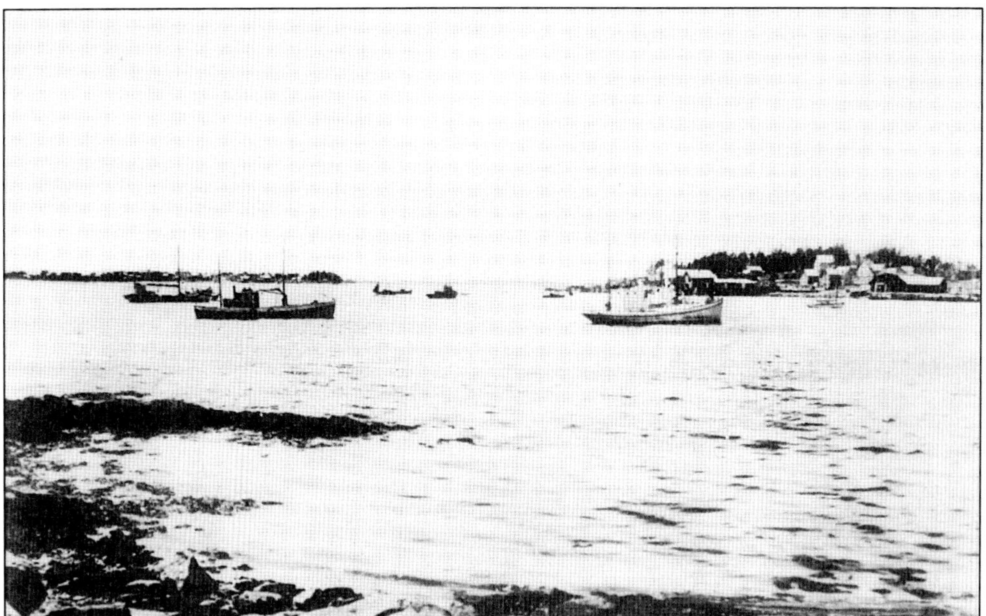

Lobster boats are shown here in Jonesport Harbor, "way down off the coast of Maine." In the 1850s, most of the traveling was done by sea; few people in town even had horses.

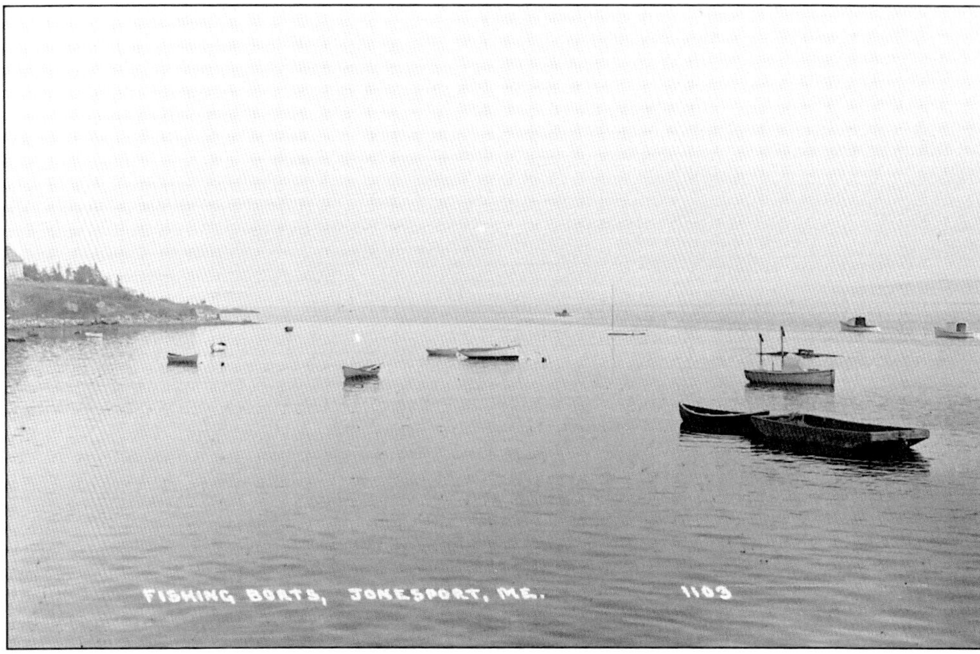

Many boats still anchor in Sawyers Cove near Henry Point. The land to the far left in the photograph is Henry Point.

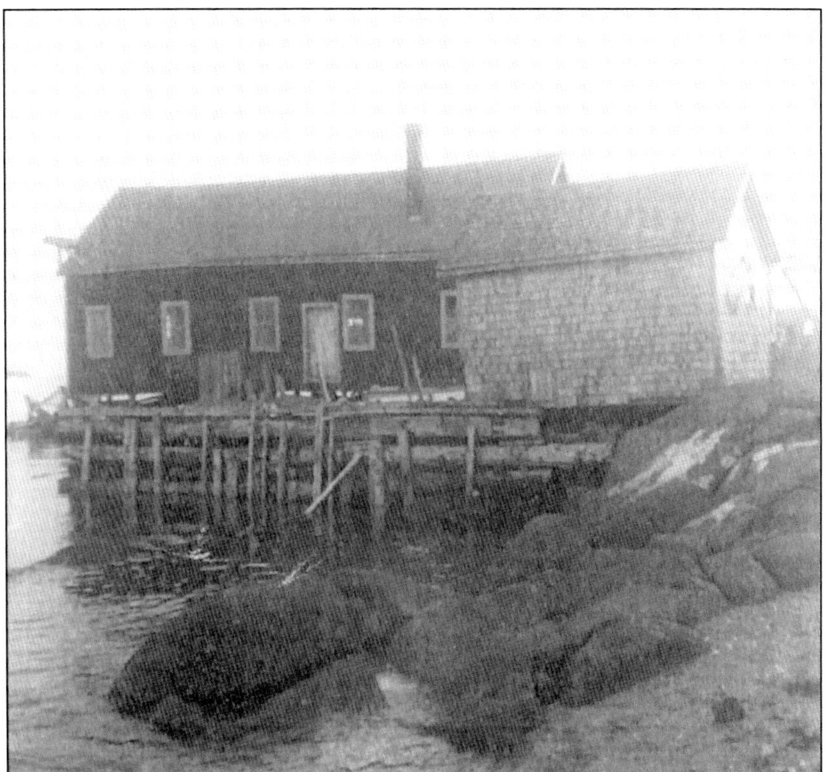

This picture of the Smith Wharf in West Jonesport was taken in the early 1940s.

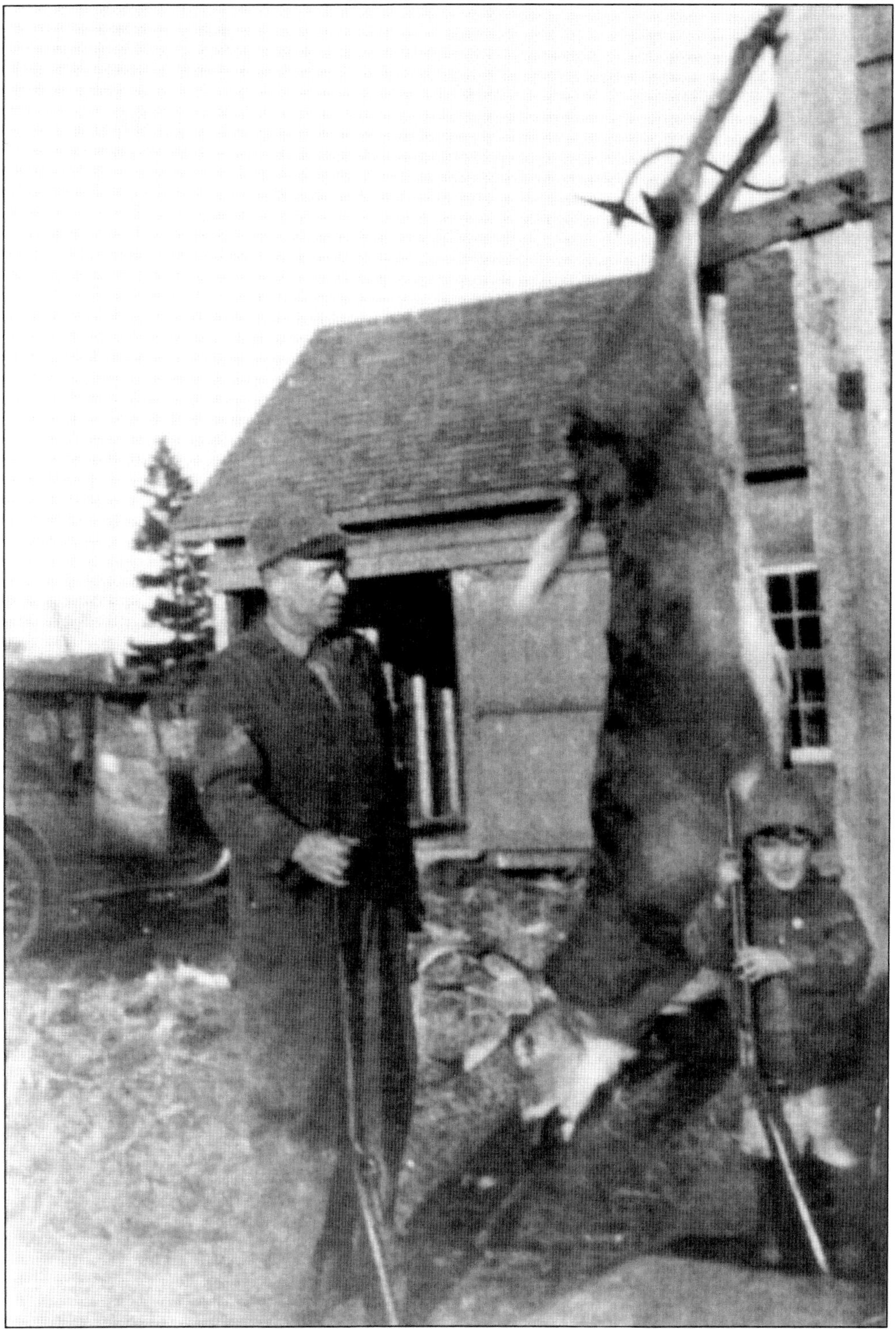

Merton Drisko and his son John pose with a trophy in front of their home in Jonesport. The deer supplied food for the winter.

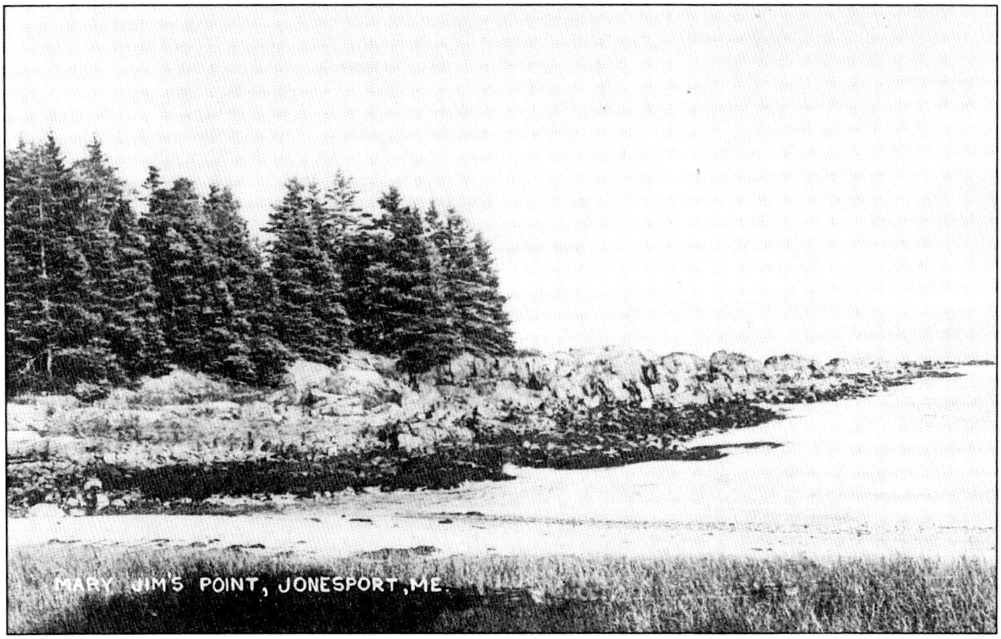

Mary Jim's Point is near the Great Bar in Englishman Bay in Jonesport. The land in the background is Roque Island.

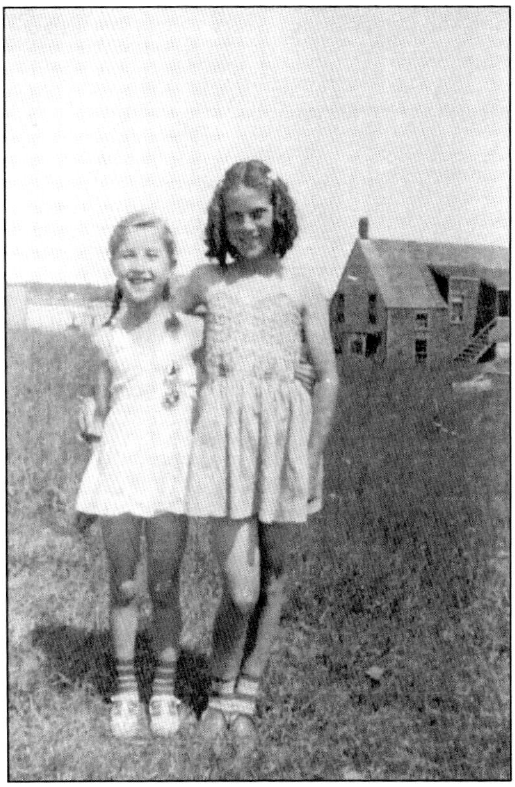

Pat (Blackwood) Stevens is on the left and Tina (Alley) ? is on the right in this photograph taken in front of Merton Drisko's machine shop in Jonesport.

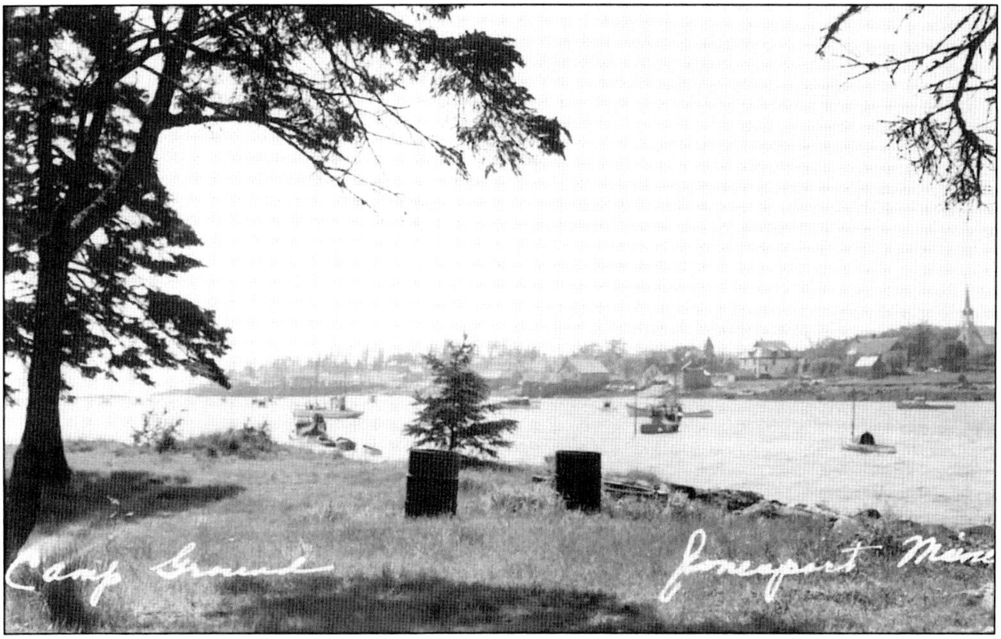

Henry Point Campground on Sawyers Cove in Jonesport is a place that you can still relax and reflect on life. The campground is open to the public for a small fee. You can boat, fish, and explore the beaches and local islands.

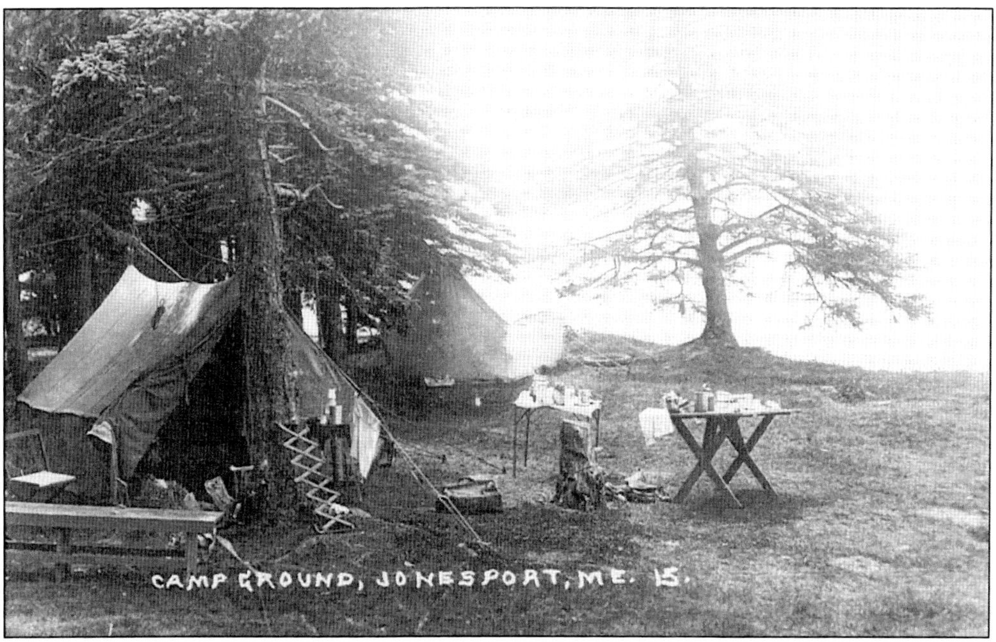

Henry Point Campground was a very popular place to camp. This picture was taken in the 1920s.

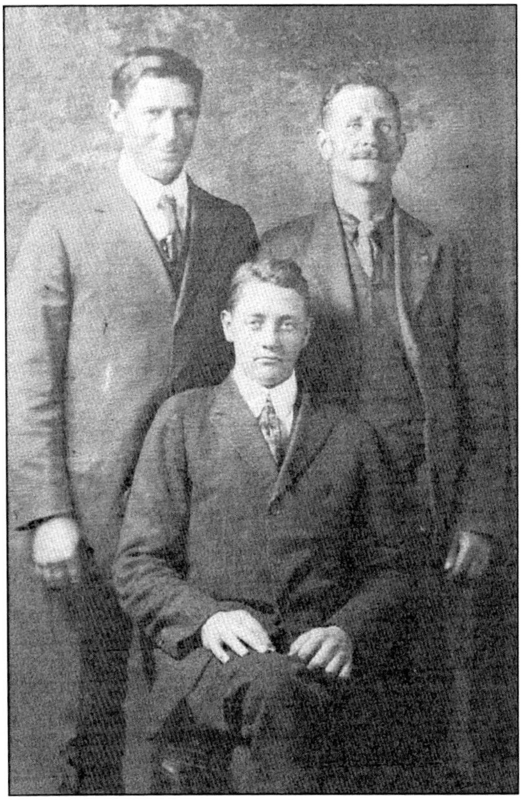

Gentlemen from Jonesport pose for a portrait, c. 1920. Seen here, from left to right, are Uncle Sherm, Millard Crowley, and Joseph Irving Faulkingham. In the 1920s, all the children called men "uncle" even if they were no relation as a gesture of respect.

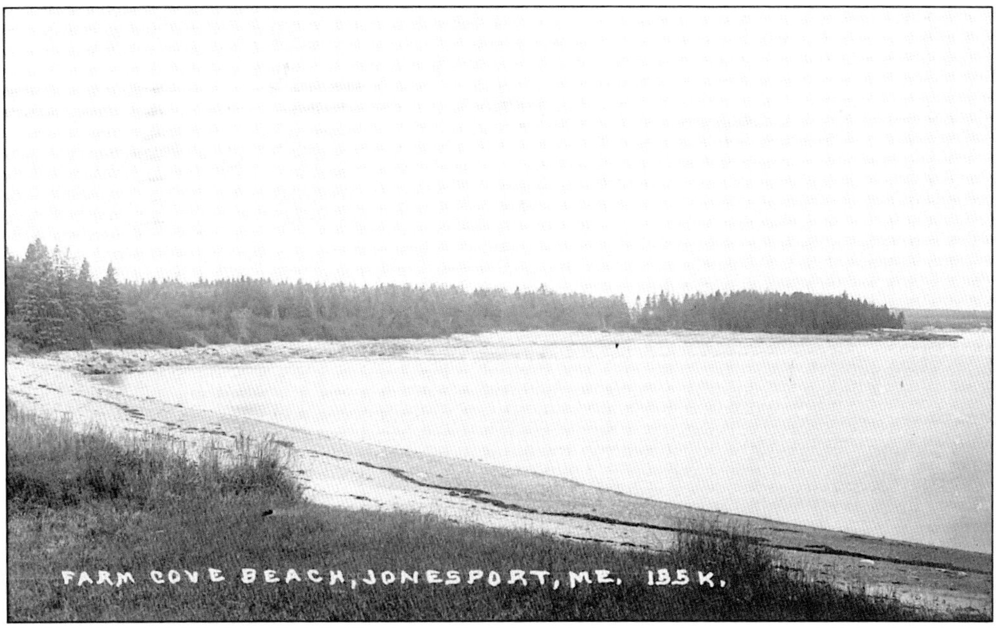

Farm Cove Beach hasn't changed much since this picture was taken in the 1930s. The Chandler Bay side of Jonesport is shown here; there is a sandy beach to swim at and a rocky shoreline to explore.

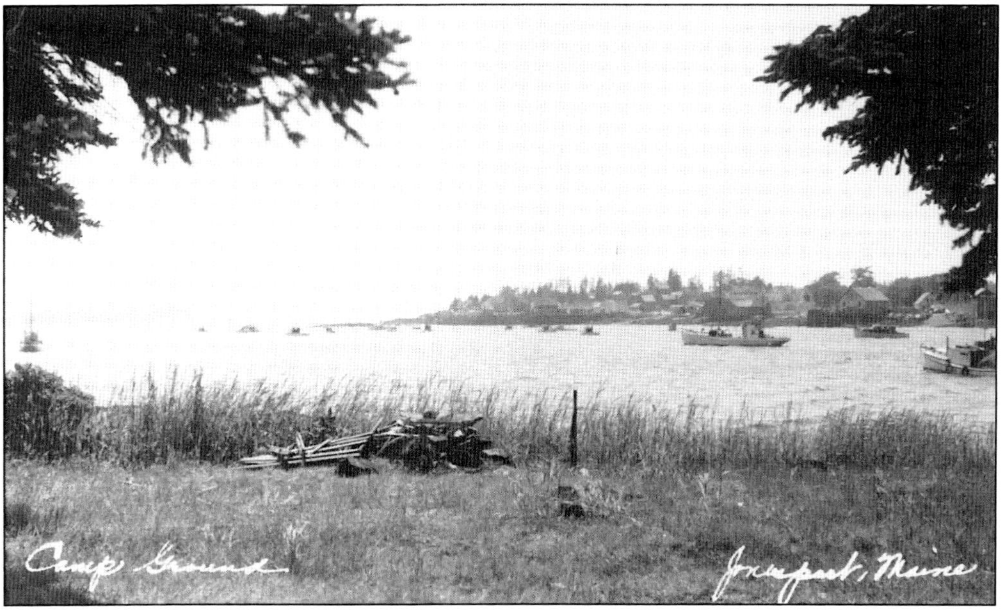

Henry Point Campground has been a popular camping site for townspeople and tourists alike for many years. The view of the ocean is spectacular from the campsites.

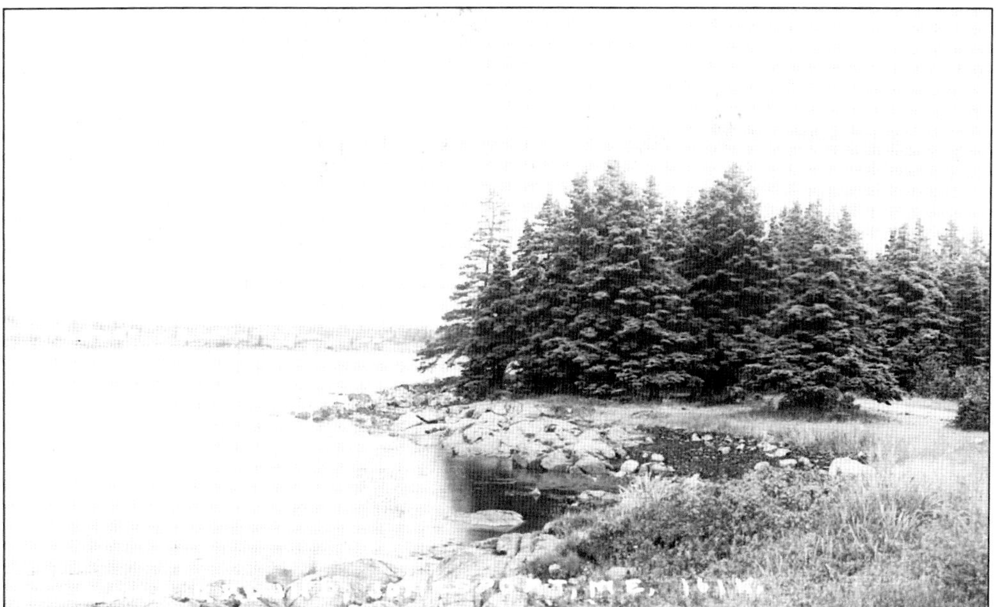

In the 1920s, Native Americans camped at Henry Point Campground in Jonesport and picked sweet grass to weave their baskets. This photograph was taken looking across from the campground toward Sawyers Cove.

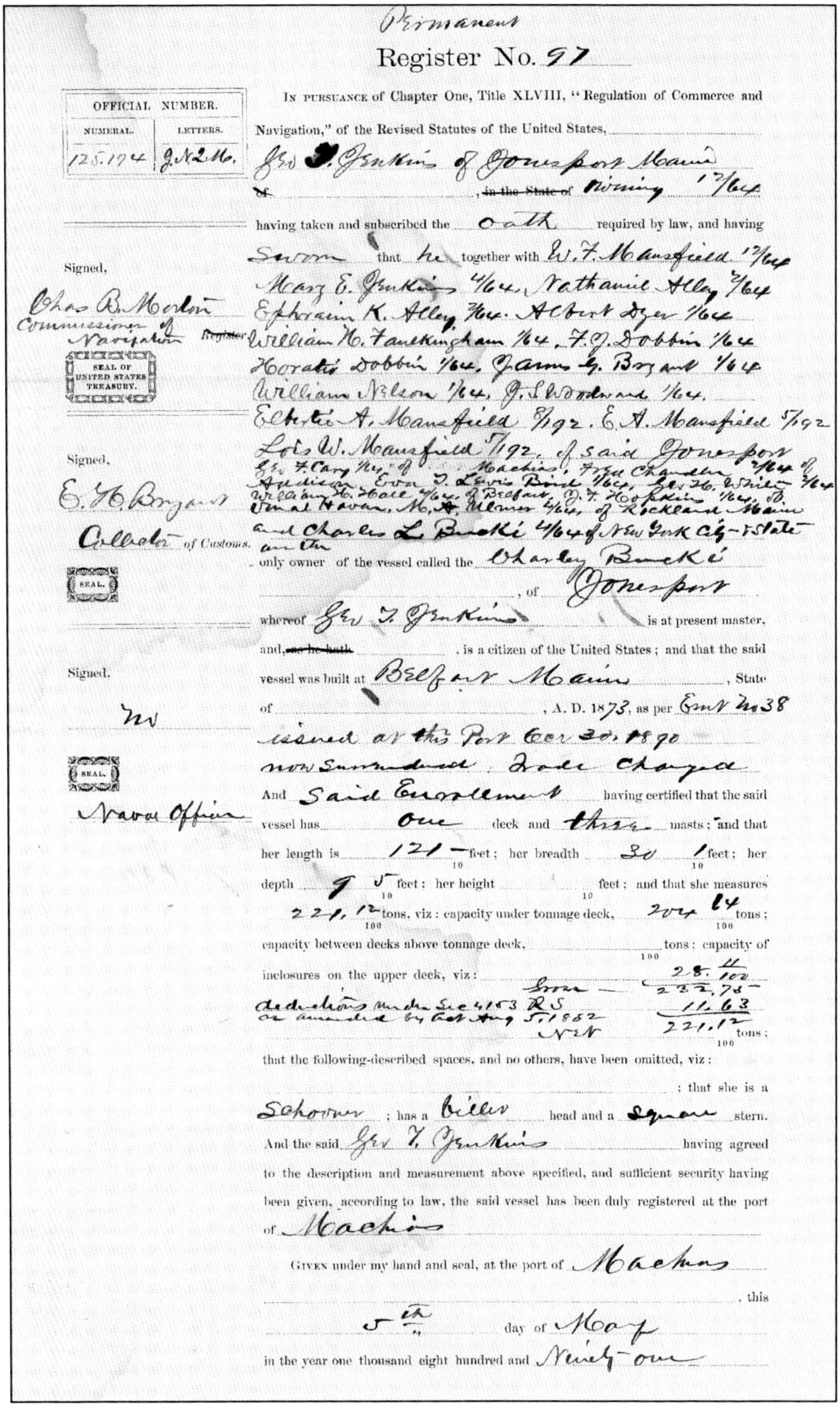
Permanent

Register No. 97

OFFICIAL NUMBER.	
NUMERAL.	LETTERS.
125.174	J.N.2.M.

In pursuance of Chapter One, Title XLVIII, "Regulation of Commerce and Navigation," of the Revised Statutes of the United States, Geo F. Jenkins of Jonesport Maine ~~&~~ , ~~in the State of~~ Owning 17/64 having taken and subscribed the oath required by law, and having Sworn that he together with W. F. Mansfield 17/64 Mary E. Jenkins 4/64, Nathaniel Alley 7/64 Ephraim K. Alley 7/64. Albert Dyer 1/64 William H. Faulkingham 1/64, F. J. Dobbin 1/64 Horatio Dobbin 1/64, James G. Bryant 1/64 William Nelson 1/64, J. S. Woodward 1/64. Elbertie A. Mansfield 5/92. E. A. Mansfield 5/92 Lois W. Mansfield 5/92, of said Jonesport Geo. F. Cary 1/64 of Machias, Fred Chandler 1/64 of Addison, Evan J. Lewis Bird 1/64, Geo. W. White 1/64 William H. Hall 1/64, of Belfast, J. T. Hopkins 1/64, of Vinal Haven, M. H. Ulmer 1/64, of Rockland Maine and Charles L. Bucki 4/64 of New York City & State are the only owner of the vessel called the Charley Bucki , of Jonesport whereof Geo F. Jenkins is at present master, and, ~~as he hath~~ , is a citizen of the United States; and that the said vessel was built at Belfast Maine , State of , A. D. 1873, as per Enrt No 38 issued at this Port Oct 30, 1890 now surrendered. Trade changed And said Enrollment having certified that the said vessel has one deck and three masts; and that her length is 121 — 10 feet; her breadth 30 1/10 feet; her depth 9 5/10 feet; her height 10 feet; and that she measures 221 12/100 tons, viz: capacity under tonnage deck, 204 64/100 tons; capacity between decks above tonnage deck, 100 tons; capacity of inclosures on the upper deck, viz: 28. 4/100

Gross — 232.75
deductions under Sec 4153 R S as amended by Act Aug 5, 1882 — 11.63
Net — 221.12/100 tons;

that the following-described spaces, and no others, have been omitted, viz: : that she is a Schooner ; has a billet head and a square stern. And the said Geo F. Jenkins having agreed to the description and measurement above specified, and sufficient security having been given, according to law, the said vessel has been duly registered at the port of Machias

Given under my hand and seal, at the port of Machias , this 5th day of May in the year one thousand eight hundred and Ninety one

Signed, Chas B. Morton Commissioner of Navigation ~~Register~~

SEAL OF UNITED STATES TREASURY.

Signed, E. H. Bryant Collector of Customs.

SEAL.

Signed, N V Naval Officer

SEAL.

This is a deed to a schooner called the *Charley Bucki* of Jonesport. W.F. Mansfield and G.F. Mansfield, part owners of the schooner, sold their share to H.A. Mansfield. The transaction took place at the customhouse in Machias, Maine, on June 24, 1891. Many locals owned interest in boats and shared in the profits and expenses.

BILL OF SALE OF REGISTERED VESSEL.

Loring, Short & Harmon, Portland.

No. 204.

To all to whom these Presents shall come, Greeting:

Know Ye, That* We W. F. Mansfield 13/64 owner and G. F. Mansfield 13/64 owner

of the Schr. or vessel, called the Charley Buck of Jonesport

of the burden of Two Hundred twenty one 7/100 tons or thereabout,

for and in consideration of the sum of one dollar and other valuable considerations dollars,

lawful money of the United States of America, to us in hand paid, before the sealing and delivery of these presents, by† Henry A. Mansfield 1/128 from each of us making 1/64 conveyed to the said Henry A. Mansfield of Jonesport Me

the receipt whereof we do hereby acknowledge and are therewith fully satisfied, contented, and paid have bargained and sold, and by these presents do bargain and sell, unto the said Henry A. Mansfield

executors, administrators, and assigns, 1/64 of the

said schr or vessel, together with 1/64 the masts,

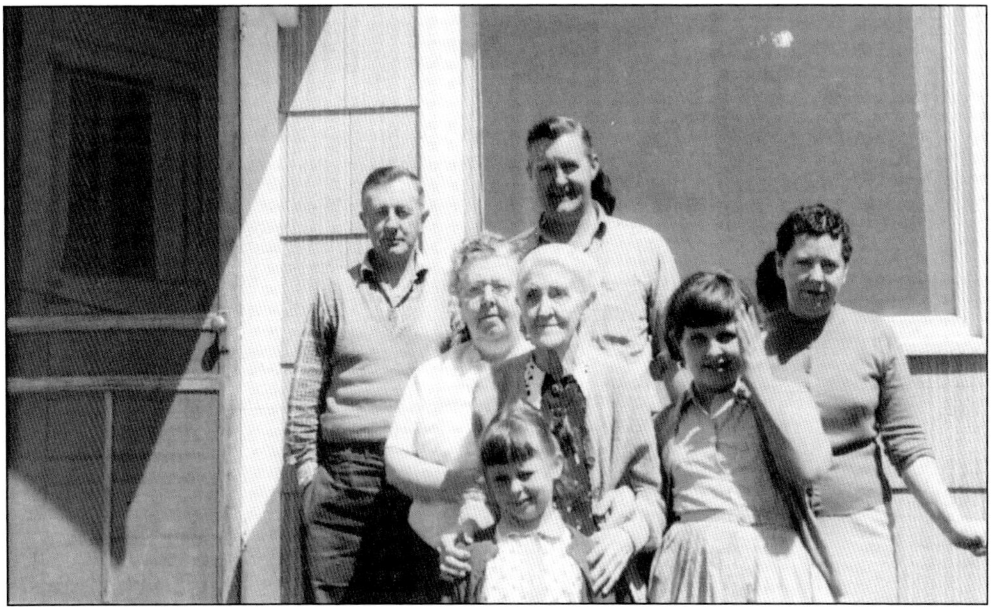

The home of Clyde and Irene Dobbins Lamson looks across Moosabec Reach toward Beals Island. Seen here, from left to right, are as follows: (front row) author Ann Kasper; (middle row) Eva Belle (Faulkingham Dobbins) Davis, Eliza Hall (Beal) Faulkingham, and Elaine Kasper; (back row) Philip Faulkingham, Clyde Lamson, and Winifred Eliza (Davis) Kasper. In this picture stand four generations.

Grandmother Davis wrote the following poem in the summer of 1957 when we were visiting her daughter, Irene Dobbins Lamson, and her mother, Eliza. It was a special time and brought back many fond memories of home.

THE NEW PICTURE WINDOW

by Eva Belle

I sit by the new picture window
And silently gaze at the sea
The picture that memory is bringing
Takes all other thoughts from me.

A little girl carefree and happy
Contentedly plays on the shore
With no thought of coming tomorrows
Or fear of what Life holds in store.

Time passes - she's now a grandmother
And pleasantly those years recall
Her hair is full of warm memories
As countless as leaves of the fall.

The pictures I view from the window
No eyes but my own ever see
For I am that happy grandmother
And that little girl was me.

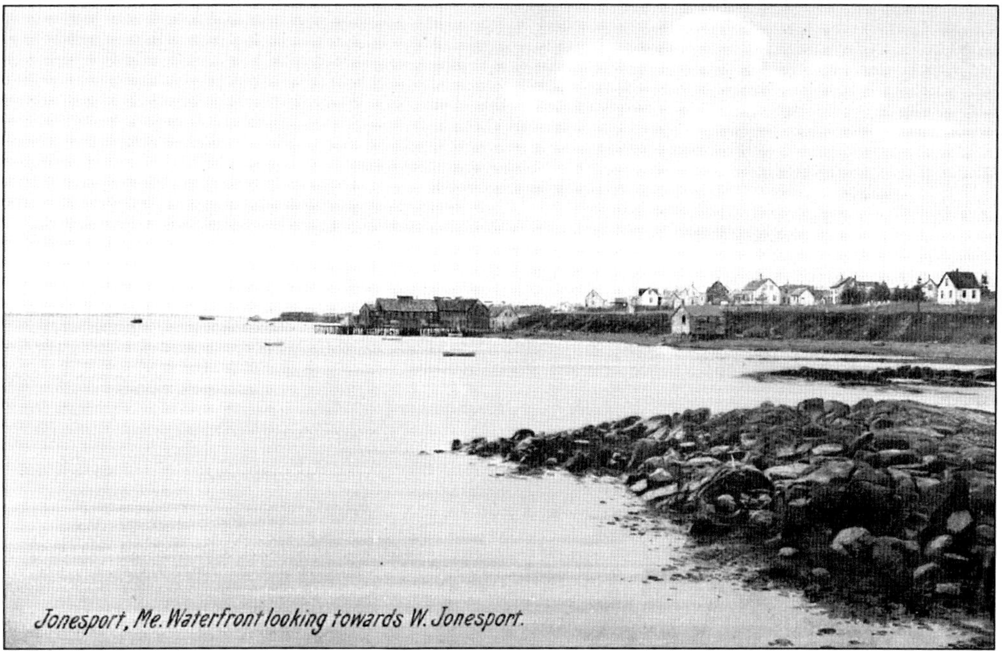

Mr. Hopkins and Mr. Hinkley ran one of the first mercantile stores at the foot of the Jonesport-Beals Bridge, *c.* 1826.

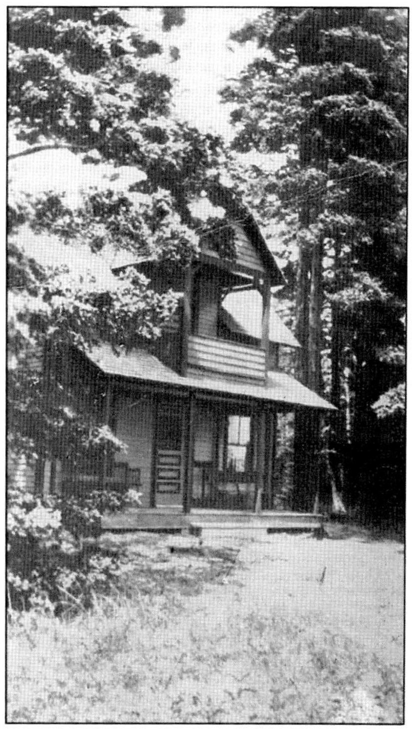

Sandy River Beach was a popular place to picnic in the 1800s; people would arrive by carriage to bake clams and swim for the day. The north end of the beach was the favorite part for swimming because the water was deeper there.

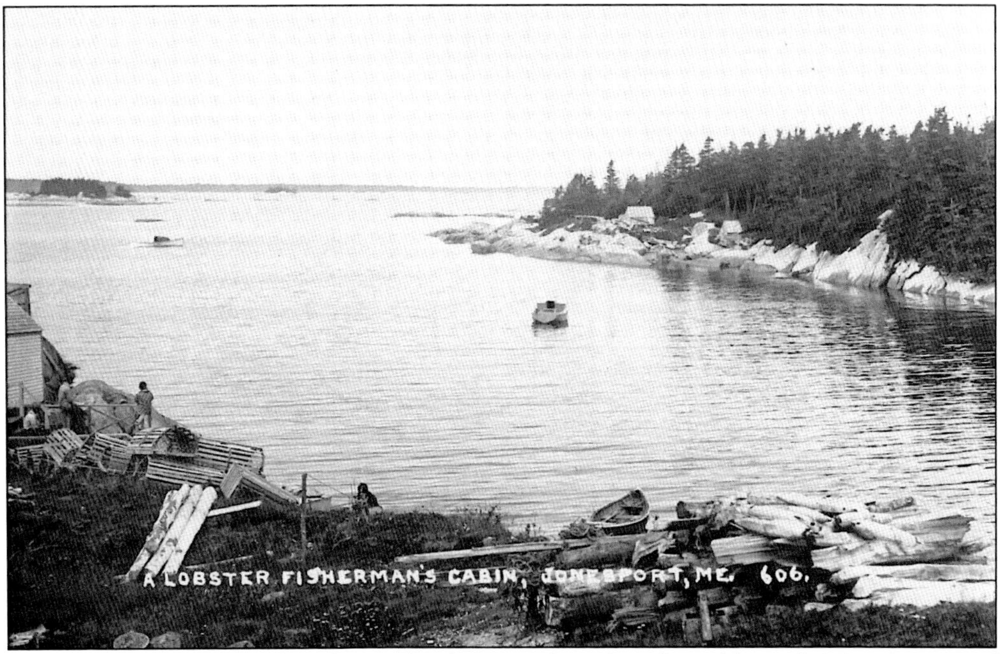

The lobster fishermen's cabins lining the shore on the right side and lower left-hand corner of the image were typical for the area. The wooden lobster traps on the shore are loaded with bait and would be hauled out to sea. The lobstermen check their traps every day or so for lobsters.

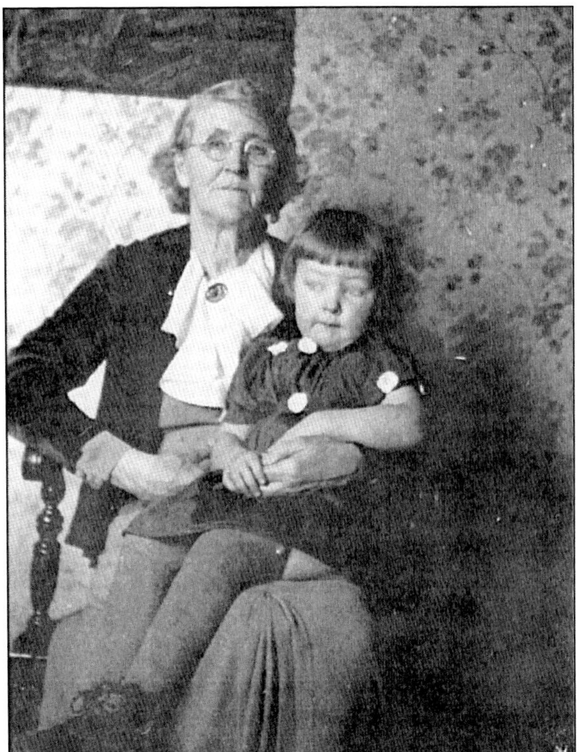

Eliza Hall (Beal) Faulkingham holds her granddaughter, Irene Dobbins, in 1918.

Five

SAWYER COVE

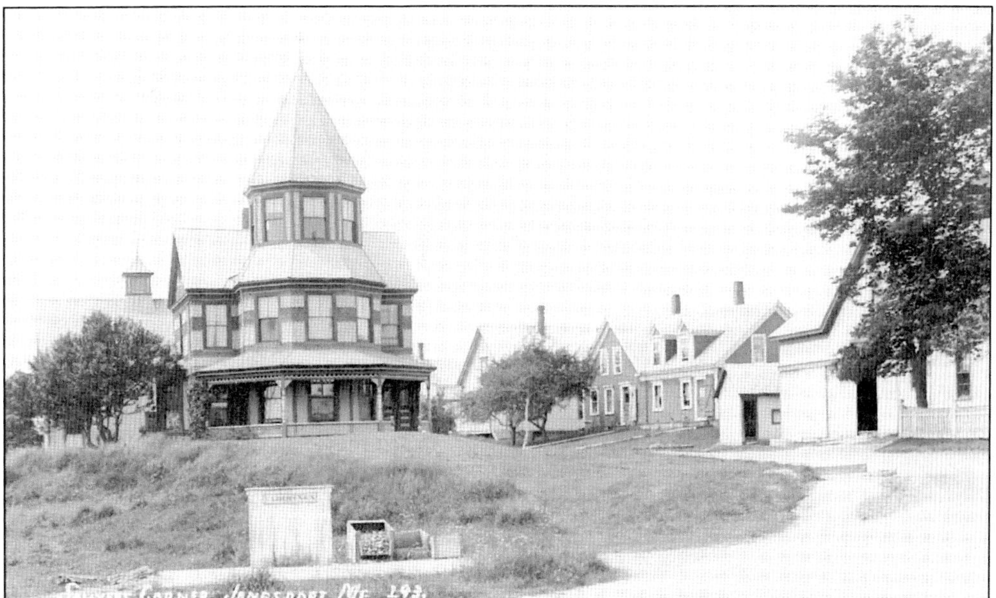

The Sawyer home, to the left, is located in Sawyer Cove near the present marina. It has been in the Sawyer family for many years. This picture was taken in 1913; the home hasn't changed much since the turn of the 20th century.

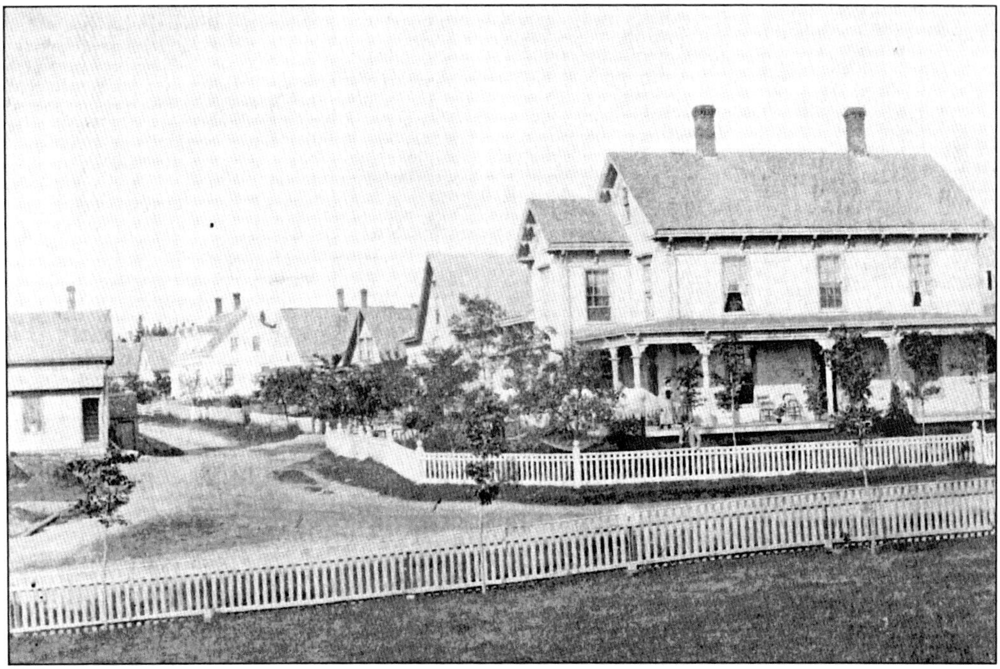

The house to the right is the Edward M. and Francis V. Sawyer's home in Sawyers Square; it looks down the road toward the Three River Company. The white house with the three dormers on the right was the Blackwood Funeral Home.

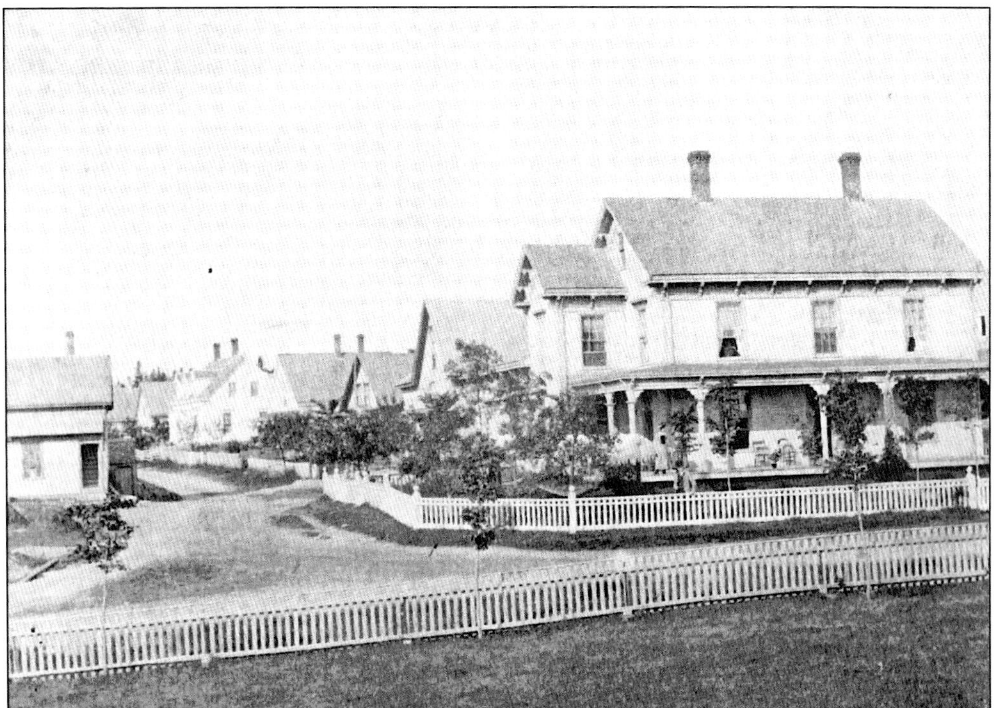

On March 21, 1814, the British privateer *Vim* chased an American cutter commanded by Captain Elliot of Machias into Sawyers Cove.

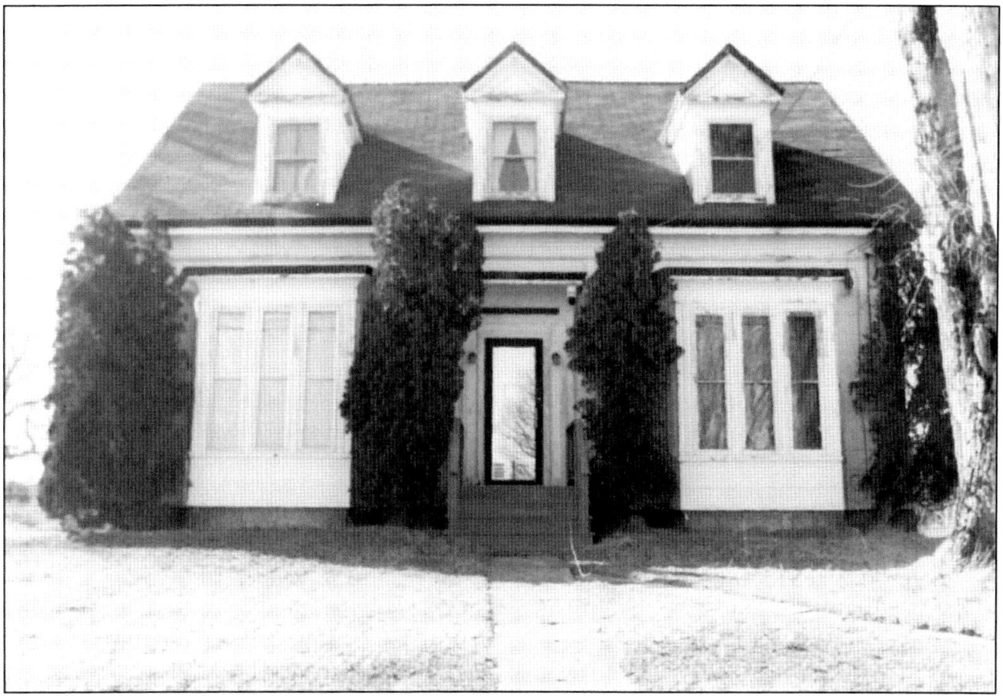

The Blackwood Funeral Home was owned and operated by Alton Blackwood from 1958 until 1964. The building is located in Sawyers Square not far from the Looks Lobster Pound.

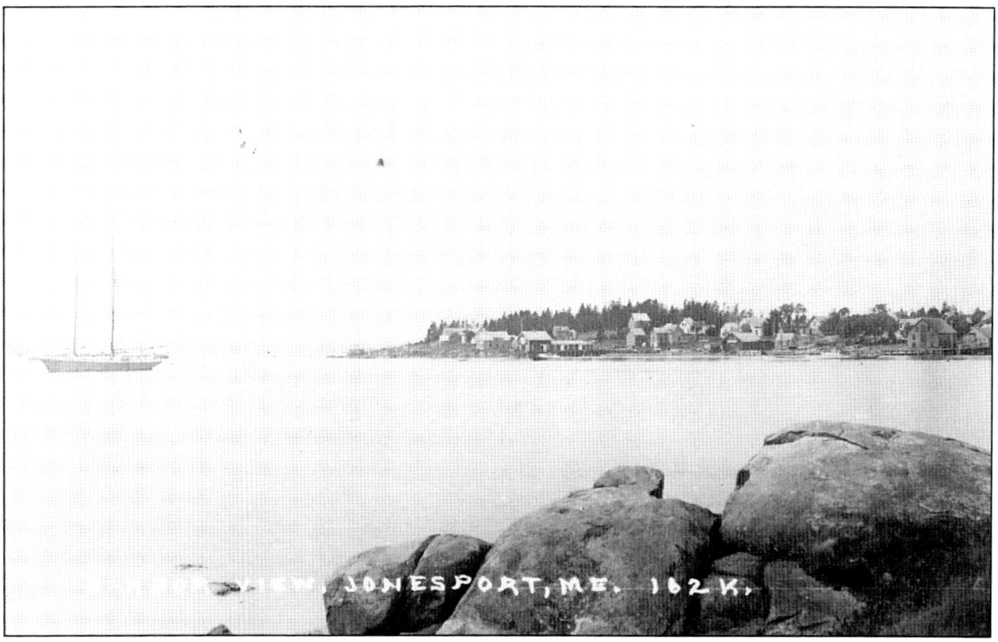

Mr. Walter Sawyer operated an ironsmith establishment in Sawyers Cove in Jonesport. He provided many general blacksmith services, including horseshoes, carriage irons, and farmer's wheels that were manufactured to order.

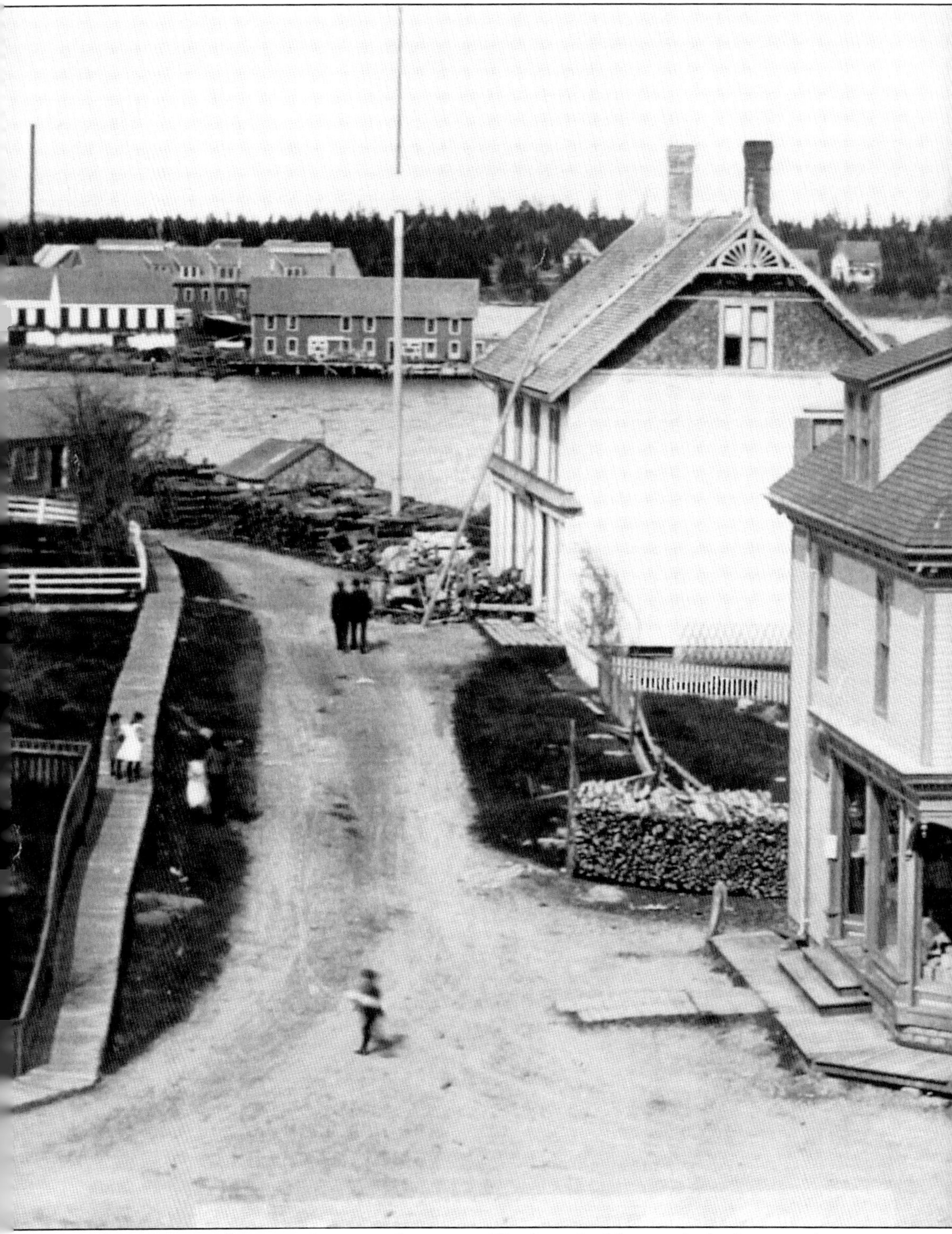

This is a view of Sawyers Square in Jonesport. The large building with the horse and wagon in front was the Sawyers building and customhouse. The next building was the Mansfield Store,

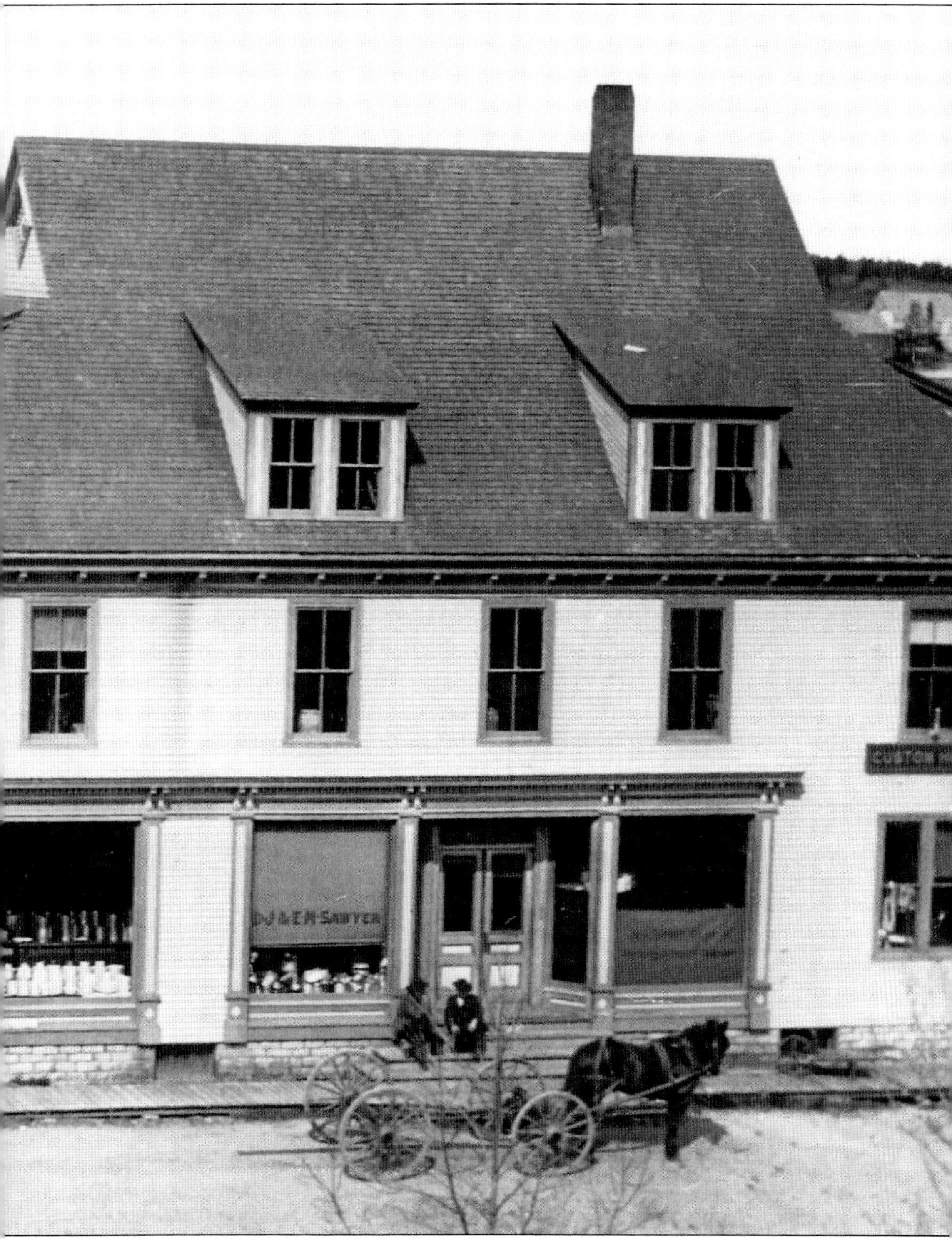

which is now the Harbor House Inn. The factories across the water are the Mansfield factories; one building processed blueberries, the other sardines.

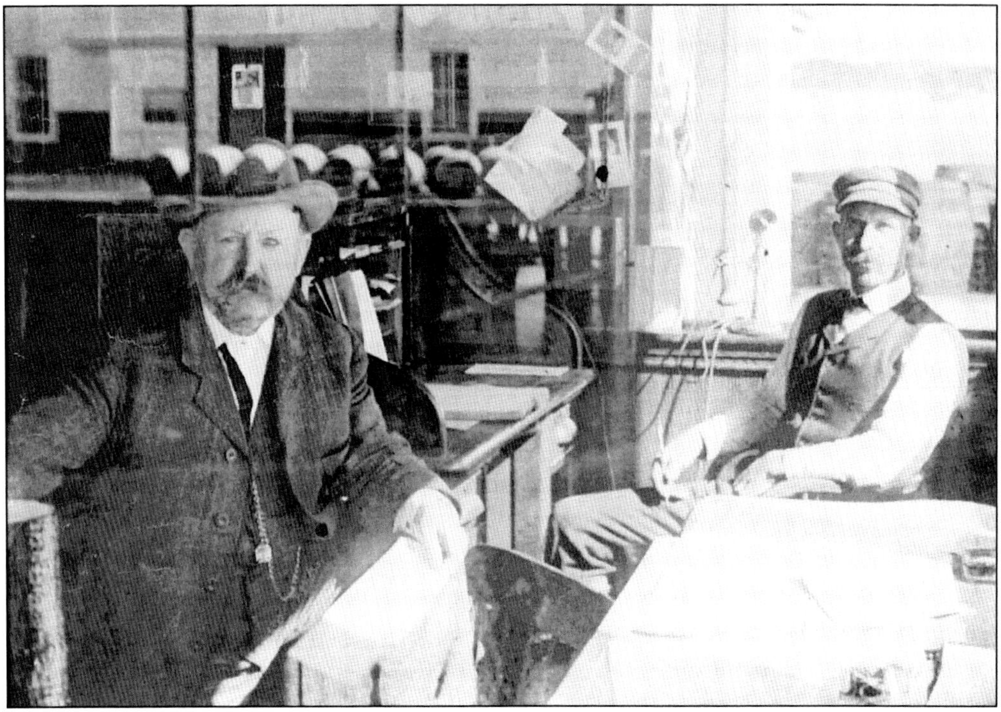

The first telegraph office in Jonesport was located at Sawyers Square. It was operated by C.H. Mansfield.

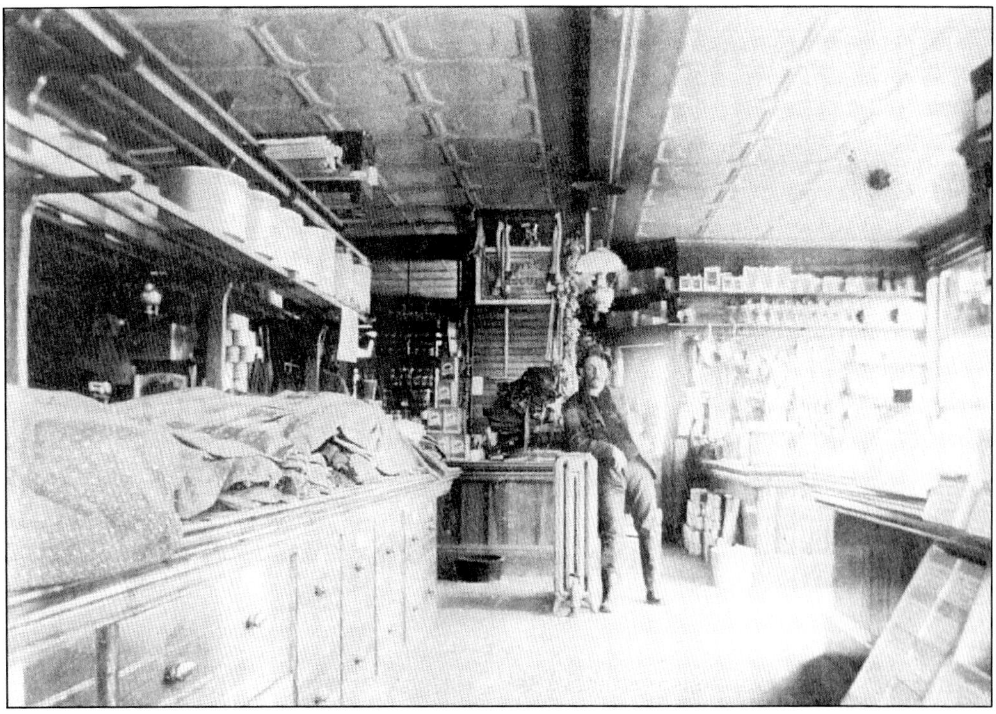

This is a view of the inside of the Worcester/Sawyers building in Sawyers Square. It is now the home of Jewel's Antiques.

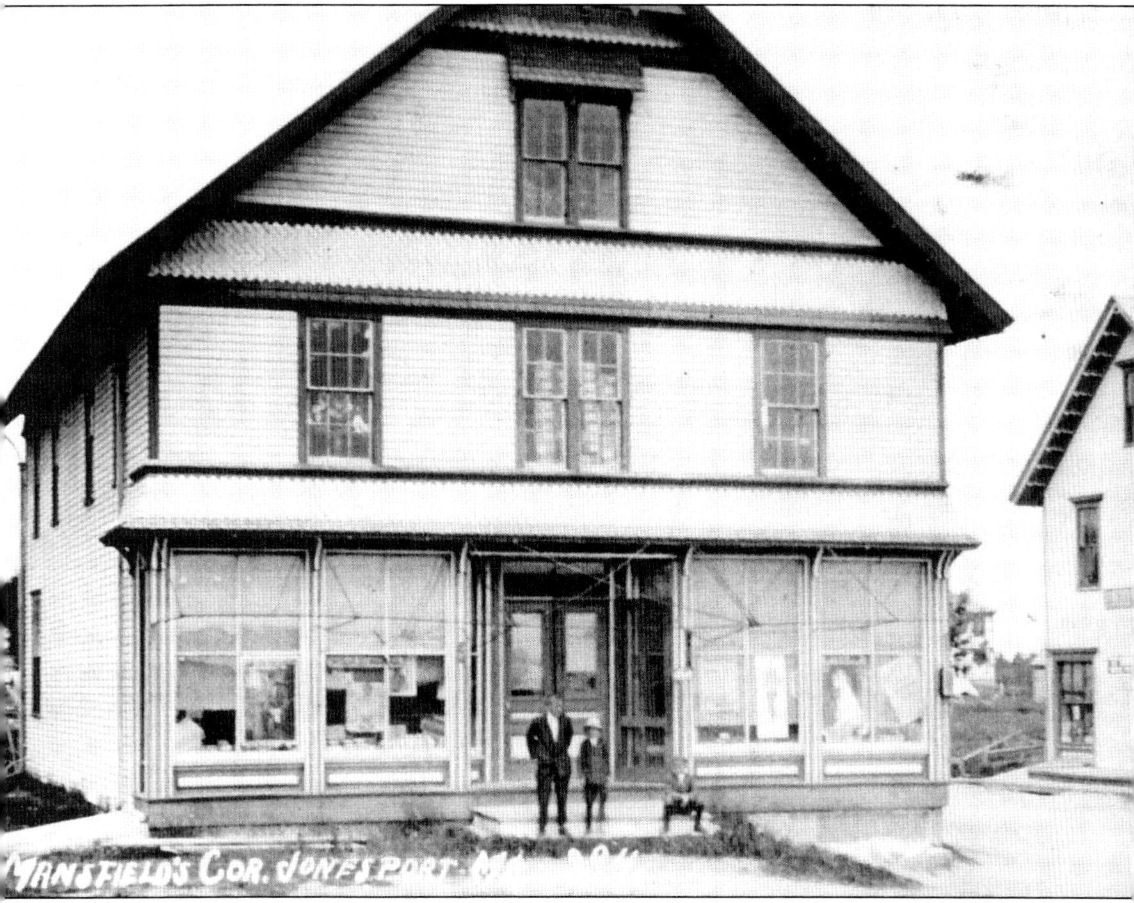

Mansfield Corner is located on Sawyers Cove. This is a view of the Mansfield Store; the first floor was a haberdashery, selling clothing and men's apparel, and the second floor was Henry Mansfield's dental office. The icehouse to the right of the building contained ice packed in sawdust for the ships and people in town.

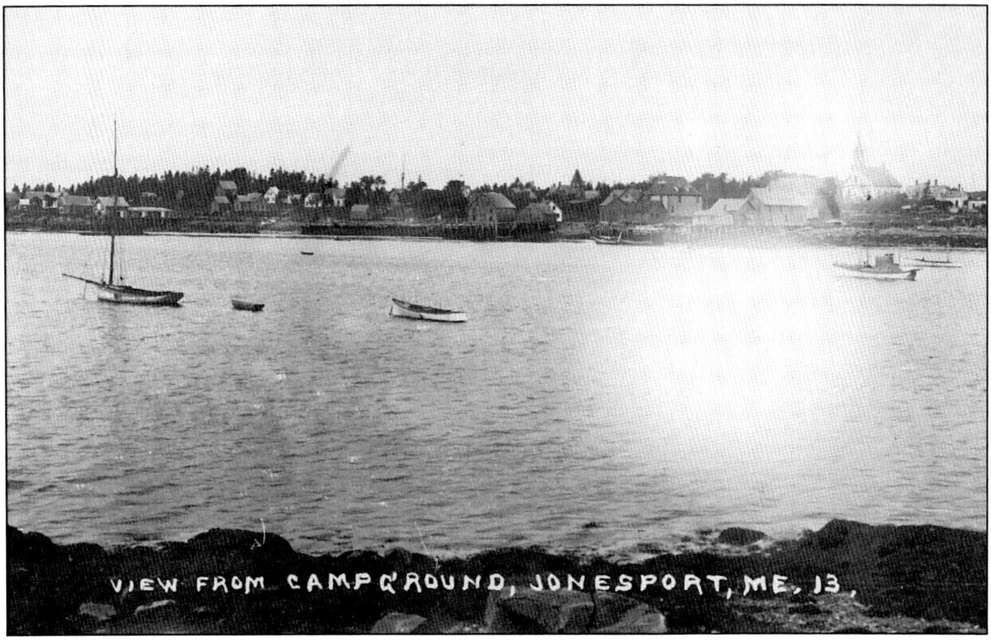

This photograph of Jonesport was taken from Moosabec Reach looking toward Sawyers Cove. The Sawyer Congregational Church is visible to the far right.

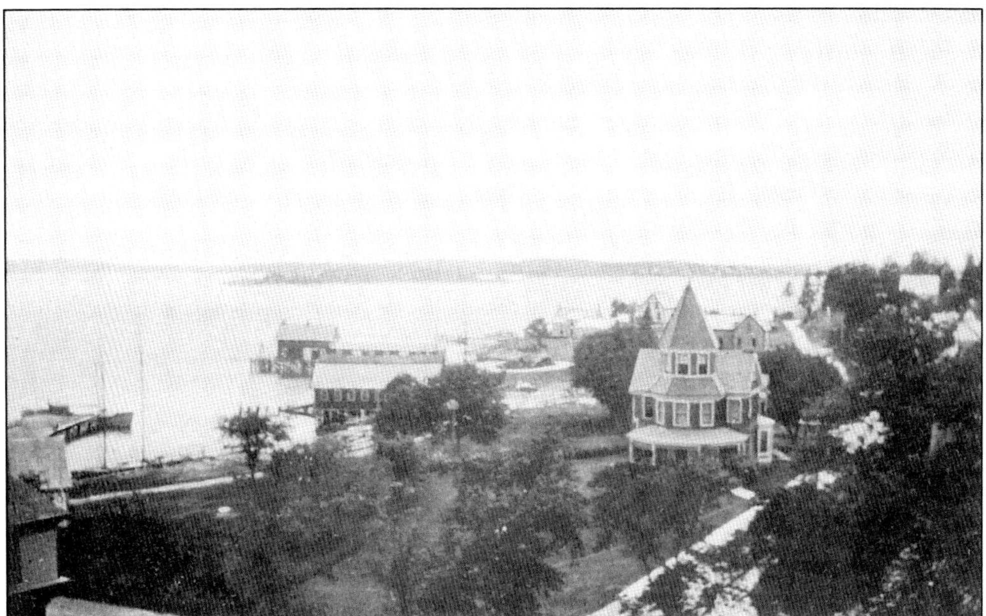

Jonesport-by-the-Sea, The Home of Seth and Mother Parker, way down on the coast of Maine.

The Sawyer home is the house with the turret in the middle of the picture. The Looks Lobster Pound is the wharf protruding into the water. Visible across the water are Beals and Great Wass Islands.

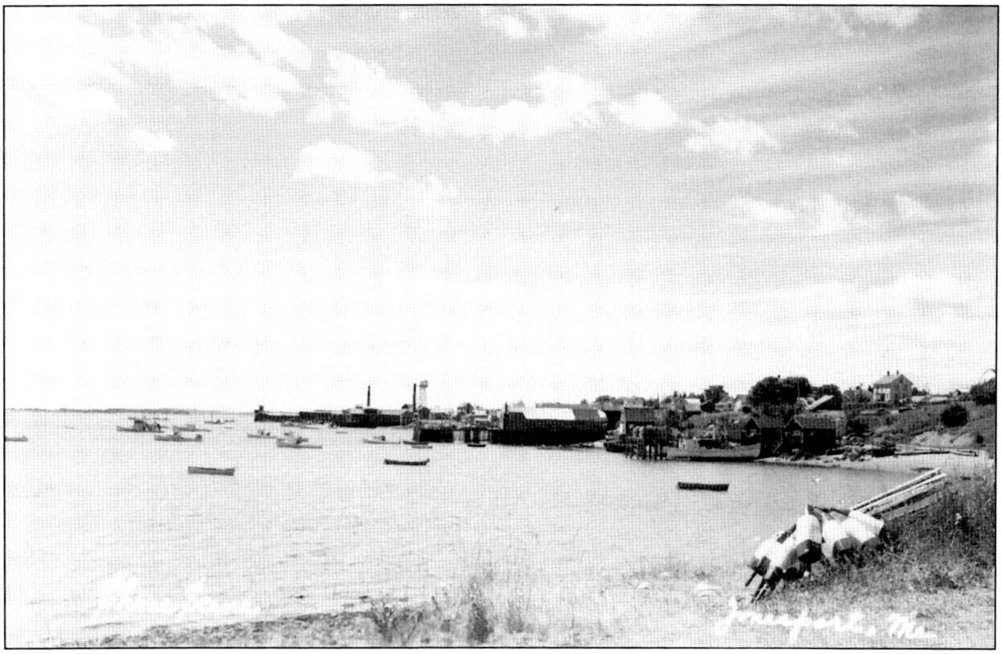

This view of Sawyers Cove was taken looking down Moosabec Reach. In 1859, Mr. D.J. Sawyer and Mr. E.M. Sawyer had a shipbuilding and general store at Sawyers Cove. The firm had control of or an interest in many of the vessels they built.

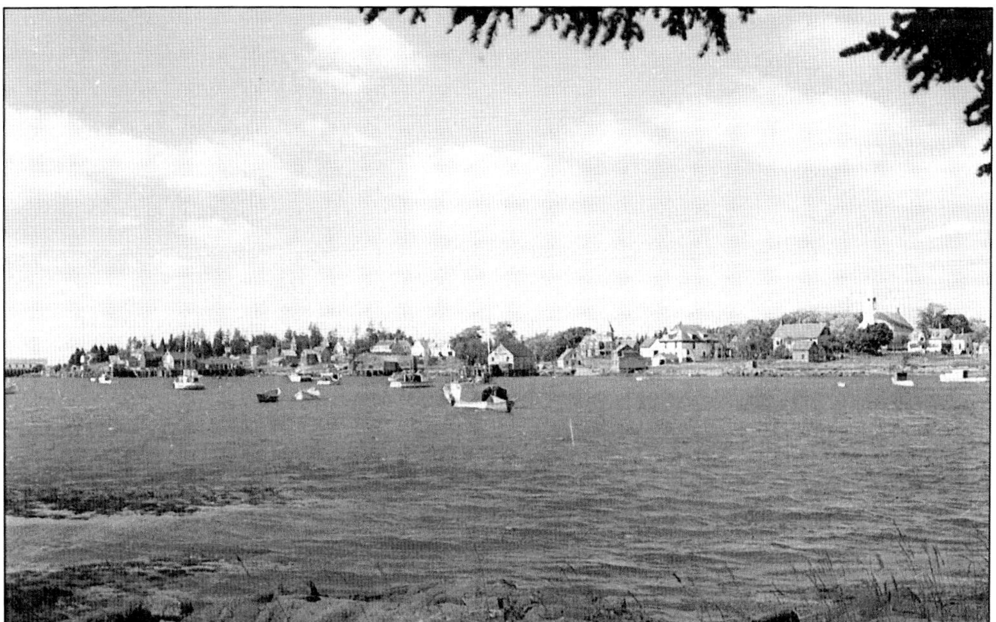

This 1960s harbor view of Jonesport was taken from Great Wass Island. You can see the Congressional church in Sawyers Cove to the far right. On the waters edge in front of the Congressional church is the present-day site of the marina.

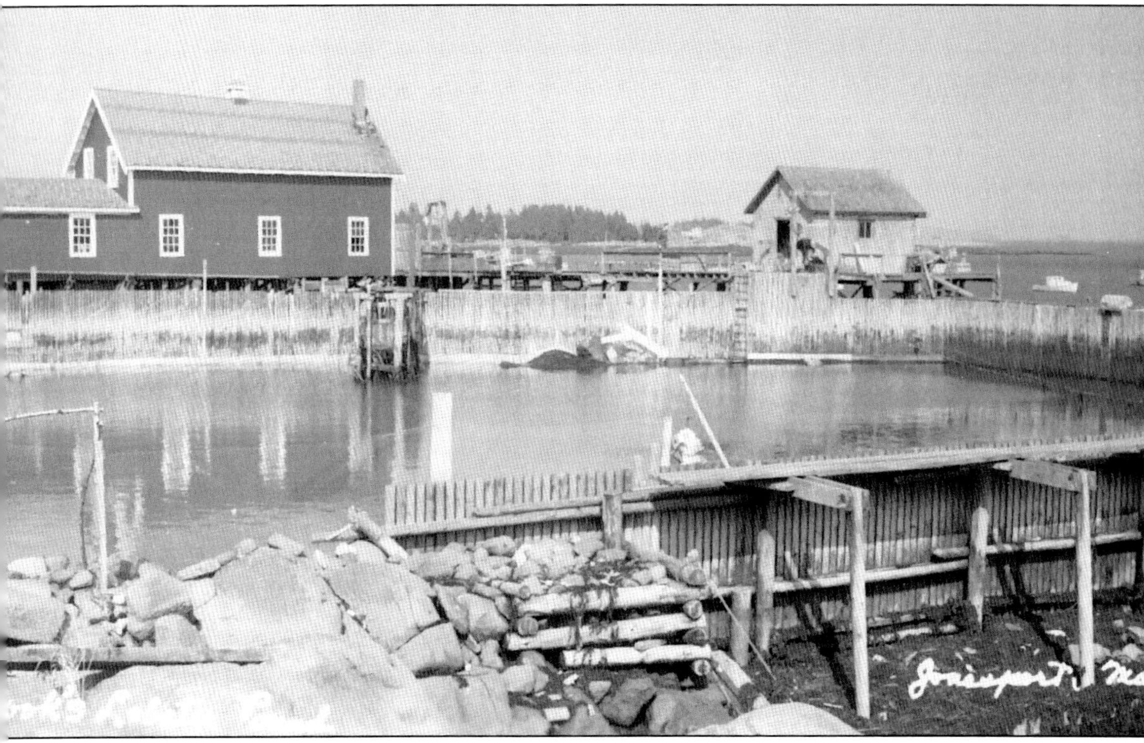

The Looks family owned the lobster pound on Sawyer Cove for over 100 years. Two of the first owners were Bert and Oscar Look.

Six

TRIVIA

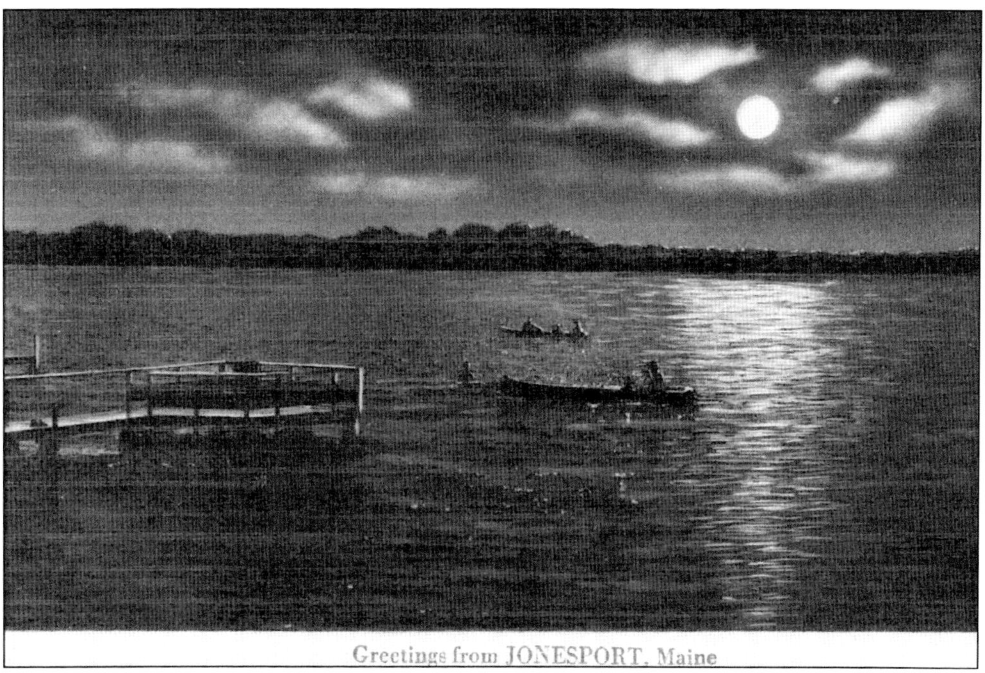

Darrel (Tubby) Trynor was the first causality from Jonesport during World War II. He died in the Battle of the Bulge; Trynor Square in West Jonesport was named in his honor.

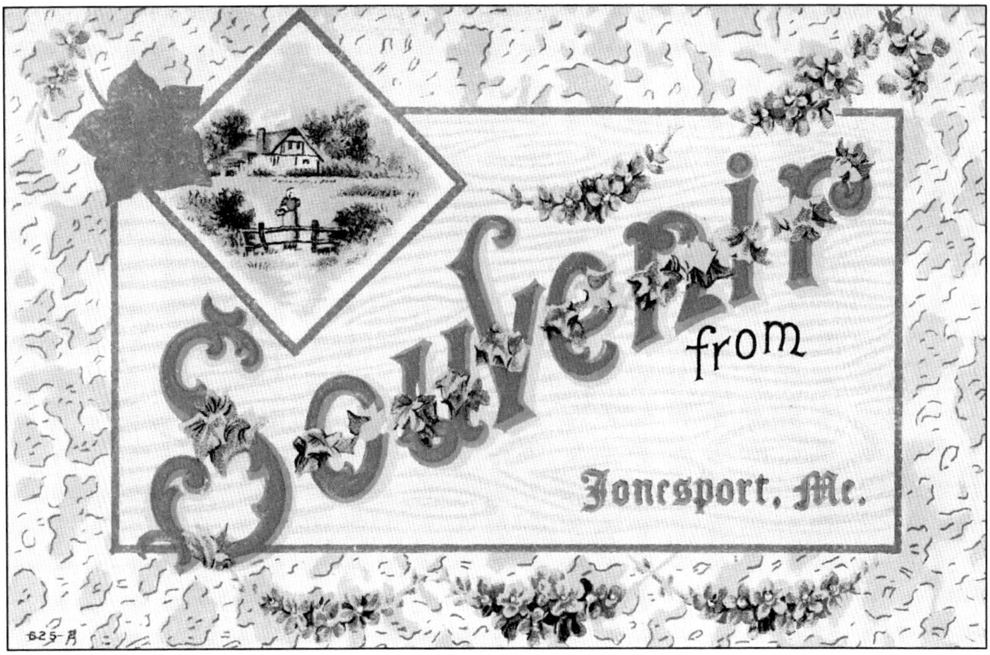

Beals Island was named for Manwarren Beal, the earliest known white person who settled on the island, *c.* 1774.

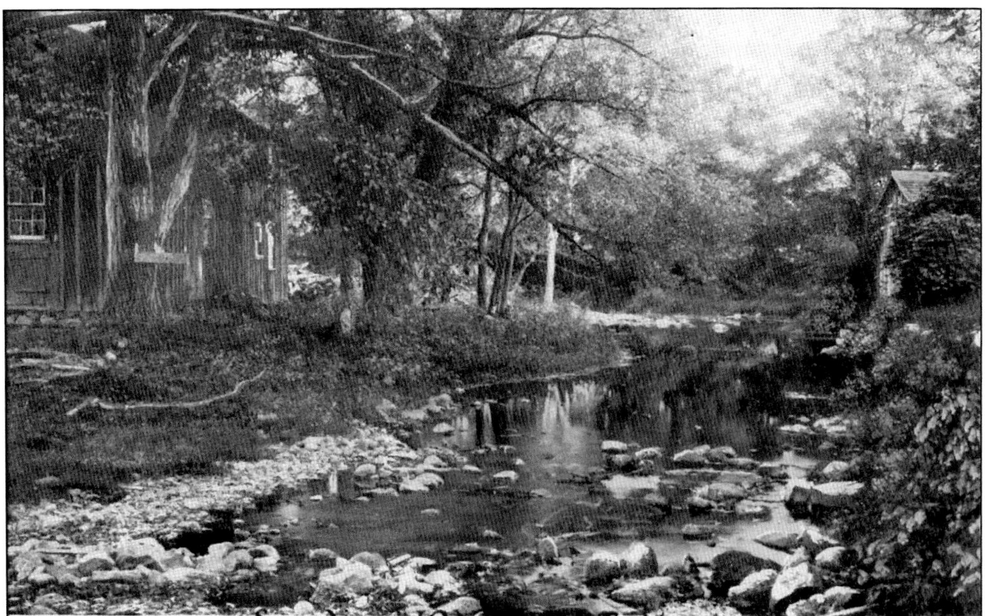

Francis Cummings was the first settler on Roque Island in 1772.

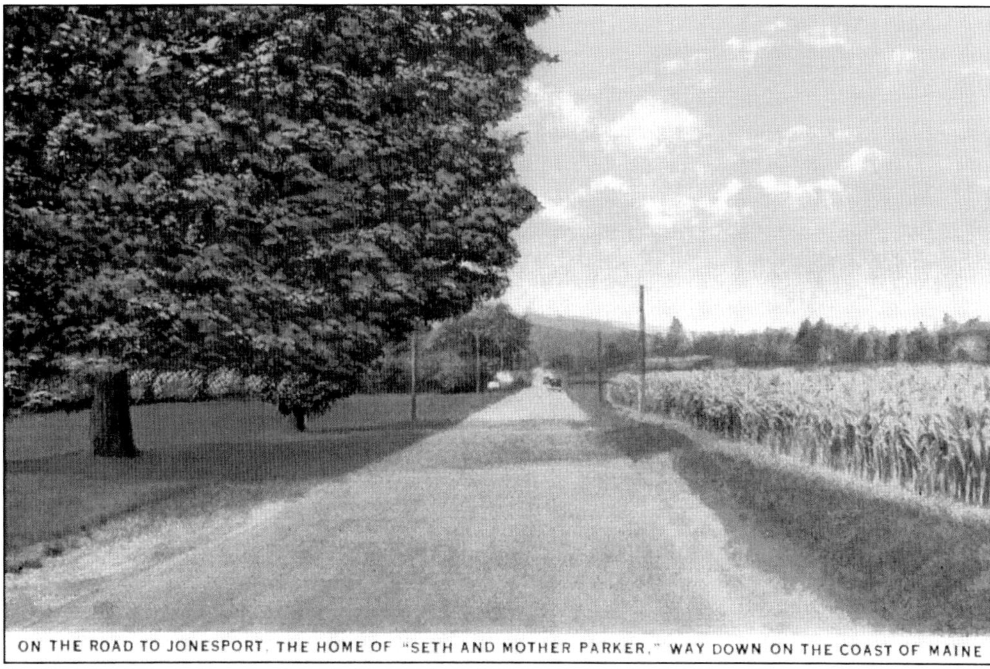

Jonesport was incorporated on February 3, 1832.

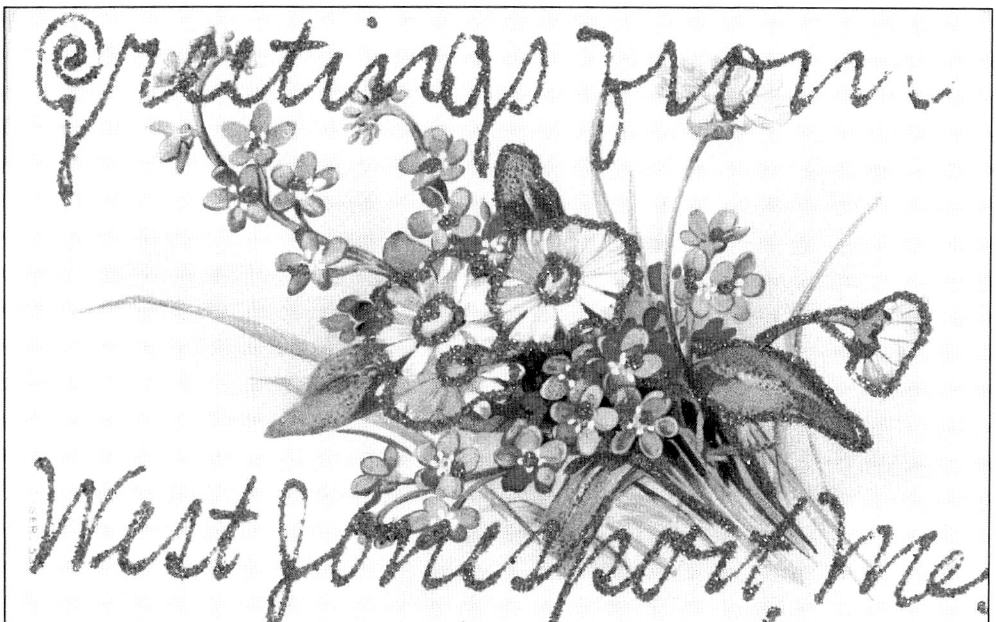

The first church in Jonesport was built in 1877.

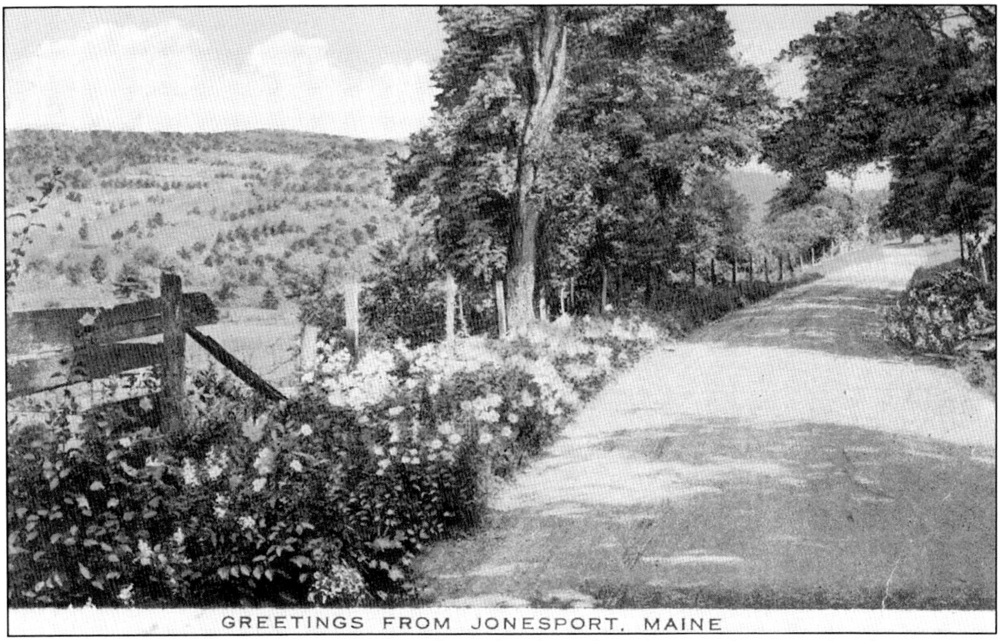

Native-American trails through the woods to the shore later became Route 187. This is a view of Route 187 in the 1930s. In the 1850s, Route 187 was nothing but a trodden path that was safe only in the winter when the swamps were frozen.

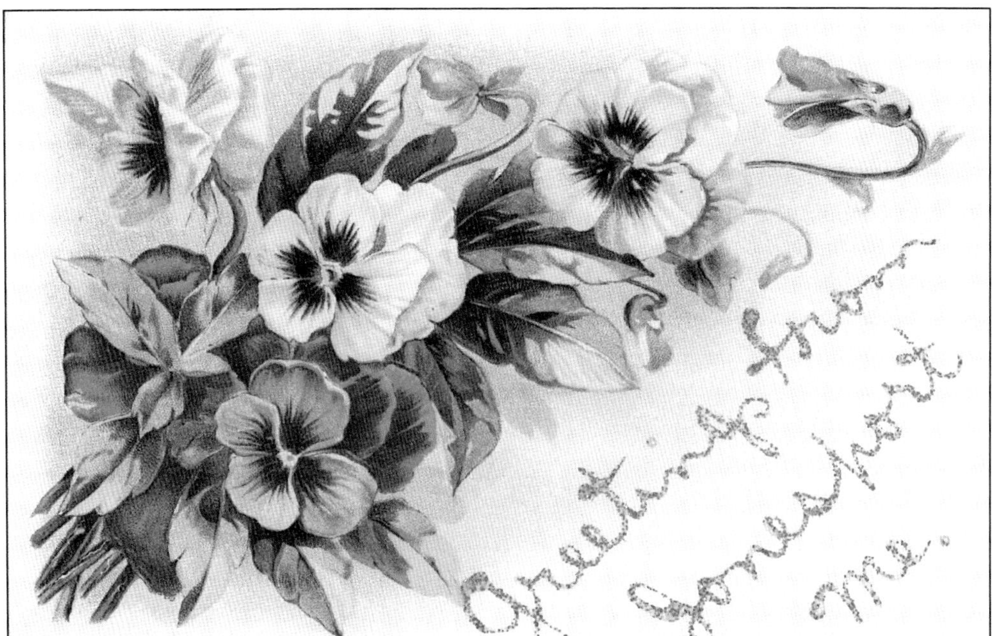

Thomas Kelly and family settled in Jonesport at Kelly Point, c. 1773.

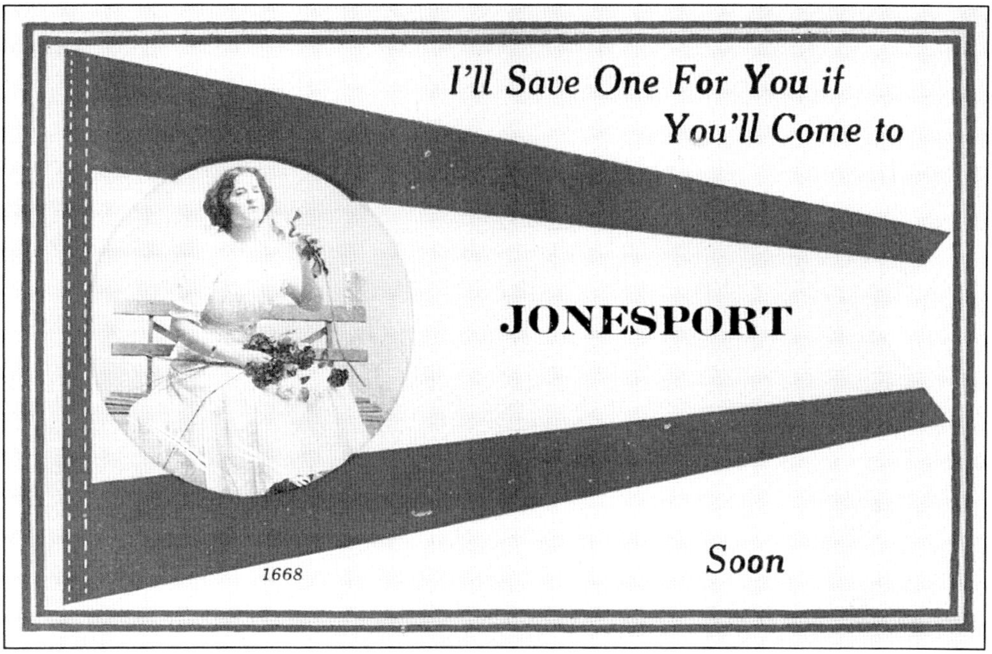

Seven brothers from Jonesport enlisted in the armed services during World War II: Allen, George, Gerald, John, Julian, Orral, and Robert Merchant. All returned home safe.

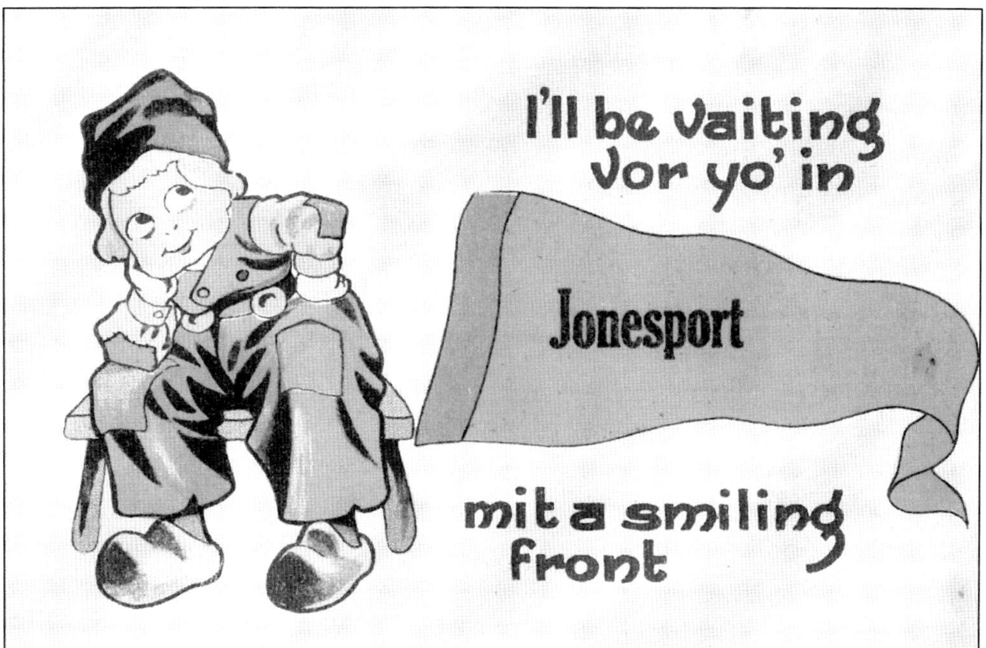

Phillip Faulkingham came to Jonesport with his family in 1850 and settled near Hay Creek.

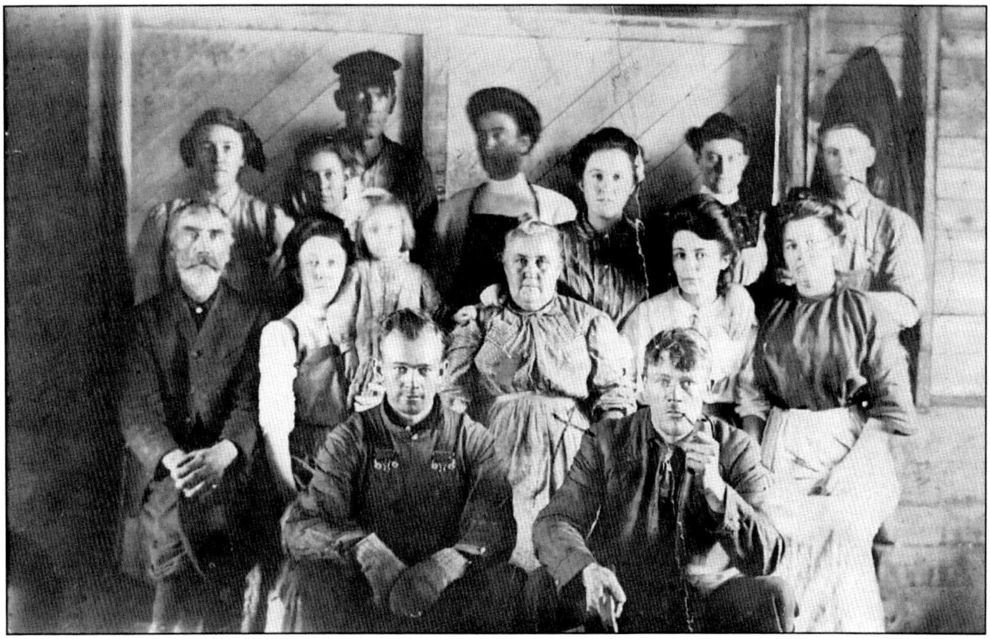

Employees of the clam factory posed for this photograph *c.* 1920s.

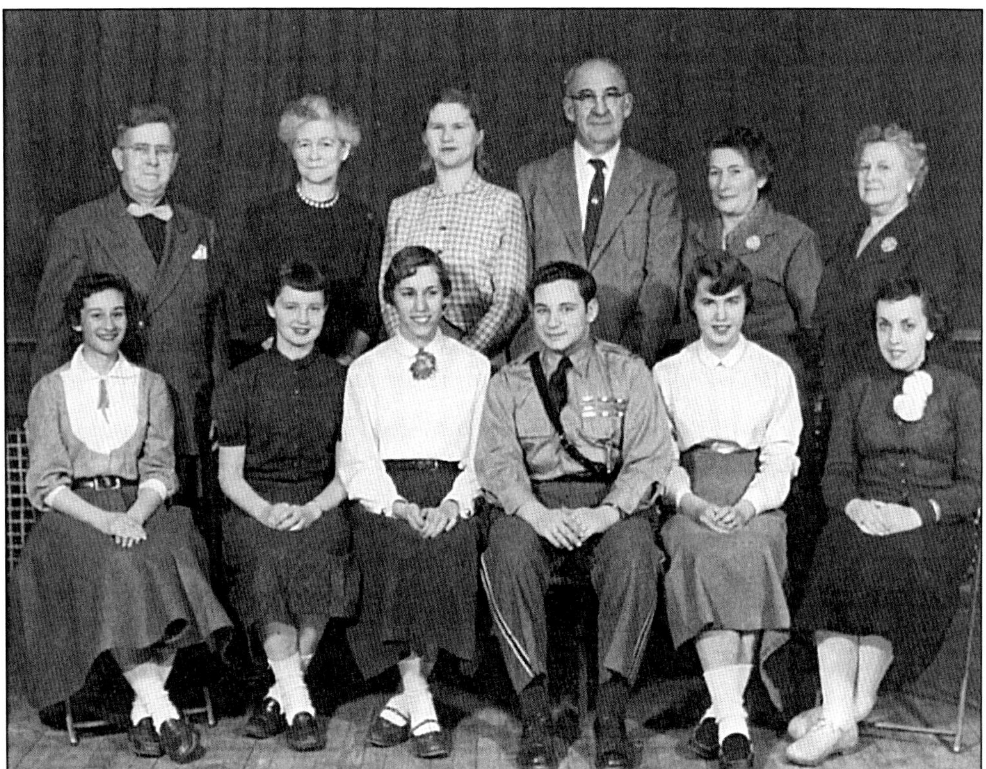

The Assembly Committee of Jonesport assembled for this photograph.

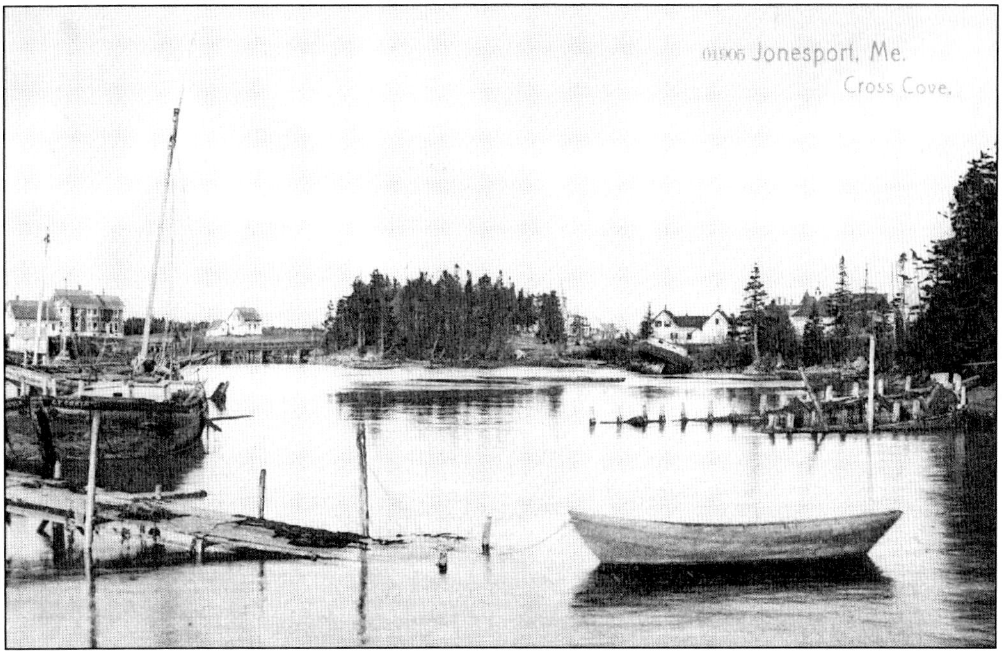

Cross Cove is shown here in 1908. It is so named because of a cross erected here by Native Americans. At the end of Cross Cove is Old House Point; early settlers spoke of a lady with supernatural powers who lived there.

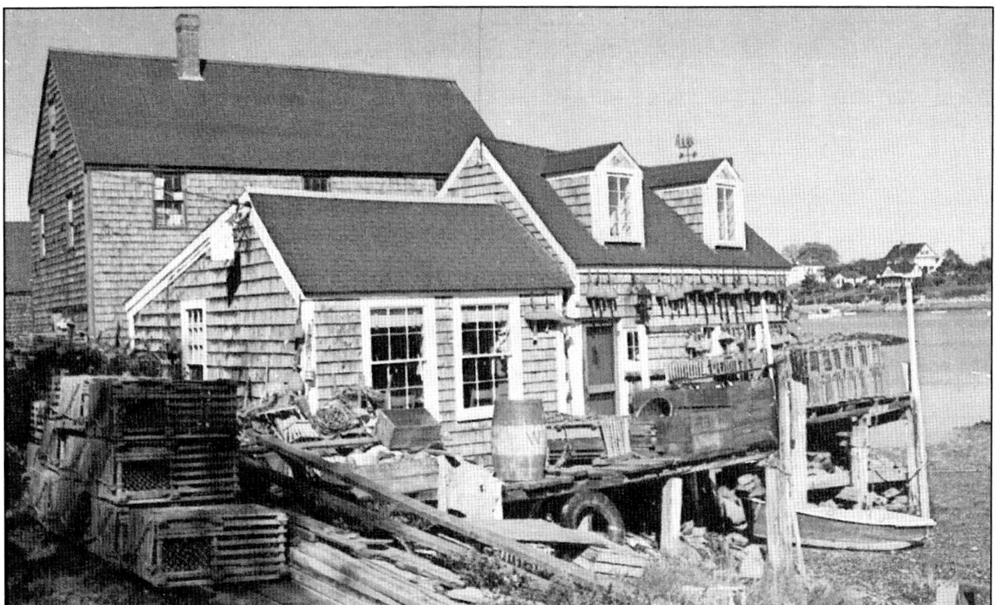

When people traveled by water instead of land, the road went behind the houses and the front door looked out to sea. Some homes had a field in front of the house that went down to the shore.

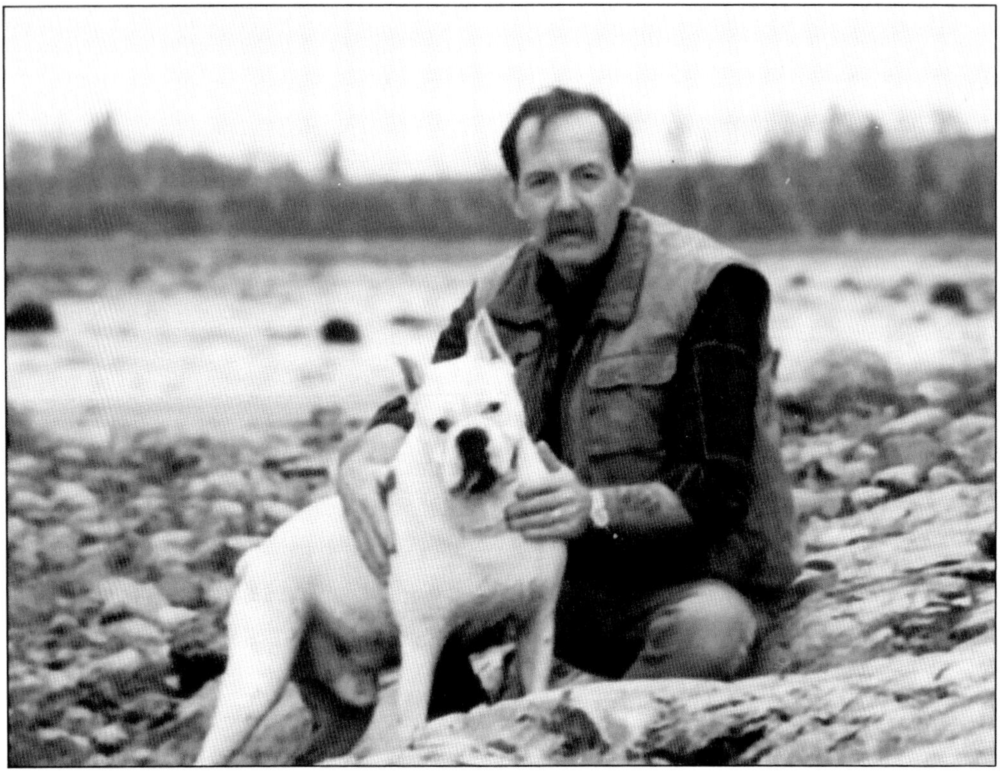

ACKNOWLEDGMENTS

This book would not have been possible without the help of many kind-hearted people. The author would like to give special thanks to the following individuals: Irene and Clyde Lamson, for answering endless questions; Richard Deegan, owner of Jonesport by the Sea Bed and Breakfast; Ronald Gray, owner of Indian River Variety of Addison; Arletta Faulkingham, Jonesport Town Clerk for many years, for her invaluable help; Maureen Hart, owner of the Harbor House on Sawyer Cove in Jonesport; Alberton Merrett; and Libby Smith.

I especially thank my husband, Woody, for the support and inspiration he has given me. He has always encouraged me in any venture that I pursued. Woody told me to reach for the stars—that I can have them, that they're out there for the taking—I just have to want them bad enough. Thanks for the endless trips he has made to Jonesport for me to do research for this book.

In addition, I would like to thank my son Billy; his precious wife, Lori; my son Shawn; and my dear Cyndi, for all their support and faith. And last but not least I wish to thank my sister Mary for the support and encouragement she has given me.